Before and After Jamestown

Native Peoples, Cultures, and Places of the Southeastern United States

Please Return To Don Swain

Florida A&M University, Tallahassee
Florida Atlantic University, Boca Raton
Florida Gulf Coast University, Ft. Myers
Florida International University, Miami
Florida State University, Tallahassee
University of Central Florida, Orlando
University of Florida, Gainesville
University of North Florida, Jacksonville
University of South Florida, Tampa
University of West Florida, Pensacola

Native Peoples, Cultures, and Places of the Southeastern United States
Edited by Jerald T. Milanich

Before and After Jamestown

Virginia's Powhatans and Their Predecessors

Helen C. Rountree and E. Randolph Turner III

Foreword by Jerald T. Milanich

University Press of Florida

Gainesville · Tallahassee · Tampa · Boca Raton
Pensacola · Orlando · Miami · Jacksonville · Ft. Myers

Copyright 2002 by Helen C. Rountree and E. Randolph Turner III
First cloth printing 2002, by the University Press of Florida
First paperback printing 2005, by the University Press of Florida
Printed in the United States of America on recycled, acid-free paper

10 09 08 07 06 05   6 5 4 3 2 1

A record of cataloging-in-publication data is available
from the Library of Congress.

ISBN 0-8130-2817-5

The University Press of Florida is the scholarly publishing agency
for the State University System of Florida, comprising Florida A&M
University, Florida Atlantic University, Florida Gulf Coast University,
Florida International University, Florida State University, University
of Central Florida, University of Florida, University of North Florida,
University of South Florida, and University of West Florida.

University Press of Florida
15 Northwest 15th Street
Gainesville, FL 32611<n>2079
http://www.upf.com

Contents

In memory of Kattie Christian,
who gave Helen Rountree her first lessons
in the joys and constraints of interethnic relations,

and

to Sarah and Robert Turner,
who gave Randolph Turner the joy of introducing
Virginia history to a new generation.

Foreword

The name of Pocahontas is well known to every American schoolchild. Less certain are the historical and cultural contexts of which she was a part. Who were her ancestors? What happened to them after the English colonization of Virginia? Where are her descendants today? In this popular account, Helen C. Rountree and E. Randolph Turner III, both scholars and experts on the Indians of Virginia, provide answers to such questions.

Drawing on the latest archaeological and ethnographic research, as well as on documentary sources, the authors tell the story of the Powhatan and other Indians who lived in Virginia in the early seventeenth century when the English colony of Jamestown was founded. They trace the Virginia Algonquians back in time for a millennium, describing the precolumbian cultures that gave rise to colonial-period Native American groups. They also tell us of the interactions among the colonists and the Indians. But that is only a part of the story. Indians still live in Virginia, descendants of those colonial populations. *Before and After Jamestown* brings us their stories as well, recording their histories through the last four hundred years literally into the twenty-first century.

Rich in ethnographic detail, well illustrated, and with information on additional readings and relevant sites that can be visited, this book is an important contribution to our understanding of our nation's Native American heritage. Best of all, it makes us aware that American Indians are not relics of the past. They are our neighbors, co-citizens of the modern world.

Jerald T. Milanich
Series Editor

Preface

We coauthors, both Powhatan specialists, had long dreamed of collaborating on a more popularly oriented book—free of footnotes and jargon—than the scholarly cultural anthropology and history books Rountree had published and the technical history and archaeology reports that Turner had produced. The University Press of Florida's series on ancient and historical Southeastern peoples, aimed at nonscholars as well as scholars, sounded like just the ticket. The Press was about to contact Rountree for a Powhatan book when Rountree contacted the press with a somewhat different project. She had already published a Powhatan culture book (*The Powhatan Indians of Virginia: Their Traditional Culture*) and a Powhatan history book (*Pocahontas's People: The Powhatan Indians of Virginia through Four Centuries*). But what about her working with an archaeologist and producing a book on eastern Virginia that covered both prehistoric and historic times? No such book had been done, so Florida gave us the go-ahead. This volume is the result.

Senior anthropologists, if they are not living the somewhat insecure life of contract scholars, tend to have risen in their hierarchies (government or university) to levels where they do more paper-pushing and less fieldwork. When they are really successful, they become upper-level bureaucrats who almost never get to go back to the nitty-gritty work that attracted them in the first place. Turner is in this position in Virginia's Department of Historic Resources. Rountree, addicted to research and knowing where her level of incompetence lay, resisted rising too far in academia first by refusing to run for department chairman, much less anything higher, and more recently by taking early retirement from Old Dominion University after more than three decades of teaching undergraduates.

Our division of labor on this book has therefore been as follows: writing and formatting of text, Rountree, with Turner checking her work; procuring of most of the illustrations, Turner, in consultation with Rountree; provision of archaeological information and interpreting it, Turner; provision of information from historical records and interpreting it, mainly Rountree, in consultation with Turner on the Early Contact period; input from ethnographic analogy, Rountree for human cultures in general and both Rountree and Turner for historic Native Americans; input from living history, Rountree (a pity; Turner has more tolerance for getting dirty, being an archaeologist); information from working with modern Virginia Indians, Rountree, though Turner is in contact with the tribes as well.

Some of the illustrations in this volume are of artifacts found in western Virginia rather than in the coastal plain. With the exception of figure 1.10, we have done this only in the case of artifact types that are found in both regions. But we have chosen items from these sites because they were in a much better state of preservation when they came from the ground, the soils in western Virginia often being less acidic than those on the coastal plain. Where we have used photographs of noncoastal artifacts, we say so in the captions.

In preparing this volume for publication, we are indebted to a number of individuals and organizations for the help they rendered us. First and foremost, we owe a debt to Jamestown Settlement: A Living Museum, whose Indian Village staff is reconstructing Powhatan practices barely noticed by the early colonists. It was the supervisor of that staff, Barbara Lynch, who gave Rountree the inspiration for a specific type of person to communicate with as she wrote the text of this book: a brand-new intern in the village who is curious about Indians but who has only the standard nonmajor's background in American history and no background at all in anthropology.

The Jamestown Rediscovery Project of the Association for the Preservation of Virginia Antiquities gave us further inspiration. Its staff allowed us to kibbitz on the excavation at close range and also supplied us with some marvelous photographs. We are especially indebted to William Kelso, the director of the project, as well as to photographer Michael Lavin and especially to Bly Straub, who discussed artifacts and also checked over chapter 4 for us. Joanne Bowen, a zooarchaeologist with

Colonial Williamsburg Foundation, supplied us with further information about the deer bones found at the site.

Keith Egloff, an archaeologist in the Virginia Department of Historic Resources, obligingly rephotographed some of that department's artifacts for us and assisted us in reviewing the thousands of photographs in its collections. Danielle Moretti-Langholtz, a cultural anthropologist at the College of William and Mary, was invaluable for her comments on chapter 3, with its reliance upon ethnographic analogy. Andrea Whitney of J & R Graphics, Inc., helped Rountree to produce figure 3.4.

Writing a book, as with everything else in life, thrives on support. Providing such support for thirty years now while the junior author pursued his dreams in Virginia archaeology is a most cherished gift. Thanks, Betsy!

Last but not least, we thank the modern Powhatan tribes, who tolerated the occasional microscope's gaze of us anthropologists, enabling us to see that in subtle ways, as well as public ones, they really are the descendants of the historical Powhatans.

Introduction

This book covers roughly a thousand years, which, allowing for earlier marriages during shorter life spans for most of that time, is about fifty generations of human life. Only for the last fourteen or so generations have there been any literate Indians in Virginia, and only in the last three generations has literacy become available to all of the Indian people. Thus we have had to rely heavily on non-Indian sources of information for this book.

There are, of course, modern Indian tribes in eastern Virginia who are descended from the historical Powhatans and their Algonquian-speaking predecessors. They have oral traditions about past times, and they are willing to share them with anthropologists and other members of the public. However, those oral traditions lose detail the farther back they go—a situation that is normal in human populations. Thus, unless they have read the same historical records that scholars use or those scholars' summaries of the records, modern Indian people's depiction of their ancestors in the seventeenth century is just as generalized as the account we coauthors would have been able to give about Stuart England (the land of most of our ancestors) before we took history courses in college. Pure oral tradition among the tribes, then, is likely after four centuries to be more useful for presenting the ancestors' point of view and general behavior than for details about specific practices or events.

This loss of historical detail is especially true, in our view, since the mid-twentieth century, with the advent of television and the admission of Indian youngsters to the public, now-integrated schools. In spite of obvious advantages through those two innovations, they still have been presenting white-dominated American culture to Indian (and other minority) young people in some very intrusive ways. Television has gone farther in recent decades by presenting a colorful, exciting, and commercially based "kid culture" (Rountree's term), which competes for children's attention with Indian ancestors and non-Indian schoolteachers alike. Major repercussions are being felt from these things in all Native American communities across the continent.

The four non-Indian sources of information we have used to flesh out the story are all open to charges of bias. Two kinds of direct evidence available to us are written records about Indians and archaeological excavation of the things the Indians left behind. The two kinds of indirect evidence we use are ethnographic analogy and living history.

Our only direct evidence of what the lives of prehistoric Virginians were like comes from archaeology. The Virginia Algonquians had no need of writing before the European invasion, since they did not have a large population running a big market system and paying taxes to support politicians and other specialists. Writing was originally invented to keep track of those things that the Powhatans and their predecessors did not have.

Archaeologists dig down through recent soil to older layers in order to find what earlier peoples left behind. The average person leaving items was usually not image-conscious, as many writers of historical documents were, so we normally need not look for bias of that kind. Instead the bias comes from two other sources: possible inaccuracies in our interpreting of recovered items and damage from poor preservation. University-trained archaeologists are in some degree Eurocentric and also live very much in the modern world. In the United States, Canada, and Mexico, they have traditionally taken courses in cultural anthropology as well as in archaeology to learn about non-European cultures in modern and historical times. But even with this mental broadening-out, they (and the cultural anthropologists) may not escape all bias. Preservation, on the other hand, creates a bias of which archaeologists are *always* conscious. Even elaborately made objects may be eaten away to nothing after years in the soil, especially if the soil is acidic like eastern Virginia's and if the climate produces almost weekly wet-dry cycles. (Deserts and cold-water submersion are the best conditions for preservation.)

The ancient people themselves can foil archaeologists. Any culture will leave an incomplete record if that record consists only of objects (which is why ancient Egypt is so beloved of archaeologists: desert tombs with plentiful everyday objects *plus written records in them*). The Powhatans' ancestors were inadvertent experts in frustrating archaeolo-

Fig. I.1. Posthole evidence of a house at Jordan's Point. Courtesy of the Virginia Department of Historic Resources (VDHR).

gists. They did not write; the structures they built were aboveground and left postholes as the only evidence of their existence (fig. I.1); the rest of the people's technology was mostly biodegradable, in soils and in a climate in which organic materials decay rapidly; and their habitation sites were on good farmland that later got plowed, near waterways that sometimes eroded the shoreline away (another plus for Egypt: burial in artificially made caves, where no one farmed and erosional forces did not intrude).

There is a further limitation on archaeology, one that the Powhatans and their predecessors unintentionally played upon in many sites: Archaeology is painstaking and labor-intensive work, both in the digging and in the analysis of the results. Even excavating a small house site and conserving and analyzing its artifacts can take weeks and cost a good deal of money. It will take longer if the site has been repeatedly occupied so that artifacts in multiple layers have to be carefully exposed, mapped, and labeled (fig. I.2). A big "dig" therefore takes longer and costs more—and time and money are often in short supply, especially if a developer owns the land and wants to begin work. But the Powhatans and their ancestors preferred to build settlements of scattered houses and fields. One village might cover all the acreage that a developer has plans for; or it might extend along land owned by several farmers—or by many homeowners, in the case of the magnificent Great Neck site in Virginia Beach. Learning about all parts of such a village is nearly impossible, given the constraints on the archaeologists.

If the village's time of occupation extended into the historic period, the archaeologist will need to become—or hire—a historian to find written records, if any, about the Indians on the site. For that matter, archaeologists who dig Late Woodland, Protohistoric, and Early Contact period sites in Virginia have usually, like Turner, acquired training in history and familiarized themselves with the early colonial records.

After 1607, there were literate people in eastern Virginia observing the Powhatans. The records they left in the early years of the colony have nearly all been published by now, as far as historians know. The printed accounts in the early seventeenth century were apt to use gothic letters that moderns are unused to (fig. I.3); the text was also couched in archaic, convoluted language that sometimes defies clarification. As a result, there have been some wonderful catfights among scholars over how to interpret certain passages. Even tougher to decode are the manuscript records, many of them county court records, that are too extensive to have been published. People's handwriting varied then as it does now; the ideal of lovely, standard copperplate writing was as foreign to the seventeenth century as it became during the twentieth. Seventeenth-century script differed considerably from that of later centuries, with "backwards" E's and occasional S's that resemble F's without the horizontal stroke (fig. I.4); there were even more differences early in the century, especially in C's and R's. Spelling tended to be freeform, in both manuscript and printed works, since standardization did not take hold until about 1700. And the combination of cheap, porous paper and a badly made quill pen could produce Rorschach-like blots that soaked straight through to the other side. Early colonial manuscript records can be perfectly maddening to read, but read them we must, for they contain gobbets of information on the Powhatans. Rountree eventually reached the point, at one time, where she could rapidly decipher a seventeenth-century court record while touch-typing a transcription.

A cultural anthropologist, trained in studying human cultures worldwide, who wants to describe the Powhatans before the present time must therefore get training in history as well (that is, become an ethnohis-

Fig. I.2. Stratigraphy at the Croaker Landing site. Courtesy of VDHR.

torian). The needed historical training does not stop with how to find and decipher relevant records; it extends to evaluating their usefulness. The people making the records grew up in very different times from ours, and they were making the records for reasons of their own that often differed drastically from our motives in reading them. Learning about their culture in addition to the Powhatan one is a necessity. For instance, the early colonists grew up in Tudor England, a culture chronologically alien to our own, and they made procolonization records about a people who were culturally alien to them and also to us. So viewing the Early Contact Powhatans is like trying to see through two sets of eyeglasses, each set made for a different person and both sets in need of cleaning. The situation does not entirely clear up as we approach present times, either, because the mid-twentieth-century American world was considerably different from today's version.

Learning two cultures in order to write about one of them, much less following those two cultures forward in time to reconstruct a longer Powhatan history, is a time-consuming, expensive project. To bring it off,

A

True relation of such occurrences
and accidents of note, as hath hapned in *Virginia*, since the first planting of that Collony,
which is now resident in the South part
thereof, till the last returne.

Inde Sir, commendations re-
membred, &c. You shall vnderstand
that after many crosses in the downes
by tempests, wee arriued safely vppon
the Southwest part of the great Ca-
naries: within foure or fiue daies after
we set saile for Dominica, the 26. of   *16*
Aprill: the first land we made, wee fell
with Cape Henry, the verie mouth of
the Bay of Chissiapiacke, which at that present we little expected, hauing by a cruell storme bene put to the Northward:
anchoring in this Bay twentie or thirtie went a shore with
the Captain, and in comming aboard, they were assalted with
certaine Indians, which charged them within Pistoll shot: in
which conflict, Captaine Archer and Mathew Morton were
shot: wherupon, Captaine Newport seconding them, made a
shot at them, which the Indians little respected, but hauing
spent their arrowes retyred without harme, and in that place
was the Box opened, wherin the Counsell for Virginia was
nominated: and arriuing at the place where wee are now sea-
ted, the Counsell was sworne, the President elected, which for
that yeare was Maister Edm. Maria Wingfield, where was
                                A 3   made

Fig. I.3. First page of John Smith's "True Relation," 1608.

a scholar needs either lush, long-term grants or else (like Rountree) a
secure "daytime job" that is geographically within the subjects' area to
support the "moonlighting." And even then, the write-up that present-
day people can readily understand will in the future be seen by the public
as archaically worded and by scholars as limited in its understanding of
the Indians.

The third source of information for reconstructing Powhatan Indian life is an indirect one, used by cultural anthropologists: ethnographic analogy. For very broad use, the method involves examining certain human physical universals (for example, very helpless and slow-maturing offspring; the Powhatans would have had these) and noting what culture traits resulting from them are also universal (for example, multiple adults spending immense time and effort to rear those offspring over a

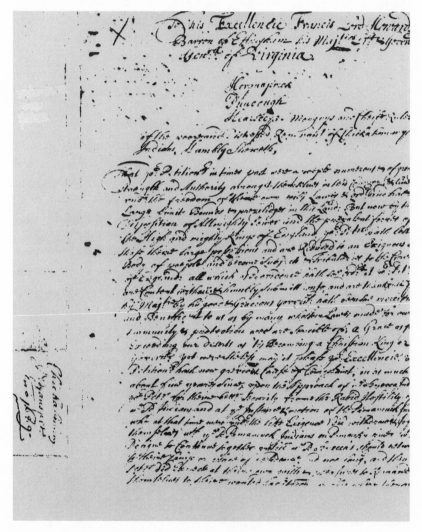

Fig. I.4. Chickahominy Indian petition of 1689.

period of decades; so the Powhatans would have done this). In order to say more specific things about a culture under study, the method involves locating better-recorded cultures whose ecology and economy were similar; examining what *general* family, politico-legal, military, and medico-religious practices stemmed from them; and then carefully generalizing by saying that the studied culture *may have* had them too. For example, other Woodland Indian groups, like the better-recorded Iroquois, Delawares, and Cherokees, had husbands and wives who did very different kinds of work and who therefore did not expect to have very much in common, much less have companionate marriages. Powhatan men and women had a very similar division of labor (see chapter 3), so it is likely that they, too, lacked companionate marriages. Ethnographic analogy does not give firm, detailed answers. Instead it adds some coarse-grained images to an incomplete picture, which is worth taking the trouble to do.

In the past few years a fourth source of information, another indirect one, has come onto the scene: living history. As the newest endeavor, it is currently the least respectable in the eyes of traditional historians. (Perhaps part of the problem is that most living historians are employed by museums rather than universities.) The method, however, is neither easy nor slapdash if it is done properly. Living history requires the careful perusing of historical eyewitness accounts, which are limited in certain ways, and then attempting to get around those limitations by actually trying to perform the tasks that the accounts only mention in passing. Some archaeologists have been doing this for decades through learning to knap flint tools. Most of the details we have about Powhatan women's work have had to come from living history (see chapter 3). The method may not tell us much about the more intellectual parts of people's lives, but it does fill in gaps. For instance, many early witnesses wrote that Southeastern Indian people traveled the waterways in dugout canoes; some witnesses also described the burn-and-scrape method most commonly used to make them. None of the witnesses, however, mentioned how long it takes to produce such a canoe from scratch, nor the fact that as the hollowing-out nears its end, it is easy to get diverted and let the fire go too long, burning a hole through the bottom of the blasted thing.

With all these techniques (oral history, documentary history, living history, archaeology, ethnographic analogy) for reconstructing the past, and the constraints they involve, the picture of the last millennium in eastern Virginia remains incomplete and still very much a matter of interpretation. New evidence will cause new interpretations; so will rereading of the "old" evidence by the same person (for instance, Rountree on the history of the Mattaponi Reservation in chapter 6). No one, Indian or non-Indian, scholar or nonscholar, has a monopoly on the truth. There will probably always be disagreements as to what "really" happened and what Indian life was "really" like. To enforce only one version would be to invite stagnation, not to mention boredom.

1

Indian Life in the Late Woodland Period
(ca. A.D. 900–ca. 1500)

The region occupied by the Virginia Algonquians, and later dominated or at least heavily influenced by the great chief Powhatan, is about 100 miles long from north to south and about 100 miles wide from southeast to northwest. Its western boundary, clearly recognized by the native people, was the "fall line," an imaginary line connecting the first occurrence as one goes upstream of outcrops of bedrock in the beds of the major rivers of the region. Today the fall line within Virginia is roughly demarcated by Interstate 95, which connects the cities (Richmond on the James, Fredericksburg on the Rappahannock, and Washington on the Potomac) that originated as depots where English ships could not go farther upstream. The eastern edge of the Virginia Algonquians' territory was the Atlantic Ocean. The northern boundary of their territory lay in the broad waters of the lower Potomac River, which were fishing grounds for the Indian people living on both sides of the river. And the southern boundary, unmarked in Indian thinking, was out in the forested hunting territory that ran unbroken from the James River to the rivers and sounds well to the south.

Climate and Land

The climate of the region today is moderately humid, which makes people feel its temperatures more acutely. Subfreezing temperatures are short lived and come mainly after New Year's, while the real heat of summer extends well into September. The millennium we are covering in this book included two periods of slightly different temperatures: a period somewhat warmer than present about A.D. 800–1200 and one slightly colder than present (the "Little Ice Age") about A.D. 1400–1800 in the Northern Hemisphere. Europeans began trying to colonize the Chesapeake area during the cold times, when frozen-over rivers were more common.

The region's rainfall averages forty to fifty inches per year, but much of it is dependent upon the tracks of large eastward-moving weather systems rather than on water evaporated from any nearby body of water to the west. When the storm systems are weak or diverted, there is a drought. Mild droughts occur approximately every three years in eastern Virginia. In the years around several early European colonization attempts—Spanish in 1570, English at Roanoke in 1584–87, and English at Jamestown in 1607–9—there was a drought of several years in progress. What horrible timing!

The territory of the Virginia Algonquians corresponded with the geological region called the coastal plain. Its soils have been deposited both by rivers from the northwest and by ocean waters at ancient periods of higher sea level. Bedrock is at or near the surface at the fall line, but it falls rapidly to the east: it is some 2,500 feet lower at Norfolk and even deeper than that (6,000 feet) at Ocean City, Maryland. The surface of the land, on the other hand, falls very gently from nearly 200 feet above sea level to less than 10 feet in Virginia Beach and less than 50 on Virginia's Eastern Shore. The Virginia coastal plain is therefore, in cross-section, a wedge-shaped compaction of muck of various kinds, and stone is not always plentiful. That shortage had a serious impact on the technology of the native people.

Thanks to the action of a number of large waterways, most of the surface land of eastern Virginia consists of several peninsulas, called "necks," extending southeastward and (with the Eastern Shore) south-southwestward into the water (fig. 1.1). The Chesapeake basin was cut in Ice Age times by the Susquehanna River and its tributary Potomac, Rappahannock, York, and James Rivers, and it is gradually being flooded by the Atlantic. Thus these four major tributary rivers in eastern Virginia are technically estuaries. Their waters consist of fresh water flowing downstream and meeting, mixing, and eventually being subsumed by salt water from the ocean. Thus a rule of thumb for Virginia waterways, big and small: the farther upstream, the fresher the water.

Several rivers well back from the ocean show meanders, such as the Pamunkey and the Chickahominy. When sea level was lower during vari-

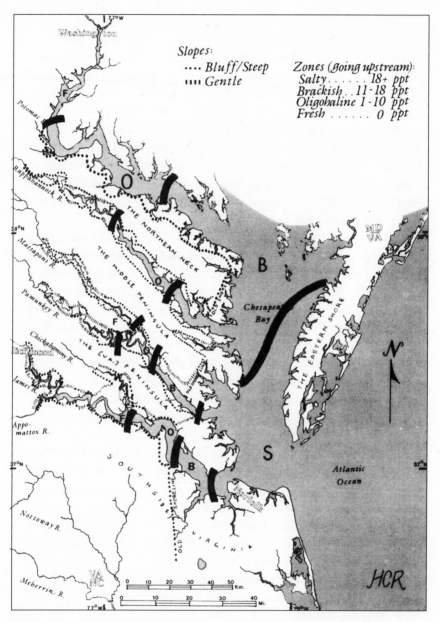

Fig. 1.1. Map of floodplains and salinities. Courtesy of Helen C. Rountree.

ous ice ages, the major rivers meandered too, across floodplains. Many exposed pieces of floodplains are still to be found, containing some of the largest expanses of the most naturally fertile soil in the whole state. Those floodplains were the preferred places for Indian farms and, for the farmers' convenience, for Indian houses and towns as well. The closeness of that soil to the waterways, where so much of the native people's life went on, was a further incentive to build on those patches of floodplain.

The surviving floodplains are the lowest of several terraces cut into the land by the higher seas of ancient times. Many of these terraces have been nearly obliterated by erosion, but the eastward faces of several have been identified by geologists. Sometimes highways run along the nearly straight line of these old oceanfronts, as do Route 10 near Chuckatuck (the Suffolk Scarp) and Route 3 north of Gloucester Courthouse. Elsewhere there are places where travelers can get a clear feeling of going from a flat piece of floodplain, up the side of the next terrace, where the countryside is hilly, and then onto a higher flat tableland. Williamsburg is on a small piece of such a tableland, and motorists can descend through eroded hills and down onto a floodplain if they drive to Jamestown via State Route 31. Towns and often extensive farms exist on the high tablelands nowadays, but Late Woodland people preferred not to settle there. That was foraging territory, where archaeologists find only temporary campsites.

Eastern North America's coastal plain narrows to a close in northern New Jersey, but it widens out as it heads first south toward Florida and then west toward Texas. South of Virginia, the plain often had unbroken stretches of pine woods before European settlers cleared them. Oak-hickory forests, rich in nuts and acorns to support plentiful deer and other animals, were not common or extensive in the southeastern coastal plain until one went inland toward the fall line. (The fall line south of Virginia is marked by cities too: Roanoke Rapids, North Carolina; Columbia, South Carolina; Augusta and Columbus, Georgia) Hence archaeologists in the rest of the Southeast find richer, mound-building cultures upstream from the fall line and smaller, poorer settlements downstream.

Virginia's coastal plain and that of the states immediately north of it had a reversed situation. Deciduous forest, much of it the oak-hickory type, covered the land almost down to the salt water of the Atlantic. Waterfront land is high enough in the northern part of the Chesapeake basin that deciduous forests reached the water's edge. Thus the forest cover was predominantly rich in nut-bearing trees in both coastal plain and pied-mont Virginia, with the coastal plain pulling ahead in richness because of all those waterways. Early English colonists observed great political com-plexity on the coastal plain but heard little about "kings" in the interior. Late Woodland settlements are more frequent on the coastal plain than in the piedmont, indicating larger human populations there.

However, Late Woodland people were far fewer on the land than the seventeenth-century English, much less modern Americans, were accus-tomed to seeing. In the area we are discussing, there were probably fewer than 25,000 people in 1607 (today there are several million). Our evi-dence comes from both archaeology and history. No really large settle-ments, even by seventeenth-century European standards, have been found in eastern Virginia. Historically, we can make a guess at the human population from Captain John Smith's rough estimates of how many fighting men were able to shoot at him in various parts of Powhatan's region. A very generous total, which allows for a bit of reduction owing to European diseases, is 25,000 people for the latter part of the Late Woodland period.

Fewer people on the land meant that the Indians were far easier on the land, just because of their numbers, than modern Virginians are. For ex-ample, they simply did not generate the same amount of sewage or trash. Much of their trash was also biodegradable—regrettably so, to archae-ologists. Further, they did not use fertilizers on their fields, judging by the English colonists' accounts, so there was no chemical runoff into the waterways. Indian settlements generated continual fogs of wood smoke in small, localized areas, but they otherwise did not pollute the air. On the other hand, small populations had their disadvantages when foreigners, Indian or European, showed up at the door, armed. We will discuss the effect of limited manpower on Powhatan Indian warfare later.

Settlements

Indian people had called eastern Virginia "home" for over 12,000 years, but for most of that time they had lived as foragers moving about on the land, probably within territories that they knew well. They moved often enough that their campsites were ephemeral, with little evidence left be-hind. In the early millennia, the people lived in a world that was mainly terrestrial, since sea level had dropped during the Ice Age and the Chesapeake Bay and its estuaries were only rivers running through wooded land. As the Ice Age ended and the climate warmed up, people had to shift their emphasis to modern-day wild animals and plants and to greater dependence on food from the waterways. These waterways were expanding as the returning ocean flooded the coastal plain, which means that many waterfront campsites from those early times are now under water. By the Late Woodland period, sea levels had more or less stabilized (though coastal submergence still continues to the present day), and agriculture (in corn, beans, and squash) had arrived. The Indians' preference for waterfront living intensified, because the riverbanks have some of the best farming soils, and the requirements of cultivating crops led to somewhat less moving around. That meant more village remnants for archaeologists to find.

During the Late Woodland period, Indian people spent several months a year in their villages, with two dispersals (in late spring and late fall) for full-time foraging. These villages, however, were not "towns" except in name, for most Virginia Algonquians preferred to live in dispersed-house hamlets. Archaeologists have found few densely inhabited sites in the region, and those sites are not large. Most villages extensively excavated so far, and there are not many as yet, are scatters of a few dozen or so houses at most, with no guarantee that they were all contemporaneous with one another. We know from historical accounts that Powhatan agriculture was of the shifting horticulture variety, so farmers came and went and came again on any one part of a riverbank. Archaeologically, we find the postholes of houses built over older, defunct houses, likewise indicating reoccupation. Figure 2.13, at a site discussed in detail in chapter 2, is a good example, showing at least six house outlines, some of which either touch or overlap each other.

Houses were built where people felt like building them. There was no rigidly standard way of aligning them, nor the door-spaces in them (shown in the foreground of figure 1.2). Houses had rounded ends to make them more wind resistant, a necessity because their frameworks consisted of rather flimsy saplings. (John Smith wrote gratefully about being waked up by the shaking of a house where he was quartered, as attacking warriors scrambled in through the door.) The postholes inside the house shown in figure 1.2 may have come from poles that braced the house further while serving as corner posts for mat-curtained beds (described by English colonists) and allowing for a drying loft above head level.

Fig. 1.2. Posthole pattern of a house at the Great Neck site, with narrow door space at bottom center. Courtesy of VDHR.

Drying in the smoke of the hearth was a major Powhatan method of preserving food. The welter of postholes along the side wall of the house probably reflects a combination of repair and extra bracing. The pit in the central burned area of the floor is a hearth. (The large, squared-off pit is a by-product of the archaeologists' work, not an Indian feature.)

There was no material to use for window glass in Late Woodland times. The only light inside an Indian house came from the doors, the central fire, and the smoke hole over it. That combination makes for poor light to work in, so houses were used mainly for sleeping and storage. It is common to find Late Woodland villages with a scatter of postholes outside the house outlines. Those holes would represent drying frames and, for working while sheltered from sun or rain, open-sided sheds like the one shown in figure 1.3. Each hamlet would have had numerous sheds, for both men and women had continual manufacturing and repair jobs to do, and that kind of work went better if done while socializing. A result of this situation, coupled with the thin mat or bark walls of the houses, would have been a shortage of visual privacy and a near-absence of sonic privacy in the people's lives.

Subsistence

The Virginia Algonquians had a diet composed of a variety of domesticated and wild foods. All of their meat sources were wild ones: deer, wild turkey, raccoon and other mammals, turtles, ducks and geese, fish, and shellfish. Historical sources add that they ate eels. The only domesticated animals the people had were dogs, which are found buried in a few archaeological sites. Bones or shells of all the animals eaten show up in

Fig. 1.3. Houses and work-shed at Jamestown Settlement's Indian Village (1995). Courtesy of Helen C. Rountree.

Fig. 1.4. Trash pit half excavated to show stratigraphy. Courtesy of VDHR.

those Late Woodland trash pits so beloved by archaeologists. Indian people buried their garbage to avoid attracting wild animals at night (bears and full-grown raccoons can be a real hazard in the dark) and to keep scavengers, like their own dogs, from spreading bones and leaving a stink where people wanted to walk. Archaeologists carefully excavate these pits so as not to miss a single fish bone, if one is lurking down there. Typically, half the pit is dug first, to establish a visual image of its shape (fig. 1.4), and then the rest is carefully unearthed, with "finds" going into meticulously labeled bags (fig. 1.5).

Many of the Indians' plant foods were also wild, though the archaeological evidence for these is much slimmer. Seeds and nutshells have a chance of preservation in trash pits; seeds and corn kernels may also be burned to charcoal in hearths and preserved in carbonized form (fig. 1.6). They and the bones of small animals may also survive in "coprolites," or dried ancient excrement. Whoever deposited the feces in figure 1.7 had eaten a meal that included a fish vertebra. However, the list of plants known to have been ingested by Late Woodland Indian people is not as long as we would like it to be. They ate nuts in large quantities; a lot of the seeds of little barley (*Hordeum pusillum*), a field plant that many Eastern

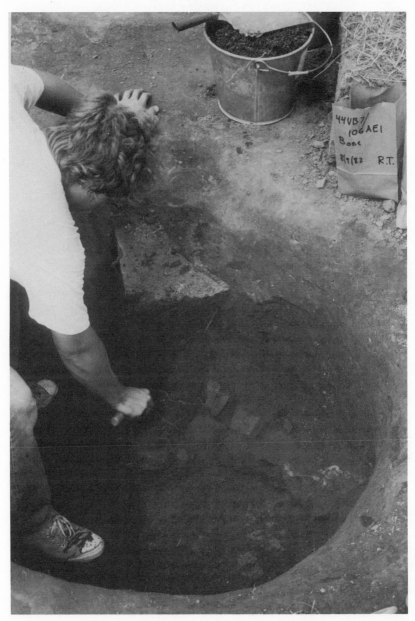

Fig. 1.5. Excavating the trash pit's other half. Courtesy of VDHR.

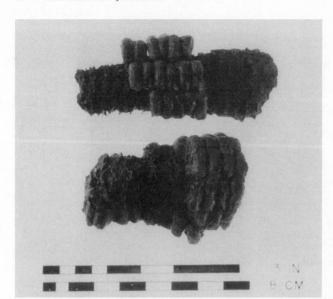

Fig. 1.6. Carbonized maize from the Trigg site in western Virginia. Courtesy of VDHR.

Woodland Indians apparently encouraged but did not fully cultivate; and corn, probably with beans and squash, since the three plants were so closely associated in the sensibilities of historical Woodland people. Other plants, such as tubers and greens, have left no evidence, and berry seeds are too tiny to preserve well for long. A more complete list of plant foods will be given in chapter 3, where historical observations fill in the gaps a bit.

Corn depletes the soil of nitrogen and other elements, unless steps are taken by fertilizing or crop rotation to make up the deficiency. Early English accounts of Virginia's natives make no mention of any fertilizer in Indian hands. Scholars have also found that the New England Indians probably began using fish only after one of their number spent time in England. Getting fish for fertilizer would have been work added to an already busy schedule for Virginia's Indians, and there is no evidence that they took the trouble. So cornfields had to be abandoned after several years, and new fields cleared (details in chapter 3). Hence the shifting cultivation that resulted in those overlapping houses.

Corn cultivation came rather late to the Virginia coastal plain: it arrived approximately A.D. 900. It was brought in from the south, a plant that was originally a small-kerneled grass native to central Mexico. Coastal Virginia's climate does not match that of the central Mexican highlands, so there were—and still are—times when corn crops failed. The main problem in eastern Virginia comes not from early or late frosts but rather from insufficient rain while the plants are growing. Corn needs at least moderate rainfall spaced throughout the 120 days or so that it takes to mature. In one summer out of three, on the average, Virginia's climate does not provide that evenly distributed watering. Hence it would have made no sense for the Powhatans and their predecessors to give up their foraging knowledge and pin all their hopes on the new domesticate. Relying on corn production would have required a horrific amount of work anyway: clearing of large fields by people who lacked large metal cutting tools or draft animals or plows to help them do it. Hence archaeologists find no evidence of heavy-duty agricultural tools or of large storage places where dried corn could have been kept.

Fig. 1.7. Coprolites, with closeup showing embedded fish vertebra and bones, from the Great Neck site. Courtesy of VDHR.

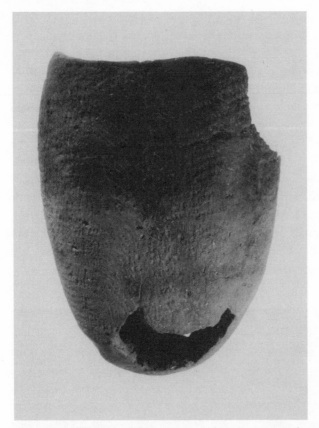

Fig. 1.8. Small Townsend fabric-impressed pot. Courtesy of VDHR.

Limited corn production also explains the reluctance of the Powhatan Indians to undertake the long-term feeding of sizable numbers of European visitors, whose foreignness demanded high-status food as hospitality. Corn, with the similarity of its ground-up version to wheat flour, was what the Spanish Jesuits (chapter 2) and the English colonists (chapter 5) wanted. But even if there had not been terrible droughts in progress when they arrived, these Europeans would soon have been out of luck. The Indian economy was simply not geared to support large numbers of nonrelatives indefinitely. As we shall see in chapter 3, even chiefs and their families had to work for their living.

The most durable objects that Indian people made during the Late Woodland period were pottery, usually found in broken pieces, and stone projectile points. Ceramics for much of the period were uniform throughout the Virginia coastal plain: the standard pottery types were Townsend shell-tempered wares with incised and/or fabric-impressed surface decoration (fig. 1.8). Virginia Indian pottery was not glazed or painted until the twentieth century, so Late Woodland pieces are more functional than decorative. The pots made were often large stewpots, with conical bottoms that could be pressed down into the coals of a low-burning open fire.

Late Woodland projectile points were triangular, coming in various sizes (fig. 1.9). Stone is limited in the soils of the coastal plain. Fieldstones are usually quartzite, which has larger crystals than are ideal for making straight, sharp edges (as shown by the rather rough sides of some of the points). Most finer-grained stone, which allows minute pressure flaking to straighten and sharpen a point's sides, had to come by trade from the fall line and beyond. Projectile points were hafted onto arrows or spears, depending on the size of the points. They could also be hafted, as in figure 1.10, onto a piece of antler to make a useful knife. This specimen, made of fine-grained chert and showing pressure flaking along the edges, comes

Fig. 1.9. Late Woodland projectile points. Courtesy of VDHR.

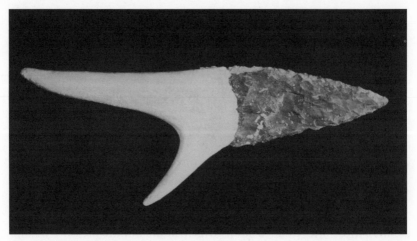

Fig. 1.10. Stone knife hafted onto an antler handle, from a site in western Virginia. Courtesy of VDHR.

from the Shannon Site in western Virginia; no hafted knife has as yet been found by archaeologists in Virginia's coastal plain, although they were undoubtedly used there.

There is no evidence, either archaeological or historical, for extensive trade specialization among the Virginia Algonquians. Each family procured the food and produced the tools and clothing it needed. However, the native people were like modern people in valuing things that were rare, usually imported objects that were also exotic. Many of the nonlocal items found in Late Woodland sites were shiny and of unusual color—special qualities in an Indian world in which most things had dull exteriors and colors that ranged from light beige to dark brown or black, sometimes with a rusty tinge included.

Status Symbols

Freshwater pearls are reported by colonist Gabriel Archer as occurring in quantity in the reaches of the James River around Weyanoke Point. Today the major pearl-producing mussel beds are in Pennsylvania and points north. Freshwater pearls, being naturally iridescent, are still moderately valuable as items of jewelry today; in Powhatan times they were considered major investments.

Copper was imported from the Great Lakes, or perhaps from a few sites in central-western Virginia and the Appalachians; archaeologists have not agreed about its source. The metal was pure copper, of a reddish color, and so soft that it could be used only for jewelry. It was fashioned into tubes like the ones in figure 1.11, which were found in one of the burials at the Paspahegh town described in chapter 2; these tubes are now reburied along with the bones of their owner.

Shell beads and larger shells made into pendants were also highly valued by the Virginia Algonquians. The shell for these came from salt water: whelk ("conch") shells for the long tubular white beads and the large whitish slabs made into pendants, and the shells of quahogs (hard clams) for white or dark blue disk beads. Both clamshells and whelk shells are very hard and difficult to work on, even with modern steel tools; the breakage rate when using stone tools must have added considerably to the value of finished items. All the beads and pendants that have been unearthed by archaeologists have lost their original shine after having

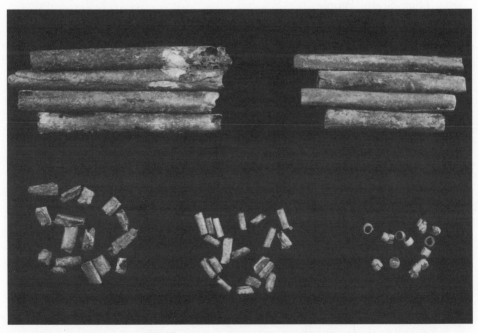

Fig. 1.11. Tubular copper beads in standard Late Woodland forms. Courtesy of VDHR.

been buried for several centuries. When new, they were not only shiny, they almost glowed, especially the clamshell beads.

Last but not least, there were dyeing roots, which show up in historical accounts but not in the archaeological record. The most highly valued paint was made with puccoon (*Lithospermum caroliniense*), which does not now and probably did not then grow in the Virginia territory of the Algonquians. According to modern botanical manuals, it is found in Sussex County, Virginia, which was Nottoway Indian (Iroquoian speakers) territory and also in several counties in South Carolina. That means that the roots were imported from the south. By 1607 a trading route, perhaps mainly for this commodity, had been established long enough for Powhatan's emissary to have learned the "Anoeg" (Tuscarora) language; the route was probably far older. Paint made of puccoon produced a mulberry-red color, according to colonist William Strachey. This was a color that did not otherwise occur in the Powhatan world, except seasonally in berries.

High-Status People

The highly valued goods described here may simply have been acquired by opportunistic people and used for personal decoration during the Late Woodland period. Or they may have been deliberately traded for by people who were becoming politically and militarily more prominent, that is, chiefs. Chiefs in other better recorded parts of the world have wealth that can be shown off to establish their claim to high status. Such validating of their importance means a certain amount of hoarding of movable wealth, as well as being able to feast guests, live in fancier houses than ordinary people, have multiple spouses, and receive special burial at death. As it happens, the archaeological record in Virginia has so far given us little evidence of these activities before the Protohistoric period (ca. 1500–1607). More elaborate houses have been found, but they date to the Protohistoric, as may the very few "status burials" of important people thus far discovered.[1] Later historic observers tell us that wealth and the bodies of dead chiefs were stored aboveground in temples; that custom would leave only a slight archaeological imprint for us to find. So the issue of whether or not chiefs were present for much of the Late Woodland period cannot be currently settled.

Warfare

The Late Woodland was probably not a totally peaceful time in Virginia. We can say this based upon ethnographic analogy. No human culture without conflict has ever been found by historians or cultural anthropologists. All human populations encountered by anthropologists or described by historians have had people with differing personalities and differing abilities to follow the rules, whatever the local rules may be. And the needs of local populations, in relation to their neighbors, can change due to natural stresses like droughts or human stresses such as overpopulation. So it is safe to say that occasionally—and only occasionally, because everybody had to work hard in order to eat—there were lawbreakers and people at odds with each other within the hamlets. There would also have been strained and even violent relations between Virginia Algonquian communities at times, like the one between the Rappahannocks and Moraughtacunds that Captain John Smith observed in 1608. Indian oral tradition, gathered by both Spanish and English visitors, further asserted a "traditional" enmity between the Algonquians and the Siouan-speaking Monacans and Mannahoacs to the west. There is, however, so far no clear-cut archaeological evidence of conflict either between language groups or between communities: no burned-down towns, no skeletons with tomahawk fractures or arrowheads embedded in the bones, no mass graves of massacre victims, hastily buried.

One thing we can safely say about conflicts during the Late Woodland period: they would have been conducted on a small scale. Small populations don't have enough personnel to spend them freely in military endeavors. So figure 1.12, with its views of masses of Indians attacking a few Europeans, goes against both Indian logic and English colonists' accounts of the usual native method of fighting. That method was guerilla warfare, a kind of competition that better allowed for the individual shows of prowess that the Powhatans are known to have valued among their people. Great deeds by individuals were rewarded with prestige and also with new personal names, culture traits found widely and therefore probably very anciently in native North America. Early seventeenth-century Powhatan men fighting in small raiding parties in order to earn new names were very likely following a male imperative that went many generations back into the Late Woodland period.

C.Smith taketh the King of Pamavkee prisoner 1608

Fig. 1.12. Robert Vaughan's 1624 engraving of a "short" Captain John Smith overcoming a "tall" Opechancanough in 1609.

The Bodies of the Dead

Prehistoric Virginians treated their dead with respect. The methods of treatment varied considerably, possibly from family to family, since multiple methods of burial are found in each area of the region and during all parts of the Late Woodland period. There are many primary burials, in which the corpse was placed directly in a shallow grave, usually in the vicinity of a house. Other bodies were given a secondary, or two-part, disposal. If not initially buried, the body was wrapped to keep out predators and kept aboveground until only (or mainly) bones were left. Then, on a certain day every few years, all the local families that had lost members gathered up their relatives' bones, cleaned them if necessary, put them into bundles, and placed the bundles in an ossuary, or common grave, that had been opened for the occasion. The custom of secondary burial serves archaeologists well, since it concentrates the dead in one small, findable area rather than scattering them separately around the houses of families who were moving up and down the shorelines as their agricultural pursuits necessitated.

Archaeologists disturb the dead, which disturbs the modern Indians in Virginia. There are no pictures of skeletons in this book, in deference to the feelings of the Indian people with whom the authors, especially Rountree, work. But skeletons, once dug and analyzed and before being reburied, can tell us many things about the lives of the people they represent.

Skeletal analyses can puncture some historical stereotypes about the Virginia Indians. Stable isotopes in bones can tell us whether the people were eating much corn or living mainly on wild foods—that is, whether they were settled or nomadic. The Late Woodland Virginia Algonquians are revealed as being settled. Skeletal measurements can also puncture the kind of propaganda that John Smith wrote and that figure 1.12 suggests: that the big, bad Powhatans were much taller than the poor, vulnerable English. The reality was less spectacular. Late Woodland Indian men from the coastal plain averaged 5 feet, 7.1 inches (170.4 centimeters) versus 5 feet, 6.5 inches for seventeenth-century London men and 5 feet, 8.5 inches for modern American white men. The Indian women averaged 5 feet, 3.5 inches (159.2 centimeters) versus 5 feet, 1 inch for seventeenth-century London women and 5 feet, 4.2 inches for modern American white women. John Smith's view was probably skewed: he himself may not have reached average height, while many of the Powhatan men he saw in the Indian towns were the chiefs' bodyguards, also not of average height.

We can generalize about Indian life expectancy, thanks to studies of skeletons in several Late Woodland ossuary sites in both Virginia and Maryland (Maryland is included to make a larger, more reliable sample). A baby's average life expectancy at birth was in the low twenties, which takes into account a high rate of infant mortality. A child who survived to the age of five could expect to live to about the age of thirty-five. Nearly all Indian females were dead by age thirty-five, nearly all Indian men by age fifty. Fewer than 4 percent of Virginia and Maryland Algonquians lived past the age of fifty. The men's greater longevity, found in all human populations before the advent of modern antiseptic practices and birthing techniques, was due to the fact that they did not bear babies.

John Smith and many other early European visitors to eastern North America reported a firmly held tradition among the native people: that women had children with ease. Once again, the reality was less spectacular. Late Woodland women were very physically fit, which probably helped during birthing. But they were as prone as other two-legged human females to breech births and other complications,[2] as well as to hemorrhaging and to infection caused by conditions that were clean but not sterile. Too much blood loss could leave a woman alive but vulnerable to opportunistic viruses and bacteria. Therefore many women died during or after a birth (archaeologists sometimes find a near-or full-term fetal skeleton buried along with that of the mother), and very few of them lived to see menopause. Infant and young child mortality was also high in Late Woodland villages: one-fifth to one-third of all children at various sites died before the age of five. The latter rate, one-third, is roughly comparable to the rate in European cities of that era.

The bones of both the men and the women were more robust than those of modern people. In fact, the women's bones were denser and tougher than those of most present-day males. That testifies to a very physical, active working life for both sexes. Early colonial accounts only describe what that life was like for the men; the use of living history enables us to do the same for the women (see chapter 3). Intense physical work does not agree with everybody. Some people become as tough as old shoe leather and stay active into their nineties. Most other people fall by the wayside, as the cemetery evidence shows. Arthritis began afflicting prehistoric Virginians when they were in their thirties, unlike modern Americans, who are first affected in their fifties. The bodies of prehistoric thirty-year-olds were beginning to wear out.

Further weakening of people we would regard as relatively young came from infections when teeth went bad, as well as from malnutrition when they lost too many teeth to chew their food. Cavities and abscesses were fairly common among Late Woodland people because of poor tooth care (stick-cleaning is not enough) combined with a fairly starchy diet. Earlier people had lacked corn and had eaten more tough wild foods, causing fewer cavities but more worn-down teeth. Seventeenth-century Europeans, on the other hand, ate mainly domesticated plants, which had been bred through the centuries to be less fibrous and to cook up into mush; their teeth were in poorer shape than anyone else's.

A significant number of Late Woodland individuals of all ages suffered from infectious diseases caused by their living more of the year in bigger villages than did their late Middle Woodland (A.D. 200–900) predecessors, who spent more of the year dispersing into camping groups while foraging. The evidence of periods of illness lies in the teeth of some individuals. In a culture that lacked tube feeding, one that also occasionally faced famines, seriously ill children could not eat and became malnourished; that condition caused a hiatus in the formation of their permanent teeth, the resulting area of thinner enamel being labeled "enamel hypoplasia." People carried that evidence of childhood illness for the rest of their lives and beyond. Late Woodland people also suffered from infections, the evidence being in their bones. Periostitis, or new bone deposited over preexisting cortex, making abnormally thick bone with a porous surface, appears in about half the skeletons at some archaeological sites. Periostitis is caused both by trauma to the bone, as in severe bruising, and by localized infections, as in scratches and wounds that do not heal properly. Late Woodland people were vulnerable to both kinds of mishap in the ordinary course of their work. Even without going to war, a man who chases deer for a living is likely to fall occasionally and hurt himself. Men and women who work part of the time in a forest will encounter briars, often without having water and medicine with them to clean the resulting scratches.

It is hard to say exactly which infectious diseases the Virginia native people suffered from. Seventeenth-century English medical diagnoses were entirely different from those made by doctors today, and much less precise. The English were more fatalistic about people dying young, so that in the case of Pocahontas's death, for instance, neither her symptoms nor their supposed cause were even mentioned by her contemporaries. (She did *not* die from the smoky atmosphere of London; she had grown up in an even smokier Powhatan house.)

On the other hand, we can say something about diseases the Indians did *not* have. Viral diseases such as influenza and the common cold, and eruptive diseases such as chickenpox, were not part of the Indian experience before Europeans began visiting American shores. The best evidence of this is eye-witness accounts from other parts of the Americas of the horrendous mortality these ailments, relatively mild for Europeans, caused among Native Americans. In places where there were densely packed cities, as in Central America and Peru, Native American mortality reached 90 percent in some episodes. There is no comparable evidence of such a calamitous dying-off of people in Virginia, where scattered hamlets were the preferred form of settlement. No mass graves with bodies pitched in anyhow and hurriedly covered over have been found anywhere in the state; the ossuaries mentioned are far more orderly. There are also no clear-cut historical records of epidemics in Virginia, except for two references in passing to high mortality. In 1608 John Smith heard about numerous people dying after viewing the recently dead bodies of two children on the Eastern Shore. In 1617 a pestilence killed some English and more Indians; the malady may have been the same one that killed nearly all the native people living near Massachusetts Bay before the Pilgrims arrived in 1620. Unfortunately, no one recorded the symptoms of either disease, so that we might have a chance of identifying it. We can say only that some infectious diseases were new to the Powhatans and caused some unusual but not disastrous mortality.

One identifiable illness remarked on by the earliest English colonists was syphilis ("the pox"), which was observed to be common among the eastern Virginia natives. There is not clear evidence of whether the lesions seen were from the venereal disease or from related but nonvenereal maladies (yaws, pinta). From skeletal evidence outside Virginia, though, one or more of these diseases appears to have existed among American Indians before the coming of Europeans.

Family, Religion, and Closeness to the Land

There are other, more general, things we can say about prehistoric Late Woodland Indian society on the coastal plain, based upon ethnographic analogy with other human cultures. For one thing, all human beings need to have a "backup system" available: There may be times of illness, injury, natural disaster, or attack by other humans. Most people produce children, and human offspring require a phenomenal amount of continuous care. Even two parents securely married to each other cannot by themselves handle all the necessary nurturing and training added to making a living for two or more decades without calling in at least occasional outside help. (Our schoolteachers provide extensive outside help.) That was especially true before the discovery of antibiotics, which can drastically shorten recovery times. There are also times when multiple adults of one or both sexes are needed just to get a necessary job done, for instance Powhatan house building, done by women (see chapter 3). For nonindustrial societies in which governments and/or religious organizations are not expected to provide many services, the family has always been the tried and true backup system. So it must have been for the Powhatans and their predecessors.

Virginia Algonquian society was a kin-based society. That means that the family you are born into determines where you grow up, establishes your main friendships in childhood, trains you to be a competent adult of whatever sex, eliminates certain people from eligibility to marry you, pushes you towards marrying other people who would fit well within the entire group, provides you with working partners in various jobs including rearing the family's (not just your own) children, makes various political alliances possible or impossible for you, protects you from being victimized by aggressive nonrelatives, forms local and sometimes supralocal groups to engage with you in religious worship, looks after you in sickness and old age, and assembles the personnel to bury you when you die from all the exertion. Details of exactly who was expected to do what in Late Woodland Virginia are missing from the archaeological record and, in large part, from the historical documents as well. But we can be certain that family membership was the pivotal identity for Powhatan people on a day-to-day basis.

Another inference can be drawn about the Virginia Algonquians, based upon ethnographic analogy with other Native Americans: Their religion was a "tribal" one, particular to themselves, geared to their homeland, and not aimed at evangelizing others. The contrast with "universal" religions like Christianity and Islam is fundamental. Universal religions aim at proselytizing their tenets while commemorating people and events that happened at distant times and often in faraway countries. The overall message of such a religion can be well worth hearing, but for many people it is far less vivid than practices based upon belief in localized forces in the here and now. The Powhatans and their predecessors had not encountered any universal religion before 1570, when the Spanish Jesuits landed (see chapter 2). Their religion would have provided them instead with holy places close to home, as well as given them rituals aimed at propitiating and then thanking the superhuman forces that affected their well-being year after year within their territory. The English did not record much about the native holy places or rituals; there is more about Indian deities and the power of the priests. But it is safe to infer the homegrown nature and the vividness of Powhatan religion in the people's lives, giving them deep attachments to a religion which in turn bound them to their territory.

Last but not least, a phrase that has become hackneyed in modern rhetoric was true for the Powhatans: they really were "closer to the land" than Europeans were then or modern Americans are now. It was not only a matter of religion (poorly recorded) and oral tradition (worse recorded) that invested various parts of the home landscape with meaning. It was also a matter of actually making a living by working with what the land produced naturally. Only part of the Indian people's diet was of agricultural origin. Literally everything else—meat, clothing, tools, houses, canoes—came from wild or naturally occurring sources. As we shall see in chapter 3, people had to know precisely where in their territory these sources were to be found, at what season they were most readily collectible, and what kind of scheduling was needed to procure and prepare them with the least expenditure of precious energy.[3]

Indian men and women knew their turf and the things on and in it the way today's "dedicated shoppers" know where various things can be bought, at what quality, and for what prices. For both sets of people, the intense interest is a response to a challenge. For the Indians, it was also a matter of survival.

Notes

1. The element of doubt about dating comes from one burial, found at Great Neck in Virginia Beach. The body was that of a grown man, interred with a wealth of shell beads to indicate his high social position. The grave was robbed the night after it was discovered, so no dating of the skeleton was possible. The Great Neck site was a Protohistoric town, but Middle and Late Woodland period elements were found there too.

2. The pelvic bone structure of erect, bipedal humans has a hole through which people excrete and women bear children. For thousands of generations, the bearing-down of a biped's body weight on the pelvis has given this hole a tendency to narrow in, a propensity at odds with the big-brained babies trying to get through. This "obstetrical dilemma" has a species-wide result: longer time in labor and with more stretching and tearing than in any other animal.

3. Indian hemp (*Apocynum cannabinum*), for instance, whose stem is a prime source of thread and string, is gatherable from ripening time in late June through late spring, when new plants overpower last year's dry stalks. However, Rountree and the Jamestown Settlement Indian Village staff have found, by "reinventing the wheel," that the only efficient way to deal with the plants is to gather them after late January, when they have naturally dried out. Before that, the tough plants require cutting of both stalks and branches, and their milky sap prevents extracting the fibers of the stalks. By altering the gathering time, we go back to the village with bundles of dry stalks ready for defibering, rather than with bulky bundles of wilting plants that have to be dried and then processed.

2

The Protohistoric Period (ca. 1500–1607)

"Protohistoric" refers to the time just before recorded history, in which there were occasional tantalizing visits by literate outsiders. In the case of Virginia, those outsiders were both Spanish and English. Our job as scholars is to flesh out the Protohistoric period using archaeology and "historical" oral accounts given by Indian people to the colonists (that is, accounts from Early Contact historic times about what had been going on before recorded history).

The Rise of Powhatan as Paramount Chief

The most important development in eastern Virginia during the Protohistoric period was the appearance of strong chiefs, including "paramount" chiefs (that is, regional chiefs who ruled district chiefs). When the English arrived, all of the Algonquian-speaking districts (tribes, to use a hackneyed term) except the Chickahominies were dominated by chiefs, each of whom had subsidiary leaders in their satellite hamlets. The district chiefs were either subjects of or, in the case of the strong Patawomeck chief, heavily influenced by, the paramount chief Powhatan. The hierarchy of chiefs is rather a complex setup for people to have when they do not practice intensive agriculture that generates large surpluses to support those politicians. If Powhatan's organization had survived longer without interference, perhaps some shift toward intensive food production would have occurred.

Powhatan's organization was a phenomenon that originated during the Protohistoric period. John Smith learned from the man himself that he had inherited six districts, three on the James River near the fall line (he took his name from the town of Powhatan, near present-day Richmond) and three on the York. Inheritance means that his predecessor, whom he never named (perhaps a taboo on the name of the dead?), was a paramount chief already. As Powhatan's heirs were his full or half-siblings through his mother, and then his sisters' children, in a matrilineal system, his predecessor would therefore have been his mother or a sibling of his mother. Nothing was recorded about how Powhatan's predecessor became the governor of six districts, or when it happened. Instead, John Smith tells us that this astute politician, born about 1540, proceeded to add districts to his original six, using intimidation when possible and force when necessary. By 1607 he had about thirty districts in his organization.

Intimidation might have been possible with the warriors of six districts to back him up, and it would have been an easier weapon to use in the face of stepped-up pressures from enemy Indians in the Protohistoric period (see below). As for taking over whole districts by force, we have several accounts of how it had been done. In about 1595 the Kecoughtans, in what is now Hampton, lost their old chief, who had consistently refused to join Powhatan's organization and who apparently had the military acumen to resist being conquered. The new chief was less able. According to colonist William Strachey, Powhatan staged a major raid on the Kecoughtans' only town. The town's chief, its women and children, and perhaps some of its surviving men were taken prisoner and transported to a central town in Powhatan's domain. Their place at Kecoughtan was taken by loyalist families headed by Pochins, a son (and therefore not an heir) of Powhatan's. These loyalists were the "Kecoughtans" met by the Jamestown colonists. The original Kecoughtans eventually made their peace with the paramount chief and in 1608 were allowed to settle peacefully at Piankatank, whose people Powhatan had just removed after a raid because they had displeased him in some way. Just before or just after the end of the Protohistoric period, Powhatan also depopulated the Chesapeake district, where Norfolk and Virginia Beach now are, in the same way. Operations like these added to Powhatan's reputation as a major force to be reckoned with.

Scholars have long tried to explain why Powhatan was able to aggrandize himself as rapidly as he did. He acted, after all, largely against the will of the people who became his subjects, a scenario that many modern Americans find distasteful. The older, easier answer was that "the Indians" sensed a serious threat from "the whites" who began to visit in the

1570s, so they banded together. However, that answer depends heavily upon hindsight and is tainted with Eurocentric perceptions. Powhatan's expansion was probably not caused by "interracial" affairs, since for the native people in 1607, there were no "Indians" and "whites." Instead there were, for instance, Pamunkeys and Nansemonds (two of the nearly thirty or so groups labeled "Powhatans" by modern anthropologists), and there were Massawomecks and Monacans, and so forth. There were "English" and "Spanish" in Indian thinking but no monolithic category—yet—of "whites," because Europeans contacted the Virginia Algonquians only about once or twice a decade after 1560. Europeans of various kinds were thus potential allies as much as potential enemies, and their intrusions along the Atlantic coast may not have seemed especially ominous. On the other hand, the Virginia Algonquians knew of enemy Indians to the west and northwest who made themselves felt at least annually and sometimes more often. Therefore it is not surprising that the earliest evidence for the development of strong chiefs shows these military leaders appearing near the fall line, on the Indian-Indian frontier, not along the Atlantic coast on the Indian-European frontier. Powhatan could do what he did because of Indian actions, not European ones.

The Protohistoric period saw Native American people moving in on the coastal Algonquian-speakers (fig. 2.1) either by means of raids or under more friendly circumstances. Either way, they exerted pressure on the local people to adapt to changed conditions. One possible movement of people, as either traders or settlers, is represented by the Potomac Creek complex of ceramics (one of their major townsites is described below). The tribal identity and language spoken by many of the incomers is unknown, so that they do not appear in figure 2.1. Early English colonists could have asked about such matters, but they took what they saw at face value, as did later historians. It is only late-twentieth-century archaeologists who have recognized a Protohistoric movement of goods and perhaps people. We coauthors discount the Massawomecks as the culture-bearers, since their warriors' means of transportation points to a home base far to the northwest. Whoever they were, the people introducing Potomac Creek wares to the Piscataways and the Patawomecks (who are included in "Powhatans" in figure 2.1) came from the Virginia and Maryland piedmont, where their pottery is found archaeologically at an earlier date than at the two sites of the Algonquian-speakers (their earli-

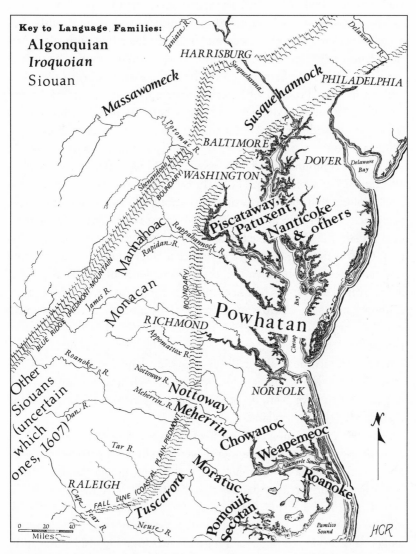

Fig. 2.1. Map of the Powhatans and their neighbors. Courtesy of Helen C. Rountree.

est dates: early 1300s). Other cultural practices may have been taught as well that do not show up in the archaeological record.

The Massawomecks and/or Pocoughtraonacks were apparently Iroquoian-speakers, though they cannot be identified either with a Five Nations Iroquois group or with any other Iroquoian-speaking tribe such as the Eries. They were known to come from the eastern Great Lakes area, and during the Protohistoric period they appeared in raiding parties along the Potomac River, wielding metal hatchets bought from French traders and paddling birch-bark canoes made back in their homeland. (The paper birch is a cold-climate tree, rarely found south or east of the Pennsylvania mountains.) The Massawomecks were fierce warriors, like all Eastern Woodland men. The early English colonists got the impression, though, that they were especially feared, and the reason must have been their canoes. Birch-bark canoes are more fragile than the log dugouts used in the Chesapeake basin, but they are far lighter in weight and therefore much faster. A war party in such a canoe could make a lightning raid on a coastal plain town and then escape without any fear at all of being overtaken. Yet the Massawomecks seem not to have wanted to encounter a new set of Europeans. After a single meeting with John Smith in 1608, they "stood him up" for a second meeting. The English trader Henry Fleet met them as late as 1632, after which they disappeared from *any* English records in either Virginia or Maryland. No more was heard from Great Lakes Iroquoian-speakers until well into the seventeenth century, when Five Nations people, especially Senecas, began making themselves felt in Maryland.

Another Iroquoian-speaking force was beginning to make itself felt from the north: the Susquehannocks were sending out parties from their lower Susquehanna River homeland, down the Chesapeake into Maryland Algonquian territory, a move that the friendly Virginia Algonquians would have heard about. Actual raids by the Susquehannocks did not take place on the Virginia side of the Potomac until the 1670s; but they had been occurring in Maryland for a century, moving gradually southward. John Smith met some Susquehannocks, and his description makes them sound like giants (fig. 2.2). Archaeology in Pennsylvania, however, shows them to have been only a little taller than the Virginia Algonquians.

Last but not least, raiding went on between the Algonquian-speakers and Siouan-speakers (Monacan and Mannahoac alliances) on a regular

Fig. 2.2. The Susquehannock man pictured on John Smith's map, engraved by Robert Hole in 1612. A wolf's head pouch similar to the man's quiver is in a Swedish museum.

basis. The Spanish Jesuits who attempted to found a mission on the York River in 1570 heard that there were native people to the west who attacked the local Indians annually, "at the fall of the leaf." It is likely that the Powhatans did the same in return. It is also probable that they provoked the Monacans and Mannahoacs further by their practice, recorded by later English writers, of conducting large-scale deer drives around the fall line. The origin of the enmity is impossible to know; it may simply have been Siouan middlemen seeming to overcharge for local or imported copper. Nonetheless, hostilities continued until 1611, the Powhatans and Monacans renouncing their enmity only in the face of a new, common enemy: the English.

Powhatan as Part of a Larger Pattern

It was probably in response to these hostile movements that some of the Virginia Algonquians began to consolidate their local groups, perhaps already led by chiefs, into stronger military patterns: widespread alliances in the east and strong, if not paramount, chiefs in the inner coastal plain. We have already described the oral tradition about paramount chiefs in Powhatan's case, and archaeological evidence also points to similar consolidations among the Virginia Algonquians in general.

One kind of evidence for the strengthening of ties is ceramic. Toward the end of the Late Woodland period, there was a change in the pottery that the women made.[1] Where shell-tempered Townsend ware had previously been the standard throughout the Virginia coastal plain, now it became a minority ware in three major areas (fig. 2.3). In each area, and in the non-Virginia area adjacent to it, a new ceramic style rose to dominance. Many female pottery-makers were perhaps now using the new styles and also marrying primarily within their own limited areas instead of moving freely around coastal Virginia. There are also eyewitness and oral-tradition accounts of chiefdoms or far-flung alliances being on the scene in these areas.

In the first major area, the inner coastal plain of the Potomac River basin, a new ware became the primary one: sand-tempered or crushed-quartz-tempered Potomac Creek ware in plain and cord-marked variants. Later historical accounts show this region to have been one of relatively heavy human population and two well-established chiefdoms, the Patawomecks in Virginia and the Piscataways in Maryland.

In the second area, sand-tempered or crushed-quartz-tempered Gaston-Cashie wares are found in a large region stretching from the fall line of the James (Powhatan's home territory) down to Roanoke Rapids in North Carolina's inner coastal plain. The version most preferred along the James was simple stamped. The region corresponds to a trading area mentioned in very early English accounts, which speak of Powhatan's

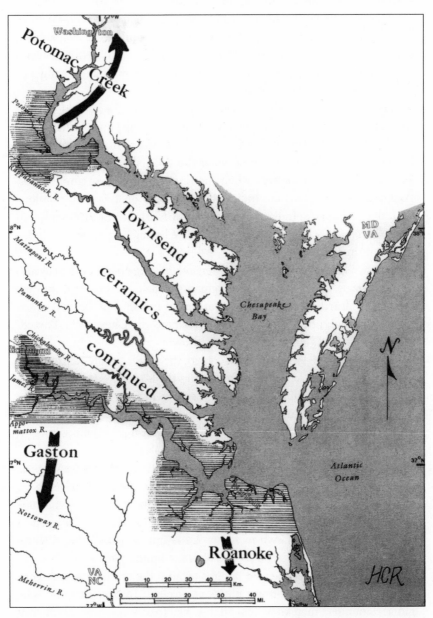

Fig. 2.3. Map of Protohistoric ceramic types. Courtesy of Helen C. Rountree.

sending the Weyanock chief as his emissary to trade with the Indians (perhaps Tuscaroras) to the south and southwest. The major commodities traded for may have been puccoon and copper, which were available by open trade to the Tuscaroras but not to Powhatan in his own territories (see chapter 1). But apparently the trade resulted in marital exchanges of women (pottery-makers) as well.

Shell-tempered, simple-stamped Roanoke ware is a kind of pottery found in the third area, from the lower reaches of the James River southward to Roanoke Island in the Carolina Sounds region. Chiefdoms were in existence in the former area when the Spanish visited in the early 1570s, and in the latter area when the English came in the mid-1580s. And various Carolina chiefs indicated to their visitors that their relations with the Chesapeake Indians in what is now Norfolk and Virginia Beach were friendly. Intermarriage appears to have been going on as well, judging from the pottery.

Another kind of evidence of a defensive pulling-together is palisades around towns. The archaeological remains of palisades are still limited, owing to a dearth of complete excavations of Indian sites, but, taken together with John Smith's observations around the Chesapeake Bay region, it looks as though densely settled towns surrounded by palisades occurred in most frontier areas. Elsewhere the native people continued to live in dispersed settlements of houses and fields scattered along the waterways. Both kinds of settlements are shown in figure 2.4, which is an early eighteenth-century engraving based upon de Bry's 1590 engravings, which in turn were based on two 1585 paintings by John White; in *all* of the versions the palisade was depicted inaccurately.

Authentic Late Woodland–Early Contact period palisades in Virginia consisted of upright sapling-stakes set into the ground a few inches apart, as John White indicates. It is lines of postmolds like these that archaeologists find at palisaded sites (fig. 2.5; see also 2.11 and 2.12). However, a palisade like the one shown in figure 2.4 is unfinished (perhaps White had his artistic reasons). The second phase of building may have been to weave durable, densely-leaved boughs around the stakes; the red cedar used in modern duck-hunting blinds is excellent for that purpose. Virginia Algonquian men knew that all they had to do was to prevent enemy Indian sharpshooters from seeing in and taking aim. A palisade—and a double one like that shown in the engraving (fig. 2.4)—made of sizable trees set closer together would require far too much time and labor with

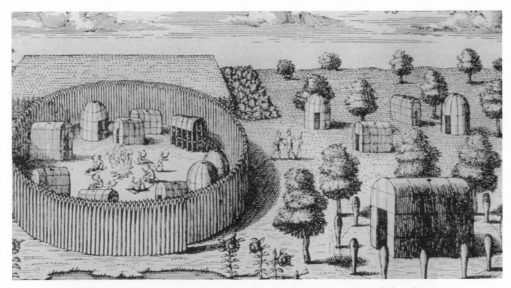

Fig. 2.4. Simon Gribelin's 1705 engraving of Indian towns, one palisaded and one dispersed. Based on de Bry originals of 1590.

stone hatchets to be worthwhile, at least until European artillery came onto the scene.

Palisades have either been found archaeologically or reported historically in the following places: Powhatan town near the falls of the James (historical); Patawomeck at the northward turn of the Potomac River (archaeological); the Buck site on the Chickahominy River (archaeological); the Indian town at Flowerdew Hundred, on the James River near its confluence with the Appomattox (archaeological); and the Great Neck site near Lynnhaven Inlet in Virginia Beach (archaeological). It is likely that more locations will be added in the future. The known palisaded sites are all in places of military significance. Powhatan and Patawomeck were both towns very close to the fall line in places where Protohistoric ceramics indicate a tightening-up of relations with adjacent coastal-plain peoples. The Great Neck site is in the third area where ceramics indicate that non-Virginia alliances had developed. The Buck site is in the Chickahominy Indian territory, and that tribe was still refusing to join Powhatan's domain in 1607, partly by being "lusty and warlike." And the Flowerdew Hundred site is near the Appomattox River, which probably was serving, as it did through the seventeenth century, as a water route into the piedmont to the southwest.

Fig. 2.5. Exposed palisade line at the Shannon site in western Virginia. Courtesy of VDHR.

In addition to local consolidation, there is archaeological evidence of chiefdoms in the Protohistoric period, though that evidence does not extend to the paramount chieftaincy that historical records tell us was developing. The evidence lies mainly in house remains and high-status goods.

Houses for chiefs were bigger and more sturdily built than those of ordinary people. One example was the largest house at Jordan's Point, which will be described later in this chapter. This building would not have shaken upon people's entry, as did the dwelling that John Smith lodged in, mentioned in chapter 1. It also cost at least twice the labor to build. Another house, this one at the Great Neck site (fig. 2.6), used saplings large enough to be considered small trees (average nearly five inches in diameter) for its framework. "Mansions" like these may reflect a community building effort, parallel to the later-recorded community work in raising a special field of corn for the chief's use.

High-status goods in the Protohistoric period continued to be imported: copper, perhaps formed into fancy pendants like the one found at the Richlands Hospital site in Tazewell County (fig. 2.7); freshwater pearls; shell beads and gorgets like the better-preserved ones from the

Trigg site in Radford (fig. 2.8); and puccoon. There may also have been rare stone items such as the chlorite pipe that was found in Nottoway Indian territory at the Hand site (fig. 2.9). Puccoon had to come from a great distance, through multiple middlemen, to arrive at Powhatan's home territory. The other materials would have been available either locally (pearls) or through one set of middlemen/allies (for instance, dealing with the Tuscaroras for copper, in the face of Monacan and Mannahoack hostility)—with the exception of shells. Large marine shells for ornaments came from coastal beaches, which were controlled by Algonquian-speakers outside of Powhatan's original six districts. Expanding his domain eastward to include them, after which he could monopolize the shells, was a sensible tactical move on Powhatan's part, and one that he was completing only as the Jamestown colony was founded.

Fig. 2.6. House pattern with larger than average timber holes at the Great Neck site. Courtesy of VDHR.

Fig. 2.7. Protohistoric copper pendant from the Richlands Hospital site in western Virginia. Courtesy of VDHR.

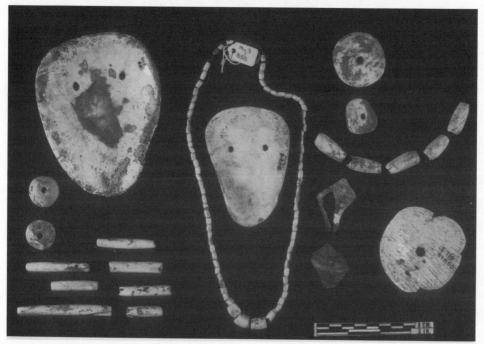

Fig. 2.8. Shell ornaments from the Trigg site in western Virginia. Courtesy of VDHR.

Fig. 2.9. Chlorite pipe from the Hand site. Courtesy of VDHR.

With chiefs now on the scene, we can hope to find evidence of their hoarding of high-status goods recorded by the English. After all, the richest man in the district would have looked more impressive than anyone else when he dressed up, and he also would have had the means of paying warriors to execute raids on enemies and disobedient subjects alike. However, most of the Virginia Algonquian VIPs—including Powhatan himself—foiled the archaeologists by storing their valuables and being buried themselves after death in temples, aboveground structures that left only postmolds behind them. Worse yet for archaeologists, many temples were away from the towns, out in the woods where finding postmolds is a matter of chance.

The major exception to this scenario of being unable to find the bodies and treasure of chiefs is at the site of Patawomeck, on the fringe of Powhatan's sphere of influence. At Patawomeck, nineteenth-century investigators (we will not call them archaeologists) found an early seventeenth-century high-status burial with a wealth of shell beads and also a large shell gorget made into a maskette (lower left in figure 2.10). The maskette's face has the weeping-eye motif that has been found widely on decorated goods throughout the Southeast, where the Mississippian culture prevailed.

The maskette at Patawomeck is only one indication that the chief of that community, at least, was part of a truly far-flung trade network, one

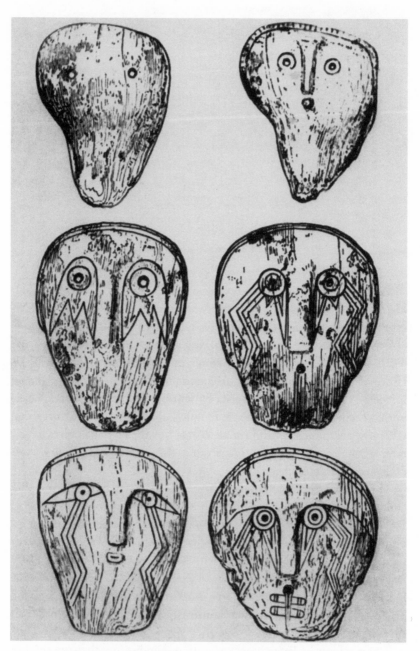

Fig. 2.10. Shell maskettes from Patawomeck and other sites. Courtesy of VDHR.

that was probably either established or enhanced by his people's contact with the bringers of the Potomac Creek complex from the northwest. The other indication of long-distance connections here is an English document of 1621 saying that one Patawomeck chief possessed a "China [Chinese-style] Boxe." It was made of palmetto and lined with taffeta, both components being regrettably biodegradable. The chief said he had gotten the box from "mountain" people far to the southwest, probably Indians who traded up and down the path that ran through the Great Valley stretching from Pennsylvania to Georgia (called the Valley of Virginia in Virginia). These Indian people had received it from other native people who lived thirty days' journey from Patawomeck and who bought it originally from a (presumably Spanish) ship that had traveled four day's reach up a river from the sea (perhaps a tributary of Mobile Bay in what is now Alabama). The English correspondent did not record how long the Patawomeck chief had had the box or how long he had been trading, indirectly, with such distant people. But by 1621 the Spanish had been active in the Mobile Bay area for nearly half a century.

European Visitors

Europeans began appearing in the Chesapeake region by the second half of the sixteenth century. The records they left behind are often sketchy, because their primary interests did not include getting to know the lifeways and history of the native people. The few who intended to settle either had religious blinders on (the Spanish Jesuits) or made records that were later lost, possibly through becoming "classified" (Roanoke colony English).

In the mid-sixteenth century the Spanish, based in Havana, considered themselves the proprietors of the Atlantic coast of North America at least as far north as what is now Maryland and Delaware. In one of their exploring trips that reached North Carolina, between 1559 and 1561, they took aboard a "savage" young man who was visiting the area. His Indian name is unknown, but it would have been in a Virginia Algonquian dialect, probably Paspahegh (one of the groups that was making Roanoke pottery). His Spanish name was Don Luis. He lived for the next ten years in various Spanish capitals—Havana, Mexico City, and Madrid—sometimes in monkish households, sometimes in military ones. Note the latter: his mentor in Havana was the military governor, and the young man would have learned from many evenings of listening what the Spanish and other Europeans thought about how to make war.

Finally Don Luis was approached by missionaries who wanted him to act as a guide for them in establishing themselves in his home territory and evangelizing his people. The first missionaries were Franciscans who had military backing; strange to say, Don Luis could not find the entrance to Chesapeake Bay, and the expedition had to turn back. The next missionaries, the Jesuits, had fewer military connections, and Don Luis did indeed lead them to his home, which seems to have been near Jamestown Island, in Paspahegh territory. But the missionaries insisted on moving overland to the York River, presumably to make it easier to contact the paramount chief, whose already growing dominions centered on the Pamunkey River. This move took them out of the orbit of their friend and guide and put them instead into the territory of a different group, the Chiskiacks. Don Luis then had to travel back and forth between the Jesuits and his relatives. He soon stopped visiting and threw in his lot with his family, because a drought was on and his kinfolks were suffering.

When the Jesuits' food supply ran out, they found they could not buy much. The local inhabitants had dispersed, having to forage all fall when they should have been able to live well on corn for a while. The Jesuits called insistently on Don Luis to help them, and at length he responded by having his people kill them. Only a teenaged boy survived, in accordance with Virginia Algonquian practice that called for sparing and adopting young prisoners. This Spanish boy was retrieved by a military expedition in 1572, and all accounts of the fate of the mission come ultimately from him. The commander of the expedition hanged five Indian men whom he had determined to be guilty of the missionaries' murder. The hanging left a very bad taste in the mouths of the native people all up and down the James and York Rivers, and possibly beyond.

Don Luis disappears from the historical record thereafter. There is no indication that the Jamestown English even asked if he were still alive in 1607, if they knew of his existence in the first place. Don Luis did *not* appear later in history (as some have suggested) as Opechancanough, Powhatan's brother and successor who feigned friendship for the English and then led the famous assaults of 1622 and 1644 on the colony. Opechancanough did not need Don Luis's experience with the Jesuits to be anti-English by 1616. Although he had been reasonably friendly before, his observations of the Jamestown colony alone would have produced that antipathy. The clinching argument against Opechancanough's having lived among Spaniards, as Don Luis did, comes from the way he conducted the campaigns of 1622 and 1644, times when he undoubtedly meant business in trying to force the English out of Virginia. An Indian who had lived with Spanish military men would have known that large-scale assaults were the norm for them and would not serve as a deterrent to their colonization attempts. But Opechancanough, with all his charisma that could have gotten Powhatan men to follow him, chose to use the old, limited-manpower Indian method: hit them hard, then withdraw for several weeks or months (it was six months both times) and let them pack up. To the English, of course, this was merely a forceful "hint" that the natives were hostile. It did not make them leave in 1622; it certainly did not make them leave in 1644. If Opechancanough had really been Don Luis, he would have known not to give the English any breathing room after the initial assaults.

Most of the subsequent European visits after 1572 were of short duration and left few records. Spanish ships sailed along the coast several times in the 1570s and 1580s. In 1588 one ship entered the Chesapeake Bay, sailed as far as the mouth of the Potomac River, and abducted a boy, soon taking another boy from the Eastern Shore. Young people like that were expected to learn Spanish and to act later as guides and missionaries. Neither of these two boys lived long enough to do either. Several English ships entered the Chesapeake in the 1580s through early 1600s. One of the Roanoke colony's ships may have gone there initially and met a hostile reception in 1584. In 1603 another ship entered what may have been the bay, and a landing party in search of water was attacked. In that same year some "Virginia natives" are known to have been in London, giving canoe-handling exhibitions; they may have been kidnapped previously, which would account for the home-people's hostility to the landing party. And around 1605 a ship of uncertain nationality sailed into the bay and up the Rappahannock River. The captain went ashore with a landing party, where he was received hospitably. But there was a sudden falling out, with Europeans firing into a crowd of people, killing the chief and kidnapping several others before sailing away. The dead chief was the ruler of the Rappahannocks; John Smith was taken to their capital town as a captive, to determine whether or not Smith was the culprit. The townsmen agreed that he was not: he was too short.

One more parcel of Europeans contacted the Virginia Algonquians during the Protohistoric period: Englishmen who were trying to colonize Roanoke Island in what is now North Carolina. In the winter of 1584–85 an expedition from the fort on the island went overland, accompanied by Indian guides, and spent several months among the Chesapeake Indians, who were allies of the people to the south. The visit passed peacefully, as far as anyone knows. John White was one of the visitors, and he probably made records of all he saw and heard. He certainly inquired about other Indian groups farther north and west, for they appear on the map he made of the whole region. The major motive for the expedition was to scout for better land to settle than the Outer Banks provided. Doing this in territory the Spanish considered theirs was a risky business, and for that reason historian David Beers Quinn has proposed that most of the records made by the expedition were "classified" and subsequently lost. Quinn has also suggested that some of the English people from the third, or "lost," Roanoke colony may have sought refuge from the Chesapeakes when the native people closer to Roanoke showed hostility. What became of these colonists if they went to the Chesapeakes is a mystery. Quinn suggests that some of them may have survived for two decades until Powhatan wiped the group out around 1607. For us it is questionable whether any of them would have survived that long, given Englishmen's documented arrogance and Europeans' lack of immunity to local "bugs."

A Closer Look at Some Indian Towns

The Virginia Algonquians who lived during the Protohistoric period inhabited a world that had still felt very little impact from Europeans. And with the exception of palisades around more sites and chiefs governing many areas, the Indians' world was still essentially a Late Woodland one. We can look more closely at that world because of detailed excavations at three sites: the Patawomeck capital town, a satellite Weyanock town at Jordan's Point, and a satellite Paspahegh town. All three sites have suffered in recent centuries because plowing of the land by farmers has destroyed the top several inches of Indian cultural remains. But enough was left of each town for it to give up its own special information to the archaeologists. Patawomeck taught us about building and rebuilding palisades; Jordan's Point and the Paspahegh town yielded up the first clear evidence of what Virginia Algonquian houses were really like (the historical accounts are a little "off"); and the Paspahegh site showed us just how a nonpalisaded dispersed-house town was laid out.

Patawomeck

Located at the mouth of Potomac Creek, at the elbow of the Potomac River's northward turn toward Washington, was the capital town of the Patawomeck Indians, the most prominent group on the Virginia side of the river when the English arrived. The town lay at a strategic place, both militarily and ecologically. The entrance to Potomac Creek has a clear view both north and east along the main river, which is a couple of miles wide at that point, so that visitors and enemies alike could be spotted well in advance of their arrival. The town lay on a twenty-five-foot-high peninsula, shaped rather like a high-heeled boot pointing upcreek, which is bounded on the south by the east/west-running Potomac Creek and on the west by its tributary, Accokeek Creek. This tract is the only sizable flat-topped terrace area within twenty miles on that side of the river. That characteristic would have attracted Indian farmers immediately. There is still a year-round beachside spring flowing into the creek, supplying water that is both fresh and clean. A natural ramp-like ravine nearby made it easy to carry water from the spring and goods from canoes up to the town.

Today the Potomac River at that point is very mildly brackish, which makes the lower reaches of Potomac and Accokeek Creeks nearly the same. Neither oysters nor clams, which prefer saltier water, occur that far upriver. Four centuries ago, when sea level was about four feet lower, the water in Potomac and Accokeek Creeks was probably completely fresh, so that spring runs of shad, alewife, and herring, which now go a bit farther upriver to spawn, would have come into the creek, close at hand. The fish available at other times of year would have been freshwater ones too, and not surprisingly archaeology shows that the town's residents occasionally ate sturgeon, garfish, yellow perch, catfish, and sucker. The marshes along both Potomac Creek and Accokeek Creek still produce considerable quantities of plants both known and suspected to have been eaten by Late Woodland Indian people: arrow arum (roots called *tuckahoe* and berries called *cuttanemons* by the Powhatans), wild rice (edible seeds, but laborious to prepare), and cattails (edible roots). The uplands surrounding the two creeks rise to over 100 feet above sea level and are covered with oak-hickory forest, with a gradation into water-loving trees such as willow and alder farther up Potomac Creek. Archaeologists found the bones of nut-eating deer (there was a vast preponderance of these bones and they were often made into tools), wild turkeys, raccoons, and gray squirrels in the town's garbage, along with those of water-loving beavers and musk-rats. People ate the nuts and acorns too, especially hickory nuts according to the excavated evidence. Altogether, the Patawomeck town was situated in a near-perfect place for Indian people to live.

There was a fly in the ointment, however: human enemies made themselves felt. The multiple palisades are direct evidence of this fact. There are actually two Patawomeck town sites on Potomac Creek. The older one (44ST2),[2] which is better known archaeologically, was about midway along the southern shore, stretching between Marlboro Point (the boot's heel) and Indian Point (the boot's toe). The newer one (44ST1), dating from about A.D. 1600 and visited by Captain John Smith, was located farther west, at Indian Point, where erosion and modern house-building had all but destroyed it before archaeologists came onto the scene. The old town, and possibly also the new one, was palisaded in the Indian manner: saplings three to five inches in diameter spaced six to eight inches apart, sometimes set directly into the ground and other times set a few inches deeper into an already-dug trench. Wooden pali-sade posts do not last more than ten or fifteen years in the eastern Vir-ginia climate, so it is no surprise that the Patawomeck one was rebuilt several times, leaving multiple concentric lines of postmolds. Recent ex-cavations indicate that some of these stockade lines were built in the four-teenth and fifteenth centuries, before the Protohistoric period proper got underway (fig. 2.11).

The smallest complete palisade found at Patawomeck's old town mea-sured about 175 feet (52.5 meters) across at the widest point in a slightly oval pattern. There were two entrances to the town, on the north and southwest sides, consisting of 20–to 30–foot-long alleyways between overlapping palisade lines. The next larger palisade was about 200 feet (60 meters) across at the widest point and featured an entrance on the west side. A 5–foot-wide ditch extended for much of the way around the stock-ade, set off at a distance varying from a few inches on the south to 5 feet on the north. This ditch was 2 feet or less deep and was filled in with garbage, which provided archaeologists with many of the artifacts discov-ered thus far at the site. The third clearly marked stockade line was about

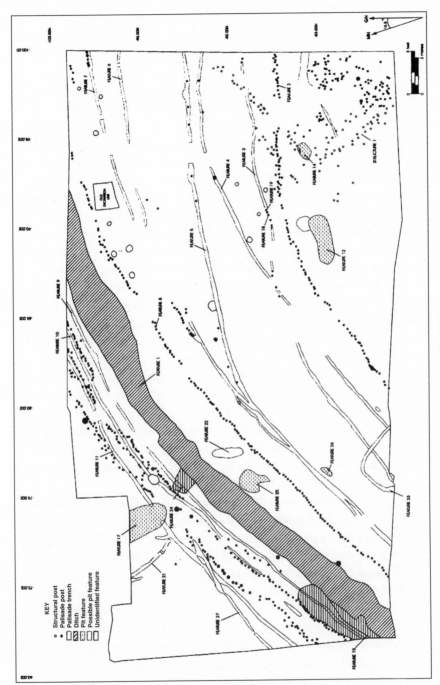

Fig. 2.11. Map of the 1996 excavation at Patawomeck. Courtesy of VDHR.

280 feet (84 meters) across and has not yet been completely excavated. So far six bastions have been found attached to it (entered across the top of the palisade, whose wall is unbroken) on the north, west, and east. Between the second and third complete palisade, besides the ditch, were a number of lengthy palisade segments, making a mazelike pattern and adding to the difficulty of recreating the construction history of the town. A further problem has arisen in recent years: archaeology indicates that the Patawomeck site was not regularly inhabited as a town or even as a hamlet before the first palisades were built by "new" people who made "new" Potomac Creek ceramics.

The origin of the settlers at the Patawomeck site is in dispute. Some archaeologists argue for a migration of people downriver, emphasizing the similarities of the settlers' pottery to that of the Maryland piedmont, where Potomac Creek–like ceramics occur earlier. Others see ceramic similarities with the Owasco culture of south-central New York State and posit a migration from there, though without specifying a workable route. We prefer to see the Patawomecks as local Algonquians who responded to some far-upriver threat (perhaps Massawomecks already staging raids) by occupying the townsite in large numbers for the first time while forging alliances and borrowing ceramic ideas from piedmont people upriver. That is what seems to have happened along the James River, though perhaps not so early: the Weyanocks were descended from centuries of unbroken Algonquian occupants of their area, but in the Protohistoric period they were sharing Gaston-Cashie pottery styles, implying intermarriage and military solidarity, with Nottoways, Meherrins, and Tuscaroras to the southwest. They were not immigrants to their site; the Patawomecks may not have been either.

The Patawomecks' language was certainly an Algonquian one by 1608. John Smith needed no intermediary Algonquian-to-Siouan or Algonquian-to-Iroquoian interpreters there, as he had with the Susquehannocks earlier on that trip. Henry Spelman became fluent in "the Indian language," as he called it, while living with the great chief Powhatan in 1609, and then he used the same language when he went to live with the Patawomeck leading family the next year. If Spelman had had to learn a second, non-Algonquian language there, or if bilingual people had been the norm at Patawomeck, he probably would have mentioned it in his account. Finally, in the case of funerary practices, which are very slow to change in most cultures, the Patawomecks showed themselves to be

Algonquians by carrying out secondary burial (see below). Ossuaries, or community bone collections, are characteristic of coastal Algonquian-speaking people from North Carolina to New England; they are not characteristic of Late Woodland sites in either the piedmont or Iroquoian-speaking areas immediately to the north.

Wherever they came from, around A.D. 1300 the Patawomecks built a large nucleated town in a place that had not been heavily settled before. They fortified their new town with an outer palisade with bastions, plus at least six concentric palisade segments making at least one maze entry, and lastly a ditch inside that. The ditch provided both soil for buttressing the innermost palisade lines and a place to bury trash without having to leave town. Multiple palisades like this are known archaeologically from Iroquoian sites to the north from the fourteenth century onward, as well as from the Patawomecks' "sister" site of Moyaone (Accokeek Creek) just upriver; they were also mentioned in 1705 by Robert Beverley, writing about Indians who wanted to be not just safe but "very safe" (fig. 2.12). People at Patawomeck would have had their houses and yard areas inside the fortifications; women would have commuted to work in their fields (men had to commute anyway to go hunting or fishing). As for what the houses were like, there were too many postholes found, in too great a confusion, for any clear pattern of building to emerge.

Between about 1400 and 1560 the "immigrants" (if that is what they were) may have become "locals"; the town's defenses shrank, according to one interpretation, to a pair of simple palisade lines inside the ditch, which continued to receive the town's refuse. Within the stockade was a single-line palisade enclosing an area nearly 110 feet (33 meters) across. The area inside this innermost "wall" may have housed political and religious VIPs, while ordinary families now lived in houses dispersed among the fields where the women worked. Ceramic evidence, meaning styles in both pots and tobacco pipes, points to the people's having connections mainly with other local makers of Potomac Creek wares, such as the Moyaone (Piscataway territory in historic times). After about 1560, the Patawomeck town was abandoned and the new town built to the west on Indian Point. The old town site was still used as a location for burying the dead.

People who died at Patawomeck town were usually given a secondary burial. The bodies were kept aboveground until only bones were left, the evidence being mud-daubers' nests inside several of the skulls. Then, on a

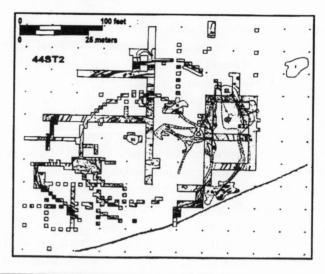

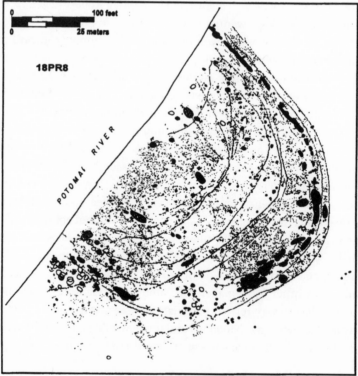

Fig. 2.12. Plans of sister sites: *top*, Patawomeck in Virginia, 1930s excavations; *bottom*, Accokeek Creek in Maryland, completely excavated by 1963. Courtesy of VDHR.

single occasion, all the corpses accumulated since the last community burial were interred together. Five ossuaries and a multiple primary burial were found at Patawomeck. The multiple burial and ossuaries 1 and 4 were within the outer palisade line of the old town; the former two contained European artifacts, indicating a seventeenth-century posta-bandonment date. Ossuaries 3 and 5, containing no European artifacts, were found within the outer palisade and were apparently contemporary with the "VIP" enclosure. It is tragic that five of the six burial pits were excavated haphazardly in the mid-1930s; many of the bones were thrown away before the Smithsonian Institution became involved in 1938. Only pre-Contact ossuary 5 received careful excavation and analysis of the bones by T. Dale Stewart.

Stewart's results showed that of 135 recognizable skeletons (not counting miscellaneous bones mixed in), 63 came from adults and 73 from juveniles, most of the latter either newborn or in the first year of life. That high infant mortality accords with what is known from other large Late Woodland sites. Eight adults or older children had long bones with signs of old infections. Many of the skeletons were associated with shell beads of various kinds. The people so honored ranged in age from adults down to newborns, indicating that the death of babies was not taken lightly, however common it may have been.

It was in a multiple burial (not an ossuary) and in ossuary 1 that the Early Contact European artifacts were found at Patawomeck. Regretta-bly, those finds were made by the laymen who preceded the Smithsonian excavators (Stewart wrote long afterward that their "explorations of the site resembled gopher activity"), so that excavation was done carelessly and records were made fitfully. As best Stewart could reconstruct it, the following European goods were found in both places:

Glass trade beads: 200 cylindrical ones (maximum length 14mm, mostly brick red) that may have come from the multiple burial, and 280 circular ones in various colors, the most common being navy blue.

Brass flushloop bells, of the kind falconers put on their hawks' legs; the color when new would have been bright gold.

Copper scissors in two different sizes.

The following were found much more often in ossuary 1: native-made ornaments of European sheet copper.

The following were found specifically in the multiple burial and therefore may indicate a later date for it:

Buttons of several types, made of various metals.

A length of fine copper chain.

A much-worn metal jeton or abacus counter that dates to between 1588 and 1612.

A pipestem whose decoration places it somewhere in the seventeenth century.

A bone comb, with teeth finer than the native people could have made, that is therefore European.

A small silver dram cup (wine taster) with a flower design in its bowl and a maker's mark that dates it to the mid-seventeenth century.

A star-shaped ornament, probably of brass and now missing from the National Museum's collection, that may have been a spur rowel.

The Patawomeck site is frustrating because of the amount of information lost through poor excavation that was little better than pothunting. It is some comfort to know that the site was too big to excavate fully, even by the rough-and-ready methods of the 1930s laymen. Although modern housing has been built over much of the site since the 1950s, parts of the town are still intact under a few undeveloped areas. But the peninsula on which it lies is only about fifty miles from Washington, D.C., so that further development is a genuine and ever-growing threat.

The next two sites were excavated in the 1980s and 1990s as salvage jobs before developers moved in. The "digs" were carefully done, thankfully with the developers' cooperation. At the Paspahegh town site, the excavations have been covered over, and thus preserved, by a golf course. At Jordan's Point, on the other hand, a residential subdivision was built that largely obliterated the traces of Indian habitation.

Jordan's Point

Cars approaching the Harrison Bridge across the James River go whizzing past the location of one of the most interesting Indian settlements excavated so far in Virginia. It was the first coastal plain site in which archaeologists found a complex of house postmolds that showed clear outlines of some of the dwellings rather than just a confusion of filled-in

Fig. 2.13. Overview of house patterns at Jordan's Point. Courtesy of VDHR.

holes (fig. 2.13). None of the Jamestown colonists specified the shape of Indian houses; John White painted squared-ended houses in the Carolina Sounds in the 1580s, but that shape might not have applied to the houses of the Virginia Algonquians. Now, for the first time, the preferred shape of Powhatan houses became clearly known—and John White had to be discounted.

Jordan's Point thrusts northward into the mile-wide James, in a reach of the river otherwise bounded either by high bluffs or occasional tidal marshes. It was a spot attractive to both Indian farmers and English settlers, so that an interesting conglomeration of sites, Indian and English, has been excavated there. John Smith's map showed an Indian village on the point, but it lacked a name. Geographically it lay between the Weyanock and Appamattuck capital towns, but archaeologists usually classify it as "Weyanock" in its district affiliation.

Jordan's Point (44PG1 and related sites) makes a triangular-shaped terrace, ten to twenty-five feet above the river, backed along its base by uplands rising to over 100 feet above sea level. These are now covered by a second-growth oak-pine forest, but they were originally clothed in an oak-hickory forest that would have served as an excellent foraging territory for Indian men and women. The low terrace is limited in extent but is better-than-average farmland, for its soil is Pamunkey sandy loam, moderately fertile without artificial additions and quick to warm up in the spring. That ancient river-deposited loam is still the best corn-growing soil in all of Virginia (it is now the official State Soil for the Commonwealth). In the seventeenth century its occurrences in the James, York, and Rappahannock River valleys attracted first Indian farmers and then prominent English plantation owners. The waterways near Jordan's Point are a fairly good source of tuckahoe and other useful marsh plants, especially up Eppes Creek to the north, and the creeks running into the James are spawning areas for shad and herring in the spring. Life could have been reasonably good for native people living at Jordan's Point, as long as not too many families tried to subsist there. The same was true elsewhere in Weyanock territory, where the people are known historically to have increased their income by acting as middlemen in the great chief Powhatan's trade with Iroquoian-speakers like the Nottoways and Tuscaroras to the southwest.

The native owners of Jordan's Point probably built their houses and planted their garden plots all over the point, though excavations were limited to selected areas not already destroyed by the old Hopewell Airport, now superceded by a residential development. The Indian houses were not quite close enough together, except in a few "hot spots," to speak of a nucleated settlement, and there was no palisade until the English settlers came in and built one of their own. The site thus conforms to William Strachey's view of Indian towns as generally being dispersed "without form of a street."

The great majority of the nearly forty (not necessarily contemporary) Indian houses found were oval in plan, with nearly straight sides and rounded ends. The majority were oriented with their long axis running roughly northwest by southeast or north-northwest by south-southeast, which helped deflect the cold northwest winds that afflict the region in winter. A small minority of dwellings were ovals running along an east-west axis, while a smaller minority yet were circular in layout. Houses usually had two doors each, let into the long sides of the oval where the straight walls began to curve around; most doors were at the northeast and southwest "corners" to prevent cold northwesterly winds from

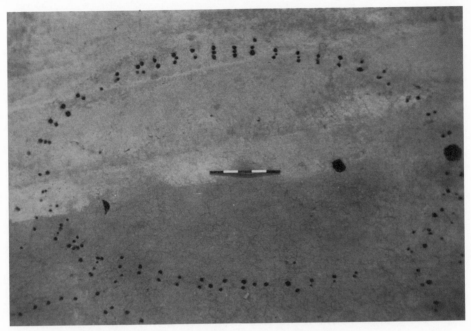

Fig. 2.14. The elaborate house at Jordan's Point. Courtesy of VDHR.

blowing into them in winter. A few houses had upright posts set inside a door, probably to support mats acting as a windbreak or a privacy partition or both. With an exception that will be described below, Jordan's Point houses ranged in length from sixteen to twenty-seven feet and in width from twelve to eighteen feet; the few circular houses were about fifteen feet in diameter. House frameworks consisted of saplings two to four inches in diameter set a few inches into the ground and about a foot and a half apart; in larger houses, the postmolds from upright central roof-bracing posts were also found. Some houses had postmolds indicating the benchlike beds described by the early English colonists, usually flanking just the long southwestern side of the house.

One exceptional house was found at Jordan's Point: the elaborate house (structure 16 at 44PG303) shown in figure 2.14, which may have belonged to a chief. It lay on a nearly east-west axis, unusual at the site. At 30 1/2 feet long and 18 feet wide, it had a greater area than any other house in town, requiring three poles inside to brace a ridgepost along the roof. It was made of slightly larger-than-usual saplings that were spaced only half as far apart as in most "ordinary" houses. Not only that, but the wall-posts were doubled, with each pair positioned carefully opposite another pair. The main door, which was four feet wide and had triple sets of saplings on each side of it, was at the east end of the building. That door was apparently sheltered by a six-foot-long vestibule, less carefully built on an unevenly placed sapling framework. The main house, however, would have been extremely solid by Indian standards.

Inside the house were found several parallel lines of postmolds, indicating a built-in bench 4 1/2 feet wide and over 10 feet long, which had been rebuilt several times. The height of the bench cannot be determined, so that it is uncertain whether it was a bed (height of about eighteen inches, according to Strachey), a higher bier for chiefs' bone bundles (though Strachey indicated that such things were in the western *ends* of buildings, "separated from the body of the temple with hollow windings and pillars"), or simply a shelf for storing food. Five sets of wall posts behind the center of the bench area were tripled rather than doubled saplings; there is no way of telling whether this arrangement represents the original building plan or a repair job. A second, narrower entrance was found in the northern long wall, near where the west end of the house began to curve around. Access to this "back" door seems to have been direct, unlike the situation near the main door.

Just inside the main entryway, between the eastern end of the bench and the opposite wall of the house, are a confusion of postmolds. These may indicate that partitions had been erected to direct traffic. Their nearness to the eastern door does not conform with Strachey's description of a temple's anteroom on the east. The site's excavators suggested that traffic was guided toward the bench. We disagree: Henry Spelman recorded that chiefs' houses had "many dark windings and turnings before any come where the King is." The post-supported partitions probably guided people from structure 16's main door into the less cluttered north half, or commoners' reception area, of the house.

The identifiable pottery found at Jordan's Point was mainly Gaston Simple Stamped, although a substantial minority, including most of the sherds found in the elaborate "chief's" house, was typed as Roanoke. No Potomac Creek sherds were found. Stone tools were limited in quantity at the site, and many of them were undatable chips made from local quartzite pebbles. The projectile points were datable and ranged in age from Middle Archaic (5000 B.C.) through Protohistoric, with the majority being Archaic. The falloff in stone projectile or knife points through time can be explained: historical accounts of the Powhatans describe people cleverly using nonlithic cutting tools like mussel shells and stout slivered reeds, and projectile points made sometimes of wild turkey spurs.

Salvage excavations at Jordan's Point produced a few individual burials and one ossuary that could be attributed to the native people rather than to European settlers. One of the individual burials was of an adult male, buried soon after death in a flexed position. He had been interred with copper beads apparently embroidered onto a mantle (long disintegrated), a piece of sheet copper, probably once attached to a leather choker, and possibly copper ear ornaments (only copper salts were left). His social status would therefore have been high. A second prehistoric grave contained the partially preserved skeleton of a woman, found with the bones of a dog (perhaps a pet; another Protohistoric dog burial was found elsewhere at Jordan's Point) and some Gaston Simple Stamped pottery. Both of the dogs found in burials were small to medium in size, conforming to Peter Wynn's description of Powhatan dogs as being the size of "warreners" dogs, or rabbit-hunting hounds. Dog burials, sometimes with human remains in what appears to be a ceremonial context, are numerous at the Hatch Site, a settlement up Powell Creek to the east of Jordan's Point.

Still another individual's burial showed a blending of native and Christian customs, pointing to a post-Contact date for the death of this Indianized white or Europeanized Indian. The person (bone preservation being very poor) was laid out face-upwards in a narrow rectangular grave, in Christian style except that the head end was to the northwest instead of the west. The native components of the burial were located in the chest area and may have been originally contained in a "medicine bundle." They were miscellaneous items whose meaning was personal to the owner and not obvious to us: a small Late Woodland triangular projectile point, an Archaic projectile point (about 5000 B.C.) that may have been reworked by the owner, a medium-large triangular projectile point similar to others dated A.D. 250–750, and a three-inch-long Miocene fossil shark's tooth (about 7 million to 25 million years old). Small fossil sharks' teeth have been found to fit the finely dotted incised decorations on many Late Woodland Indian clay tobacco pipes, so the collection of such teeth by Powhatan Indians need not surprise us.

The Jordan's Point ossuary was small, only a little over five by six feet, but it contained the poorly preserved bones of at least seventeen people buried during Late Woodland times (the small amount of pottery found in the pit was pre-Protohistoric Townsend ware). Amid the dense jumble of bones, seven of the skulls had been arranged in a semicircle, for reasons unknown. There was considerable evidence of cuts on the bones made during defleshing, indicating that when the community's burial day arrived, some of the accumulated corpses had not been completely reduced to bones. Such defleshing, unpleasant as it was, was an expected part of secondary burial customs, and people put up with it. Of the seventeen bodies, the age could be determined for only twelve: there were seven adults (two female, three male, two undetermined) and five young people ranging from newborn to mid-teens.

Native American skeletal material from the burials at Jordan's Point was limited, but there were enough teeth recovered to compare with those taken from early seventeenth-century English burials on the same site that we can safely make one statement: the English settlers had been far less healthy during childhood than the Indians had been. Four-fifths of the adult English skeletons, but none of the Indian ones, had teeth with enamel hypoplasia, indicating prolonged disease or malnutrition in early childhood (see chapter 1). It seems clear that the English who built their settlement on top of the Weyanock one at Jordan's Point in the 1620s had good reason to be seeking a better life across the Atlantic and/or upriver from Jamestown. But they did not find a better life there: their skeletons indicated that 43 percent of them had died as teenagers, 32 percent in their twenties. The intruders may have taken control of the land, but the aboriginal owners possessed better immunity to the local "bugs."

The Paspahegh Town

John Smith's map of 1608 shows an unnamed town, clearly within the Paspaheghs' territory, on the eastern side of the mouth of the Chickahominy River. The land there is a box-shaped point with two terraces on it: a swampy one, one to five feet above river level, in the southern half and a ten- to fifteen-foot-high one in the northern half. The point is surrounded on three sides by waterways: the James River on the south (about two miles wide at the point), the half-mile-wide Chickahominy on the west, and Mattapamient Bay on the north.[3] Like the previous two sites, then, this one is situated on a fairly low, relatively flat-topped but two-tiered peninsula that is backed up by a higher terrace, twenty-five to fifty feet above sea level, that forms the mainland.

Today both the peninsula and the uplands to the east are covered by a residential and golfing community styled The Governor's Land at Two Rivers. The developer of that community agreed to a historical and archaeological survey of the entire tract before building began. The survey showed that English colonial and later Anglo-Virginian living areas were concentrated along the edge of the highest terrace, which would have been foraging but not living territory for the Paspaheghs. The Indians' living areas centered on the middle terrace, out on the peninsula. Initial grading revealed that in most of that part of the point, Indian town remains several inches deep still existed. So construction was halted, and the archaeologists were brought in to do a meticulous excavation of the 2.75 acres (out of 31 on the point) that were in immediate danger. That meant not only uncovering pits, burials, and house postmolds but also carefully removing their contents while making detailed records, which was necessarily somewhat destructive in the case of burials. To mitigate the sense of desecration involved, the developer set aside a nearby plot as a cemetery; the archaeologists had the human skeletons and their grave goods analyzed within two years (by agreement with Indian representatives), and then in 1993 the bones and goods were reburied in a private ceremony by members of the modern Virginia tribes. Native Americans, archaeologists, and developers *can* work together.

This town of the Paspaheghs (44JC308) had everything a Woodland Indian family could want: plentiful deciduous forest nearby for hunting, nuts, and firewood; fairly flat land with some good Pamunkey loamy soil on it for the women's corn crop; lush growths of tuckahoe up the nearby tributaries of the Chickahominy (and possibly back then along that river itself: the water is a tiny bit brackish today); spring runs of shad and herring heading northward past the point to spawn in those same tributary creeks; and shallow bay waters in which to build sapling-and-reed weirs to provide fish at other seasons. For reasons that will appear in the next chapter, the waterways would have been bustling with people of both sexes and all ages: people from this town and other Paspahegh ones not far away up and down the James River; people from the friendly though autonomous Chickahominy towns up that stream; and people from the fellow Powhatan-allied Quiyoughcohannock towns across the James.

There was no need for the townsmen to huddle together or build fortifications, so the town could spread out over the point in an intermixture of houses, gardens, and fallow fields, all within easy reach of the higher terrace of forest or the waterside canoes in which the people's other work was continually done. The town's houses were therefore scattered across a considerable area (fig. 2.14).

Forty-eight complete or partial buildings were found in the excavation area, most of them presumably dwelling houses and some perhaps storage buildings. A number of parallels with houses at Jordan's Point emerged. These Paspahegh houses were also oval in shape and ranged, in their long axes, between 14.5 and nearly 31 feet long. Owing probably to lessening flexibility in longer (and therefore thicker) saplings used as posts, the width of houses ranged only between 10.3 and 14.4 feet, with wall posts usually set 1.2 to 1.95 feet apart and upright ridgepole supports down the center of the longer structures. Structures' orientation along their long axes usually varied from north-south to northwest by southeast, with a few examples veering toward northeast by southwest or going east-west. Doors, often two in number, were located opposite each other (for example, in the northeast and southwest "corners"), in the long sides where an end began to curve; several houses had three and even four doors. There was, however, less consistency in which "corners" were used for doors than at the Jordan's Point houses.

Next to no traces of central hearths were found inside the houses. Since the English observers were adamant about their existence, it would seem that the hearths were not set into pits that survived archaeologically. Evidence of built-in benches was also scarce in the Paspahegh houses, but two of the five structures showing benches had them along both sides of the house instead of just one. Three houses had four or more interior postmolds that aligned perfectly to make a rectangle in the center of the floor; the rectangle in structures 8 and 43 covered a sizable part of the floor (7 x 4 feet in number 43, whose maximum dimensions were 22.8 by 13.6 feet) The best explanation for these upright posts is that they supported the sapling framework around their houses' smokeholes. They probably also supported crosspieces (long disintegrated) that made a strong storage loft above the occupants' heads.

Three houses (structures 29, 30, and 33) stood out. They were significantly longer (26.8 to 30.7 feet, compared to 23.7 feet for the next longest); they were not double-posted, but structure 29 had wall posts set a little closer together than "normal"; the three were placed close together on the highest spot on the middle terrace; and they and a few outbuild-

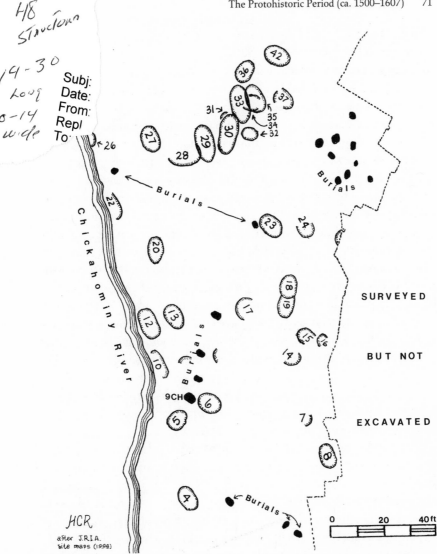

Fig. 2.15. Plan of the Paspahegh town (central portion). Courtesy of Helen C. Rountree.

ings were somewhat isolated spatially from other, more scattered house remains.

Structure 30 had interior postmolds that may indicate a bench or corridor along the west side and a room on the north end set off by partitions. Structure 29's interior postmolds seem to form a more intriguing pattern (fig. 2.16). The house was oriented north-northwest by south-southeast and had doors on the southwest and southeast "corners," with some kind of partition making a baffle north of the southeastern entry-way that may have created an anteroom at that end of the eastern half of the house. A narrow bench seems to have run along the central straight part of the western wall. The central open room containing the bench was truncated on the north by more partitions, offset from each other to form an angled corridor: visitors went to the northern end of the narrow bench, where the house's third doorway was, then turned east-southeast into the corridor, then east where it widened out briefly, and then north-northwest into the end room of the house. Accounts of English colonists indicate benches or "beds" for chiefs to sit on across the end of the houses, but this room lacked one. Instead there may have been a bench along the room's east side, past which visitors walked to enter the room. The northern room was thus irregularly shaped, ranging from five to nine feet north-northwest to south-southeast and a maximum of eleven feet east to west, and it may have contained a narrow fourth door-way to the house in the northeast "corner." It would have been a rather cramped audience chamber, even for someone who was only a town (not a district or a paramount) chief. The room could have been the "chancel" area of a temple, yet the structure's whole north-northwest by south-southeast orientation argues against that interpretation (temples being built on an east-west axis, according to Strachey).

The occupants of the Paspahegh village used two different burial prac-tices for their dead. Some corpses were put directly into the ground, in a primary inhumation, while others may have been kept somewhere aboveground until their bones were placed with those of other people in an ossuary. In either case, the pits dug for burials were often shallow and bowl-shaped (flat floor, curving sides), but generous in length and width; the shape was usually oval. In the primary burials, people were laid out straight, on their backs, with their heads usually to the east (a practice echoed among the burials found at the Protohistoric Great Neck site in Virginia Beach). Historical accounts of the Powhatans' beliefs about the afterlife included the idea that souls traveled toward either the setting sun (James River groups) or the rising sun (Patawomecks). Grave goods occasionally accompanied the dead. Some burial pits contained pottery, others jewelry consisting of copper and shell beads. The copper in one ossuary was found to be both native and European (for the method of

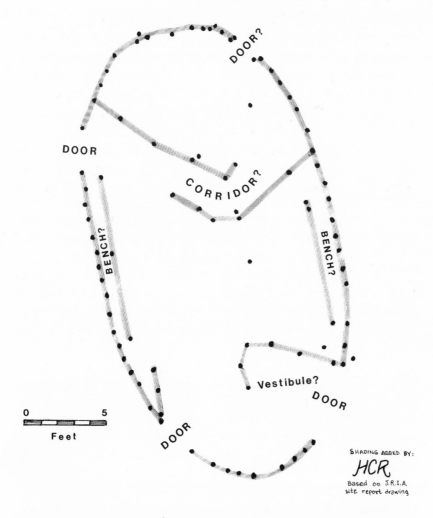

DOOR?

DOOR

CORRIDOR?

BENCH?

BENCH?

Vestibule?

DOOR

DOOR

0   5

Feet

SHADING ADDED BY:

HCR

Based on J.R.I.A.
site report drawing

Fig. 2.16. Structure 29 at the Paspahegh town. Courtesy of Helen C. Rountree.

determining the copper's origin, see chapter 4). The native pieces were buried with the adults, the European ones with three preteenagers. European copper was also buried with a man (burial 9CH) who was in a class by himself.

Burial 9CH was a man over 35 years of age who was interred alone in a large pit; he lay on his back with his head to the east and a necklace of tubular copper beads around his neck. Minute X-ray and chemical analyses were made of the dark substances found around his bones, with as little disturbance to them as possible before he was reburied. The copper found with him—and also with the bone bundles in the ossuaries—had oxidized enough that it partially preserved some fabric that had been wrapped around him (and the ossuaries' bone bundles). The fabric consisted of unwoven strips of cedar-like bark (those in the ossuaries had been woven into mats). That mostly decomposed bark in burial 9CH retained impressions of another, now completely disintegrated, fabric, apparently woven in a wicker or herringbone pattern, which indicates at least a double wrapping before burial. Below the body was a dark thin layer that may have been a mat or mantle. All of this accords with English colonist accounts of "corpses being lapped in skins and mats with their jewels." This corpse bundle had been brought to the pit on three stakes; their decomposed stains remained beneath the body, perpendicular to it at head, feet, and hips. What analysis of this burial has not shown is whether the interment was a primary one, with the corpse being fresh, or a secondary one, with the man's bones carefully re-articulated. If he was of high status, the second scenario is expectable, judging by Smith's and Strachey's writings.

At the time this middle-aged man died, he had only four cavities; given his age, that was a good state of dental health in the Indian world and a sensational one by European standards of the time. He may also have had a mild case of rickets in his youth, for one of his femurs was bowed a little. Enamel hypoplasia in the teeth of a few of the people in the site's ossuaries show that they had had nutritional problems.

People who look for "hidden geometry" in archaeological remains often find it, whether the natives of the area intended such a thing or not as they went about their business. The excavators of the Paspahegh town found that many of the burials at the site could fit a master design: individual burials including 9CH lined up with each other, north-northeast by south-southwest. An extension of that axis could form the downstroke of a "Z" with a fifth burial occurring exactly at the midpoint. Other burials lined up along parallel lines that intersected the axis perpendicularly to form the top and bottom strokes of the "Z," with yet another burial at the end of another parallel line running through the downstroke's midpoint and perpendicular to it, in the manner of a European "zed." There is no way of telling whether the townspeople buried their dead with such a design in mind, but the alignment is so close that it reduces the chances of their being coincidental.

Microscopic analysis of apparently unexciting things produced other interesting bits of information. The soil inside the tubular beads from the ossuaries retained evidence of the cordage used to string them. It was probably made from the stem fibers of several native wild plants. The thread through one bead used fibers made from Indian hemp (or "silk-grass"; see chapter 3), while that in most others utilized milkweed or nettle or red mulberry. Tiny bits of food plants were found as well, mainly in the soil from the town that drifted into burial depressions after they had settled (the graves were "out in the yards," after all). The plants included two cultivated ones, domesticated maize and semiwild little barley, plus a number of wild ones. Hickory nuts and acorns were the most common nuts, occurring more frequently in the soil than maize (not uncommon at Late Woodland sites); black walnuts were a distant third. There were also some seeds of chenopods, persimmon, [wild] strawberry, and maypop, the last-named known historically to be encouraged around Powhatan fields. The seeds listed become ripe at varying seasons, showing that the Paspahegh townspeople were present and eating meals there at least during all the warm months of the year, even in the spring and early summer when John Smith recorded that people dispersed from the settlements to go foraging before the corn crop came in.

The occupants of the town got the protein in their diet partly from the maize and nuts, but primarily from wild animals that were hunted and fished. Stable carbon and nitrogen isotope analysis, run on human teeth and bone fragments from burials, suggests that in the people's overall diet wild plants and land animals took a backseat to cultivated plants (contradicting the nutshell evidence) and aquatic animals. Exactly which animals were brought in by hunters and fishermen was determined by identifying the food bones, some of them tiny, found at the site. People in the town were eating deer, raccoon, grey squirrels, box turtles, oysters, striped bass, several kinds of catfish, and long-nosed gar. The oysters had to come from at least ten miles down the James River, which is as far upstream as they occur with today's higher sea level. Getting oysters from that distance may have meant either trading for them or going downriver to get them, which was allowable in a "public" foraging area. Missing from the list but very probably eaten frequently by the locals were sturgeon, which migrate up the rivers to spawn in spring and which weighed an average of 150 pounds back then (they are fewer and smaller nowadays). Really big fish like that may have been butchered at the town's waterside, which has eroded away in the succeeding four centuries.

The pottery found so far at the Paspahegh town was nearly all Roanoke Simple Stamped ware. That points to a Protohistoric date for the settlement and also indicates close contacts, at least before Powhatan's paramount chiefdom overwhelmed the group, with people downriver and southward to the Carolina Sounds. Wider excavation on the point may eventually show more Townsend ware from an earlier Late Woodland occupation; some projectile points from both the Archaic and Woodland periods (spanning over 7,500 years) were collected on the surface of soils on the point. A small amount of Townsend ware had already been found during survey, along with some bits of pottery that may be Gaston. The whole story of the site's occupation and outside contacts has yet to be unearthed.

By no means has all of the Paspahegh town's area been uncovered. Only the part subject to immediate tearing up was examined closely, and even then the developer modified the construction plans to allow some of the discovered pits and house postmolds to be protectively covered up again, unexcavated for the foreseeable future. To give the entire site better long-term protection, the developer has had the land placed under a historical easement. All of this means that more Paspahegh remains are still there on the point, underground, protected and waiting for future archaeologists who will be armed with even more sensitive and perhaps less destructive ways of extracting information about the past.

For the native people of eastern Virginia during the Protohistoric period, the few episodes they experienced with the overdressed foreigners in peculiar boats would have been insect bites compared to the injuries and anxieties they were being caused by various hostile Indian groups. The expanding "Powhatans" worried about enemies from the west and northwest; the more easterly Algonquian-speakers worried about the ambitions of the Powhatans. Physical clashes took place: Monacan and Massawomeck versus Powhatan, Powhatan versus Kecoughtan, and (just before or just after Jamestown was founded) Powhatan versus Chesapeake. Our hindsight shows us that in the long run, the Europeans were a far greater threat to Indian well-being, but Indian people who actually lived during the period could not know that. Thus when the English arrived to settle at Jamestown, the Powhatan organization, now reaching to the Atlantic shore, was not immediately hostile. Instead the district chiefs were allowed to make their own decisions in dealing with the strangers, and Powhatan himself was initially friendly. It is because of these reactions that the more curious of the English colonists had the chance to find out as much as they did about the culture of the Virginia Algonquians.

Notes

1. Archaeologists pay so much attention to pots, broken or whole, because pottery is an almost indestructible product composed of many varied elements: clay (which varies from source to source), tempering material, shape and thickness of bottom and sides and lip, handle treatments (if any), method of smoothing outside and inside, method of decorating outside and inside. In traditional cultures, where even the most highly decorated pottery was for utility rather than art, these elements tended to be dictated by custom, which made for uniformity within tribes and very slow changes in styles.

2. For plotting on a master nationwide map, archaeological sites today start with a number (Virginia is the forty-fourth entry down an alphabetical list of the lower forty-eight states), followed by two letters representing the county in which the site lies (ST means Stafford County), and a registration number in the order in which the site was reported to the Virginia Department of Historic Resources (the Protohistoric Patawomeck town was the second town reported from Stafford County once the system was set up).

3. See Helen C. Rountree's "Powhatan Indian Women: The People Captain John Smith Barely Saw," *Ethnohistory* 45 (1998): 1–29, for a detailed map of the area around this point, with plant cover and elevations indicated. The article reconstructs the work of the women in this Paspahegh town in April 1607.

3

Powhatan Indian Culture
When the English Arrived

The way of life of the Powhatans was described in considerable detail, albeit with gaps, by several Englishmen connected with the early James-town colony. One, Henry Spelman, lived among the native people and learned their language, but he was in his early teens at the time, which by his own account limited his observations. Another, John Smith, visited many of the Indian districts around the Chesapeake Bay before war broke out, but he was a bachelor focused upon his military career and that, too, limited his observations. The third, William Strachey, was a scholarly man and also a married one who took an interest in the women's world (Smith and Spelman did not). He had the good fortune of an already-fluent Henry Spelman as interpreter and the bad fortune to be in Virginia during a time of strained relations, which limited his travels in the region. All three men left far more detailed descriptions of the native people, who were "new" to the English, than would later colonists with the exception of Robert Beverley (see chapter 6). The early days of the English colonization effort also produced the most detailed map of the Indian towns: John Smith's "Virginia Discovered . . . 1606" (fig. 3.2).

All these descriptions come from observers who admitted that native people lived in a culture, not a vacuum. All of them contrast with the religion-soaked accounts characteristic of the New England Puritans (Roger Williams being an exception) by reflecting a genuine interest, extensive or not, in what the Powhatans' existence was like. The result was a written record in the lower Chesapeake region that sheds far more light on Indian ways than does any collection of records made elsewhere along the Atlantic coast of North America during early colonization.

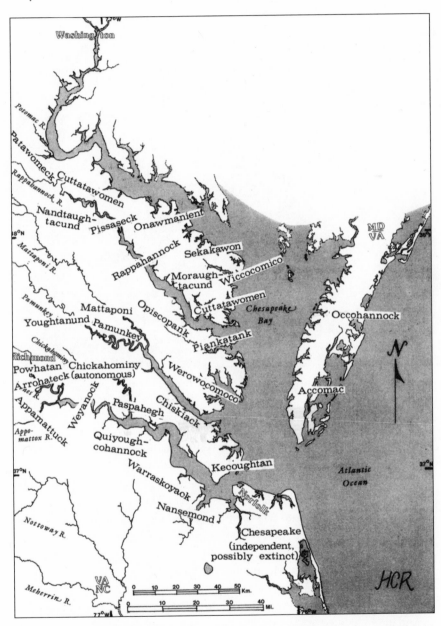

Fig. 3.1. Map of the Powhatan paramount chiefdom in 1607. Courtesy of Helen C. Rountree.

Fig. 3.2. John Smith's map of the Chesapeake region, compiled in 1608 and published in 1612.

There are still gaps, of course, in areas such as kinship, about which the English either did not ask or did not comprehend the answers they got; women's lives, which the male colonists probably could not have found out about even if they had asked (it was none of men's business); and religion, which required first-rate interpreters. The best we can do nowadays to fill the gaps is to use the other three methods discussed in the introduction. Archaeological investigation of the Powhatan area is still limited, as mentioned already. We can get closer to seeing many intangible aspects of Virginia Algonquian life by using ethnographic analogy. Its use requires eyewitness descriptions of various cultures, either in writing or by oral communication with other cultural anthropologists. And living history, at least the Virginia version with its strong basis upon early colonial descriptions, also becomes an essential tool in bringing the working lives of the Powhatans in the "traditional" period (that is, early contact) into focus.

There have been several modern write-ups of traditional Powhatan culture, the major ones by Christian Feest and Helen Rountree (see the bibliography at the end of this volume). All of these versions describe the culture one part at a time, an artificial depiction since all of a culture's parts are interrelated and functioning simultaneously (it is the written word that has to proceed linearly). This chapter will differ: after reconstructing more of the physical world in which the Powhatans lived—a world very different from the Virginia that Americans know today—we will follow a Powhatan male and female from birth to death. This view of a culture through the life cycle is less artificial.

The two Powhatans we will describe were real people, appearing briefly in the Jamestown colony's records around 1610. Their names were Winganuske (perhaps pronounced "wing-a-NOOS-ki," idiomatically "Pretty Woman") and Machumps (put the accent where you will; translation unknown). They were a brother and sister who were born somewhere in Powhatan's domains during the Protohistoric period. They reached young adulthood by 1610, had their "fifteen minutes of fame," and faded out of the limelight again, presumably following a reasonably ordinary course of life thereafter. Their prominence stemmed from one major fact: the sister married the great chief Powhatan. Her brother came into favor as well and even traveled to England as a guest of the colony, a trip that will not figure in our account of his life's course. We know little of their personalities, other than that when he was away from his own people, Machumps could be hot-tempered to the point of murder (he killed a compatriot, Namontack, on the way home from England in 1610, a murder that he and the English concealed from Powhatan). But this brother and sister became important only because of a temporary connection with eastern Virginia's paramount chief: Winganuske's tenure as wife was limited by custom, and Machumps's fortunes seem to have faded along with hers, since he was only one of several young Indian men who learned enough English to become an interpreter for his people. Instead the pair was in many ways representative of Virginia Algonquian people of their time. Powhatan culture had very little occupational specialization, and the lives of nearly all males and females followed certain well-defined paths. Winganuske and Machumps are as good a choice as any to follow, and their names are not the usual yard-long Algonquian ones.

Further Environmental Considerations

The native people of eastern Virginia lived in a dual world of water and land, as had their ancestors ever since sea level rose after the last Ice Age. Both water and land were extremely important in their lives. Both elements also had their hazards to human life, so that they had to be treated with respect, which included making offerings and prayers. John Smith wrote that "All things that were able to do them hurt beyond their prevention, they adore with their kind of divine worship; as the fire, water, lightning, thunder, our ordnance, pieces [guns], horses, etc." Smith and most of his readers would see such rituals, aimed at local or tutelary deities, as superstition. More likely, to the Powhatans the prayers and offerings were not only heartfelt but also a perfectly sensible precaution to take before going to work.

Waterways permeate eastern Virginia. Their waters and marshes provided the Powhatans with a variety of food plus a major transportation route, so tribal territories either spanned both sides of a major river in the inner coastal plain or surrounded the drainage of large tributaries to an estuary. Fast-moving floods in spring or after hurricanes are only a minor danger that occurs along narrower watercourses. Most of the region's waterways are wide enough to have a considerable "fetch," so the danger comes instead from wind and lightning. The Chesapeake Bay area can get pounded by horrific squalls at most seasons of the year; they occur almost daily in some years in the late spring and early summer. Even modern ships with powerful diesel engines can be blown onto shoals or into bridges in winds well over seventy miles per hour if anchoring precautions are not taken in time. The Powhatans, in their dugout canoes, knew enough to head for shore early on and stay there until the blow was over. If a storm went on too long, so that no canoes could be launched and waterborne business came to a halt, there were rituals the priests performed to try to quell the winds. Storm-raising was also in the hands of the priests: the English saw such a ritual on the Nansemond River in 1611, when the local people wanted the forces of nature to soak the enemy's guns.

Fig. 3.3. Replicated dugout canoe paddled by the Jamestown Settlement staff who made it. Courtesy of Helen C. Rountree.

Dugout canoes were slow in the making and cumbersome to maneuver (fig. 3.3), as living historians have found out at both Jamestown Settlement and the Mariner's Museum in Newport News. Dugout hulls were rounded on the ends and very heavy, which made them sluggish and tippy, though hard to capsize completely. There was no keel, so that in any wind they tried to come about broadside to the wind and sit there lolloping. Henry Spelman's derogatory depiction of their shape, "the form of a hogs trough," is roughly accurate, and it definitely feels apposite to anyone trying to paddle one somewhere today. It was not the Powhatans' fault: they lacked metal other than soft copper and were short of hard rock that would make sharp, straight edges for anything like a workable chisel, much less a saw for cutting ribs and boards. Instead, the most efficient cutting tool they had to transform a large log into a dugout was fire: burn a piece and scrape out the charcoal with a shell; burn another piece, and so on. It was a slow process, rather like paying on the installment plan *before* getting the boat. But without a dugout, or if the old canoe gave out before a new one was finished, then the family faced either borrowing another from busy relatives or else doing without a lot of crucial things for a while (for lists of the things procured by men and women, see below).

Land was the other world in which the Powhatans lived. The uplands away from the rivers were left in mature forest, where firewood and certain plant foods were to be found and whose nut trees provided necessary food for animals and for the people who hunted them. Terraces near the waterways were used for farming and houses, as mentioned in chapter 2, and they were also used for foraging. Abandoned fields produce various wild plants useful to humans at various times after cultivation ends (fig. 3.4), some of which the English saw the Powhatans using (like blackberries), so people would have gone collecting there. All things that people foraged on land had to be brought back under human power: like all other peoples in the Americas before the Europeans came, the Powhatans had neither draft animals nor wheels for carts.

The Virginia Algonquians would have faced several kinds of danger as they went about their work on land, so they went in groups and made offerings before leaving home. Human enemies might attack them suddenly, since guerilla warfare was the norm back then. There were also several large predator species still on the scene before the English drove them nearly to extinction within Virginia: bears, packs of wolves, and bobcats. (These predators also reduced the deer population, making deerskins even harder for Indian families to come by.) In the mature forest, there could be danger from large dead limbs falling. Aside from the rattlesnakes and copperheads lurking in that forest and also in the old fields (they are *not* extinct today), it was possible to trip and fall, if one were not careful, and get a sprain or even a fracture perhaps far from home. And in the overgrown fields and edge areas of the mature forest there were tangles of briars, some of them with long enough thorns to pierce through one's leggings. William Strachey was told that "many of them are divers times (especially offenders [who had not made offerings]) shrewdly scratched as they walk alone in the woods." Scratches that were not cleaned soon enough, especially in the warm weather that promoted bacteria, often became "putrefied" (Strachey's word) with the infections mentioned in chapter 1, the results being pain and debilitation for the victim.

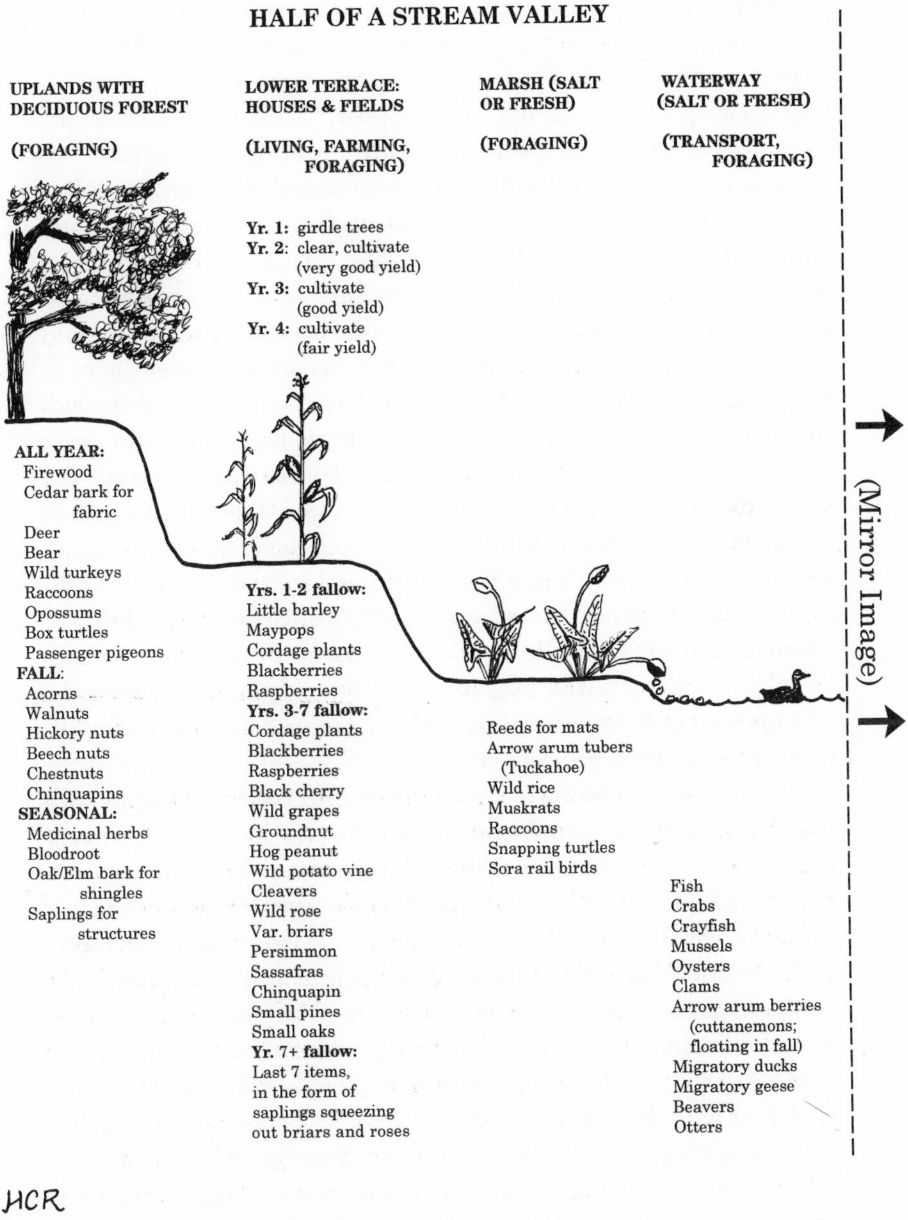

HALF OF A STREAM VALLEY

UPLANDS WITH DECIDUOUS FOREST	LOWER TERRACE: HOUSES & FIELDS	MARSH (SALT OR FRESH)	WATERWAY (SALT OR FRESH)
(FORAGING)	(LIVING, FARMING, FORAGING)	(FORAGING)	(TRANSPORT, FORAGING)

Yr. 1: girdle trees
Yr. 2: clear, cultivate (very good yield)
Yr. 3: cultivate (good yield)
Yr. 4: cultivate (fair yield)

ALL YEAR:
Firewood
Cedar bark for
    fabric
Deer
Bear
Wild turkeys
Raccoons
Opossums
Box turtles
Passenger pigeons
FALL:
Acorns
Walnuts
Hickory nuts
Beech nuts
Chestnuts
Chinquapins
SEASONAL:
Medicinal herbs
Bloodroot
Oak/Elm bark for
    shingles
Saplings for
    structures

Yrs. 1-2 fallow:
Little barley
Maypops
Cordage plants
Blackberries
Raspberries
Yrs. 3-7 fallow:
Cordage plants
Blackberries
Raspberries
Black cherry
Wild grapes
Groundnut
Hog peanut
Wild potato vine
Cleavers
Wild rose
Var. briars
Persimmon
Sassafras
Chinquapin
Small pines
Small oaks
Yr. 7+ fallow:
Last 7 items,
in the form of
saplings squeezing
out briars and roses

Reeds for mats
Arrow arum tubers
    (Tuckahoe)
Wild rice
Muskrats
Raccoons
Snapping turtles
Sora rail birds

Fish
Crabs
Crayfish
Mussels
Oysters
Clams
Arrow arum berries
    (cuttanemons;
    floating in fall)
Migratory ducks
Migratory geese
Beavers
Otters

(Mirror Image)

HCR

Fig. 3.4. Cross-section of half a stream basin, with human use areas shown. Courtesy of Helen C. Rountree.

Altogether, the land and the waters that ran through it were sources of both sustenance and danger. People had to know where the plants and animals were, and they also had to be on the lookout, with the deities' help, for dangers that were quite real. It was a rich world, but humankind was not in charge of it, so people had to treat it with great respect.

Powhatan houses, and the limited cutting tools they had with which to make those houses, show another facet of the people's working with, rather than against, the natural world. Indian men wielded smallish, not-very-sharp axes in the Late Woodland and Early Contact periods. Those small axes could be used either to finish off a wounded enemy (quickly) or to cut down trees (laboriously). Cutting larger trees might have to be done to clear a field desired by the women, but that was done with the people's other cutting tool, fire: burn off the bark around the tree's base and give it a year to die and dry out. Houses required trees that were numerous and also green so that they could be bent and cured in that shape (see the account of women's housebuilding below). Hence the use of saplings for house frameworks and for the uprights in palisades. Houses were not covered with the clapboards that the English preferred; clapboards required saws that the Indians did not have. So bark shingles or reed mats were used to weatherproof them, with wind-resistant rounded ends and placement of the framework under trees for further protection from the elements.

William Strachey wrote that properly covered Powhatan houses, with fires burning in the central hearths, were "warm as stoves albeit very smoky" even in the depths of winter. They were kept smoky in the summertime too, to ward off mosquitoes as people slept. It took a lot of labor to build a "good" house like that, and continual labor to keep it in repair, as the Indian Village staff at Jamestown Settlement has discovered. The work was most probably done in groups, very likely by members of the extended family ("from 6 to 20 in a house," in John Smith's words) who lived in each house. The people worked in groups by day; by night they made love with their spouses and slept cheek by jowl with their relatives or in-laws; they were almost never alone. Ethnographic analogy with . other populations living in one-room houses and working constantly in groups indicates that people who have never had privacy do not miss it.

Each family made what it needed, with materials for house furnishings, tools, and clothing all coming from the foraging territory that the tribe held in common. People accustomed to making their own implements, even those that are expensive in terms of time to manufacture them, do not view their possessions in quite the way we do. Things are made to be used, and as they wear out, they are replaced. (Many American families used to feel that way about handmade quilts, until those became "folk art.") When the cutting and smoothing tools are necessarily primitive like those of the Powhatans, many items would take time and patience to make. However, repetitive labor does not require all one's attention, as some modern women like Rountree who read while knitting or crocheting can attest. So Indian women making pottery by the coil method (wheels being lacking) and men scraping bone into fishhooks would have established enough muscle-memory that their hands would go on "autopilot." They would consciously be doing other things with other members of their sex sitting nearby: visiting, watching toddlers, telling stories to older children, reporting things they saw while outside the village, and making plans for future expeditions. Older men would be politicking. And the children who saw these adults would know that "good" people were *never* idle.

The Powhatan annual round involved two major "desertions" of their towns. Men and boys went on trips away from the village to fish and hunt at all seasons, but the fishing was done more intensively during the spring fish runs and the hunting was done much more intensively in the late fall. Those two seasons corresponded to things the women were doing away from home, for women and men were complementary providers of food for their families. Serious nut-gathering went on in October and November, a job made more urgent among people who lived along saltwater streams because they lacked tuckahoe to gather in the spring. The women among those people did raise more corn than did the inner coastal plain women, but no Powhatans seem to have chosen to farm intensively enough to live on domesticated plant foods year-round (for reasons given in chapter 1). The spring and early summer, then, after last year's crop of corn and nuts had run out and before the new corn crop came in, required women and girls to forage for wild plants to supplement the men's fish. So both fall and spring saw whole families leaving the towns and dispersing into temporary camps around the rest of their territories.

There were always jobs to do, whether they be collecting materials to work on in the village or repairing things already made. One way these industrious people reduced the workload was to live simply, unlike us.

Houses were furnished sparsely, with built-in bed platforms doubling as sitting places and bedding of mats and skins being rolled up out of the way during the day. Housecleaning seems to have been rudimentary, leaving certain insects in charge: colonist Ralph Hamor reported being driven out of the house assigned him for the night by the attacks of fleas. The year was 1614 and his host was the great Powhatan himself, who had plenty of people available to keep the house "clean" by Indian standards.

Clothing was very expensive, requiring hunting and killing deer (bringing down one could take all day), plus skinning the carcasses and then stretching, scraping, and tanning the hides (several days' work). Clothing was kept from being more expensive by keeping it simple; there was no tailored clothing, with sleeves and the like. Children went nude, which is why a prepubescent Pocahontas was described as turning cartwheels "naked as she was" all over the English fort. Breechclouts for men and aprons for women, hung on cordage belts, used one deerskin or less each. To repel insects, people smeared on animal-fat-based paint. For foraging, people added deerskin moccasins and leggings, all sewn by their owners, male or female. When faced with a get-filthy job, like that of the warriors Powhatan ordered to carry some visiting Englishmen ashore through frozen mud in 1608, most if not all clothing was discarded.

Judging by the hardiness observed by the English, everybody practiced the ability to acclimatize their bodies so as not to feel cold except in truly arctic conditions. Daily baths in nearby waterways, whether salty, brackish, or fresh, were a requirement for living like a "human being," and in cold weather that meant immersion in cold water. What people had to ward off bitter weather the rest of the day was impractical if one had to be active: the forerunner of the woven "Indian blanket," a mantle made of multiple deerskins—if the family had enough left over for such a luxury. A family with poor hunters would have to do without even that in the winter; in fact, its members would be so short of deerskins year-round that they would have to make loin coverings out of "grass, the leaves of trees, and such like." And very likely the wives would be seriously considering divorce.

Childhood

Winganuske and Machumps were born into a world where infants were rarely separated from their mothers. The Powhatans, like so many other

Native American peoples, put their babies into cradleboards, so that they could go out and about with their busy, working mothers. Babies were exposed early to the elements. For one thing, they took daily baths along with their families, no matter what the weather. For another thing, Powhatan cradleboards were not elaborate, judging from a later engraving made for Robert Beverley's book: a wooden slab drilled with holes at top and bottom, so that the deerskin thongs passed around the baby's shoulders and feet could be fastened securely. In very cold weather, the baby must have been wrapped first, to prevent hypothermia, but the engraving shows a naked baby. The child was also smeared with animal fat and paint to "tan their skins, that after a year or two, no weather will hurt them," as John Smith reported. Early European visitors to North America had seen people thus tanned and dyed a reddish color and assumed that these "red Indians" (as some British people still call them) were born that way. John Smith and William Strachey did their best to dispel that myth.

Only hardy children, as Machumps and Winganuske would prove to be, survived as long as two years. The rate of infant and early childhood mortality in the Late Woodland Chesapeake region has already been noted in chapter 1. One form of infant death, however, was apparently not condoned: the deliberate killing of a baby. Henry Spelman witnessed the public execution of a woman who had killed her presumably healthy infant, along with the two men who had helped her do it (the method is not mentioned) and a third man who had seen the goings-on but had not reported them.

Winganuske and Machumps, if they were full siblings, were probably several years apart in age. The evidence for this supposition is indirect and relies heavily upon ethnographic analogy. Strachey noticed that the Powhatans' population was lower than elsewhere in his travels, and he blamed it both on the attrition of warfare and on men's tiring themselves out through an "immoderate use and multiplicity of women," which he implied lowered the birth rate. The Powhatan birth rate probably was lower than among the English gentry and Turkish diplomats that Strachey had known.[1] But part of the difference may have been due to the mothers' lengthy breast-feeding of children, recorded for many American Indian peoples, which would have caused a prolonged lowering of fertility. Mrs. Strachey and her friends used wet-nurses, which allowed for more frequent pregnancies. Another contributing factor, also reported in many better-recorded Eastern Woodlands tribes, may have been the fathers' periodic absences from the marital bed for a variety of reasons. Hunting could mean several days away; warring could mean several weeks. And before engaging in either one but especially the latter, most Woodland men went through ritual purifications involving sexual abstinence and other self-mortifications. Wives also separated themselves from all men while they menstruated (recorded for the Powhatans) and during and after giving birth (length of time not recorded for the Powhatans). Men might have been hard warriors, but they were also brittle creatures who could be harmed by blood from a woman's womb. (Early twentieth-century Iroquois medicine included a prescription to cure the shriveling-up that could afflict a man's "fifth leg" if he slept with a menstruating woman.) All of these practices reduced the number of nights that marital partners could spend together, which must have lowered the birth rate somewhat. The active life that Powhatan women led would have made them desirous of using all of these methods to space out children. In a society that lacked wheeled strollers, having children too close together in age made for genuine hardship.

Virginia Algonquian people had several names during their lifetimes, some of them borne simultaneously. Very personal secret names were given early in life and not divulged easily for fear of malicious use by a sorcerer of a possession so personal. The only reason we know this much about the Powhatans is that Samuel Purchas wrote that when Pocahontas converted to Christianity in 1614 and took on the new "powerful" name Rebecca, she revealed that her secret name up until then had been Matoaka. Her "proper" yet public name as of 1610 was Amonute, whose meaning is unknown; it may have been a child's name, differing from an earlier "proper" baby name. In later childhood her father called her "Pocahontas," meaning "little wanton"—the early seventeenth-century meanings of "wanton" being "capricious" or "teasing" as well as "lewd." Thus it is safe to say that Winganuske and Machumps had other secret names and probably also different public names in early childhood.

Machumps especially could expect that his future names would be a serious matter. Strachey tells us that boys and young men were supposed to "aspire to many names," which they had to earn by deeds. Powhatan names were composed by parents and others, so that, like names in so many other Native American cultures, they had clear meanings, as opposed to European ones whose meanings had become buried by time and translation. So for up-and-coming Powhatan males, one's name reported something one had done or seen fairly recently. Names could become a source of pressure: a twenty-year-old who was still called "Killer of Rabbits" was a permanent bachelor.

The pressure toward performance from parents and other adults was probably indirect, though. John Smith's only statement about child-rearing, which was corroborated and added to by Strachey, was that "they love children very dearly." One interpretation is that Smith and Strachey were a bit surprised that Indian parents insisted on rearing their own children and doing it gently. The English, on the other hand, had long had a tradition of "fostering out" among people from the tradesman level on up. One's own children were sent to live as apprentices or servants in a more highly placed family, to learn their trade and their manners and to make "higher" connections that might result in social mobility for the other relatives. Correspondingly, one took in the children of other, more lowly families. The result for the children was a "better" education gained under harsher conditions, the parents being deemed too likely to pamper their own children, a "bad" thing. Powhatan parents were offered the chance to "foster out" their children to English families throughout the seventeenth century. But they steadfastly refused to cooperate, partly because they saw it as an unwelcome assimilation attempt and partly because, in the Indian world, proper parents trained their own offspring.

Another interpretation of loving children "dearly" is that the Powhatans probably resembled other better-recorded American Indian peoples in using minimal lecturing and very little physical discipline with their progeny. Under this system of tutelage, children are assumed to be thinking creatures who can deduce—sooner or later—that the adult behavior they see is the proper "human" way to be. That is a system which works when there is no separate, exciting "kid culture" to deflect children's interest from the respectable but essentially workaday world of the adults. Before the modern industrialized world developed a "kid culture," it was true in all societies that one gained self-worth and a measure of autonomy only by becoming a full-fledged adult. Children aspired to be "grown-ups" rather than adolescents. So it was with Powhatan youth. No one put them on clock-time in their development, for the culture itself did not have clock-time. But they were expected to absorb what was expected of "proper" human beings, and they were to do it with a minimum of being lectured to. Many traditional Native American societies emphasized learning by observation, with the learner not attempting the new skill publicly until he or she felt fully ready to perform. That was possible under conditions of close watching of one's elders, in very small groups of people, rather than under classroom conditions. Fortunately, plenty of adults were available in such traditional cultures, since all parents expected to be teachers.

When Winganuske and Machumps reached the age of about three, their paths in life began to diverge seriously. Winganuske remained physically and emotionally close to her mother, at least until she married, for she would spend her life in the women's world, which was strenuous but companionable. Her toys were miniatures of the women's pots, carrying bags, and so forth. Machumps, however, was male, and he had to prepare to belong to a different milieu. He was expected to grow up to resemble his father and other male relatives, who lived in a world of competition: with his own people for wives and for the chief's approval, and with enemy tribes for glory and captives to bring home. Boys' toys were smaller versions of the men's weaponry, for constant practice was needed to achieve competence as a stalker and bowman. The male world was exacting, exciting, and potentially lethal. Machumps had to identify himself with that world while distancing himself from that of his mother; later there would be a final, drastic severance at the hands of the older men.

Let us first examine what Winganuske's girlhood would have been like. Much of what we can say about it comes from living history. Then we will turn to Machumps's boyhood, which will rely more upon the writings of his fellow males among the English colonists.

Girlhood

Winganuske was trained to become a woman with a strong body and a good memory. The tough bodies of Powhatan and other Woodland Indian women were noted by European observers; a huge mental database would have to be learned in order to carry out all the jobs that are merely listed by those writers. Girls, and also boys when young, helped their mothers do their work, according to John Smith. And Smith's list of the work is fairly comprehensive: "They make mats, baskets, pots, [wooden] mortars, pound their corn, [plant, weed, and] gather their corn, bear all kind of burdens and such like." The real list probably went farther: in better-described Woodland tribes, women gathered a large variety of edible wild plants and were also responsible for the carrying of water, cooking of food, and collecting of firewood to do the cooking. They were not, however, the only ones responsible for rearing children; men were involved too, during their rest periods at home.

Being the main providers of fuel in Powhatan society would by itself have demanded physical fitness in the women. A wood fire had to be kept going continually in the house, according to Strachey, or bad luck ensued. Other fires were made from it: cook fires, fires to dance around in the evening, fire to hollow out canoes and mortars. The need for firewood was continuous and heavy. It did not take many trips into the woods by an extended family's women before the daily collecting excursions lengthened considerably. John Smith wrote that "near their habitations is little small wood or old trees on the ground by reason of their burning of them for fire. So that a man may gallop a horse amongst these woods any way, but where the creeks or rivers shall hinder." Firewood once gathered must have been a burden both heavy and cumbersome to transport home. At least the women's outdoor hearth cooking did not require anyone to chop the wood into smaller pieces.

Winganuske would not have grown up assuming that women "stayed home" to do their work. Like most societies that lacked plow agriculture, the Powhatans probably had no "domestic sphere." Instead women and children had continually to go out and get things in order to do the jobs in John Smith's list: water from the stream for cooking; water from a spring for drinking, if the stream were at all salty; firewood wherever they could find it; farm crops when they came in; wild plant foods perhaps from miles away when crops were not available; other wild plant materials to make things, including the carrying baskets and tumplines that continually wore out; clay to make pottery; little fossil shells to embroider a chief's robe.

The list just of *edible native* wild plants encompasses some 1,100 species in eastern Virginia, several dozen of them being productive enough to be worth the women's time. The variety of the preferred habitats of those plants meant that any women who gathered them had to travel, sometimes by canoe, to many parts of their territory at various seasons of the year (see table 3.1, which is only a sample of the usable species). John Smith was wrong when he said that the Powhatans lived "near 3 parts of the year . . . from hand to mouth." The amount may have been right in the drought years he saw, but the method was wrong. Wandering around,

Fig. 3.5. Arrow arum (*Peltandra virginica*), whose tubers the Powhatans called *tuckahoe*, and berries *cuttanemons*. The distinctive two veins growing downward from the indented base of each leaf are characteristic of the species. Courtesy of Helen C. Rountree.

aimlessly searching, would have led to hunger. The women not only memorized where which things normally grew; they had been trained, as professional botanists are, to recognize even temporarily useful plants at *all* seasons. Thus they could make mental notes during their trips out into the tribal territory about which species were making a new appearance where.

Some wild foods were available all year if needed. The most prominent in English accounts was tuckahoe, a major source of starch and therefore of carbohydrates in the months before the corn crop came in (if it did that

year). Modern botanists guessed which marsh plant John Smith was talk-
ing about: *Peltandra virginica*, arrow arum (fig. 3.5), a distant cousin of
the taro from which Hawaiians make poi. It can form large stands along
meandering freshwater streams (fig. 3.6). But no botanist that Rountree
interviewed felt certain about that identification until she and a culinary
arts teacher and some of the Jamestown Settlement Indian Village staff
waded out into a marsh, dug some up, and tried eating it both raw (ouch!
. . . too acidic) and prepared (blah . . . no real taste). That led the culinary
arts man, who teaches courses on foods around the world, to speculate

Fig. 3.6. Arrow arum growing along a meandering freshwater
stream. Courtesy of Helen C. Rountree.

Table 3.1. Major native edible wild plants of eastern Virginia by season

Ecozone[a]	Spring	Summer	Fall	Winter
SALTWATER MARSH	Glasswort plants ———————————			
		Salt-marsh bulrush (various parts) ———————		
BRACKISH MARSH	Cattail rootstocks			
	Glasswort plants			
		Salt-marsh bulrush (various parts) ———————		
		Great bulrush (various parts) ——————		
	Reed shoots ————————————————————— Reed rootstocks ———————			
FRESHWATER MARSH	Reed shoots ————————————————————— Reed rootstocks ———————			
	Cattail rootstocks			
	Tuckahoe tubers ———————————		Tuckahoe berries ———————	
		Wild rice ———————		
		Pickerelweed seeds		
		Great bulrush (various parts) ———————		
			Cow lily rootstocks ———————	
			Duck potatoes	
	Jewelweed shoots and leaves ———————————— Water parsnips ———————			
SWAMPY WOODS	Tuckahoe tubers ———————————		Tuckahoe berries ———————	
	Groundnuts ——————— Wild rose hips			
	Reed shoots ——————————————————		Reed roots ———————	
	Jewelweed shoots and leaves ———————————		Jack-in-the-pulpit tubers ———————	
	Knotweed leaves ———————————		Skunk cabbage tubers ———————	

Habitat	(Greens)	(Berries)	(Berries, Nuts)
FALLOW, OVERGROWN FIELDS (see fig. 3.4)		Wild grapes Various berries	Water parsnips Acorns Persimmons
PINE WOODS	Pine trees' inner bark (emergency food; year-round) Pine needles (for tea: vitamin C) Briars' leaves as greens	Persimmons Wild plums, some berries	
WOODLAND EDGES	Briars' leaves Bracken Violet leaves	Wild rose hips Various berries	Persimmons Hog peanuts Black walnuts Wild grapes
DECIDUOUS FOREST	Briars' leaves Indian cucumber root Jewel weed shoots and leaves Violet leaves	Various berries May apple	Pawpaws Jack-in-the-pulpit tubers Acorns Nuts[b] Hog peanuts

a. For a longer, more detailed list, see appendix C of Rountree and Davidson's *Eastern Shore Indians of Virginia and Maryland*. Much of the Maryland Eastern Shore's vegetation parallels that of the inner coastal plain of Virginia.

b. Beech, chestnut, chinquapin, several kinds of hickory, two kinds of walnut.

that like other peoples who ate a great variety of wild foods without seasoning them, the Powhatans were more attuned to texture than to taste as they filled their stomachs.

Smith never said whether men or women gathered tuckahoe, only that "a Savage" could gather enough in one day to last a week. Since it was a plant food, it probably fell to the women and girls to dig it. Trying to dig that plant was enough to enlighten Rountree about the women's physique (confirmed by a physical anthropologist who has examined their bones): many of them must have been built like piano-movers. The tubers are large, but they are buried up to two feet down in the mud and held fast there by a few fleshy roots and a myriad of thin, steely rootlets that dulled the culinary arts teacher's toughest kitchen knives. The best extraction method found by the self-styled "grunts" from Jamestown Settlement was for two or three people to sit down on the muddy bottom at high tide and attack a single clump of plants, alternately removing the surrounding mud (which will float away) with hands and feet and prying at the clustered tubers with both feet and a long-handled chisel-ended stick until the rootlets had all been snapped. The cluster was then cleaned further and set aside. It was a genuinely get-filthy job, but since we were a mixed work crew, we had to remain clothed. Powhatan female diggers probably did it sensibly, in the buff.

When a tuckahoe party was in progress, there was probably a canoe nearby, for that was the most efficient way to transport people to and from the marsh and also to get a large load of food home. Tubers tossed into the canoe could be given their first stage of processing: slicing off their rinds and throwing those overboard. Arrow arum plants are permeated with oxalic acid; all parts of them, when bruised or cut, can sting hands that are not callused, as both of us professional teachers found out. Older women and any children sitting in the canoe would, like the Indian Village staff at Jamestown Settlement, be immune because of hands toughened by the work they did daily. But it made sense not to create stinging piles of garbage near the homeplace, so the tuckahoe tubers were probably peeled while the younger women attacked the next clump of plants. We found that a large clump's tubers could be dug out in about twenty minutes, yielding nearly fifteen pounds of edible material. John Smith was right: a day's work could feed a family for a week.

Peltandra tubers tasted exactly like a beesting when Rountree nibbled a raw one for the good of science. So their acid has to be neutralized by either of two methods given by John Smith: by cutting the tubers into coins and sun-drying them, or by baking them for twenty-four hours in an earth oven or hot coal pit containing tubers covered by oak leaves and ferns and covered further by earth. We tried sun-drying and found that even after neutralization of the acid, arrow arum resists being pounded up into fine flour, according to the culinary arts teacher. But somehow Winganuske's kinswomen reduced the stuff to a usable consistency. Smith wrote that it was used "ordinarily for bread," especially in June through August [of 1607 through 1609, when a drought delayed the corn crop]. Smith did not mention that the districts in which the waterways were brackish or salty lack arrow arum, so that the local people had either to trade for it or make other arrangements. The Kecoughtans and Accomacs, at least, were accustomed to farming more intensively: William Strachey remarked upon it for the former, John Pory for the latter.

Winganuske would have learned her people's cooking techniques much sooner than she mastered the edible plant list. The methods were basic: roasting over a fire, grilling by using a hot, flat stone as a griddle, and stewing. Since the English noted that the people ate when they were hungry, rather than on a schedule, the most efficient way to feed an on-the-go family in a world that lacked refrigeration and microwave ovens was to keep a large stewpot simmering all the time. A later colonist called it the "hominy pot," but into it could be tossed any tubers, greens, or skinned animal carcasses that family members procured during the day. Even the smallest children could contribute and feel they were helping to feed the family.

A pot in constant use was in danger of breakage, with a hungry aftermath. So Winganuske's womenfolk very likely scheduled in the activities needed to produce a backup pot before the current one broke. They had long since memorized where the pottery clay was in their territory. Now, as they passed by on some other errand (always save energy by combining errands), they collected clay and also the shell or quartz to crush for temper, so that they were ready to begin the several-day process of making a pot by the coil method (fig. 3.7). The actual coiling would only take a couple of hours for a working mother; but the clay had to be cleaned and the temper crushed and added beforehand, and then the completed pot had to be dried out over several days, followed by firing for several hours (extra firewood needed). It was a job that had to be chipped away at while doing other tasks.

Winganuske probably grew up in a women's world that was free of clock-time but involved a great deal of thought about scheduling ahead. The building of a house, for instance, took only a day or so if enough people worked at it. But the preparations began *months* before, since all the materials that went into the house came from plants, and these had to be gathered—at the right season—and processed from scratch.

A new house required a couple of miles of cordage, since its parts were lashed together, not nailed. Cordage could be dug up, in the form of rootlets, around trees like pines, but John Smith observed women making it out of fibers, which they twisted. The fibers had to be extracted by hand from the mature (late summer onward), previously dried (nature-dried, in winter and early spring, is easiest) stems of certain plants, such as the Indian hemp (or dogbane, *Apocynum cannabinum*) that grows in abandoned fields. That plant's fiber can be smoothed enough that the English colonists referred to it as "silk-grass." Twisting the fibers into long

Fig. 3.7. Rolling out a coil to add to a pot's conical base. Courtesy of Helen C. Rountree.

Fig. 3.8. Making opposite-twist cordage that will not come apart. Courtesy of Helen C. Rountree.

lengths of cordage was probably something that Winganuske and her female relatives were constantly doing, just to keep ahead of the family's requirements. Once the fibers were twisted correctly, as shown in figure 3.8, so they did not come apart, they could be woven into household items (fig. 3.9) or used to lash things together.

The things lashed immediately for the new house would be reeds, gathered from the marshes during the cold months when the reeds were dry and lighter in weight. A canoe would still be necessary, not only to get to and from the marsh but also to haul enough reeds, in many trips, to make a great many mats. The Powhatans are known to have used mats, of reeds or woven cordage, for a wide variety of things: house coverings,

Fig. 3.9. Twining two lines around "ribs" to make a bag. Courtesy of Helen C. Rountree.

doors for houses, clean places to sit or work on the ground outdoors, part of the bedding people slept on, even shrouds for corpses. The stiffer reed mats, in two layers, could weatherproof a house if applied properly, as John Smith made clear, and they last several years when constantly exposed to wood smoke, as the staff at Jamestown Settlement has discovered. But it took a tremendous amount of work for the women to produce enough reed-and-cordage mats to cover a house, and starting well ahead of time was the only sensible proceeding.

One more set of materials had to be prepared as well before building day arrived. Virginia Algonquian houses had barrel-vaulted roofs whose shape was established by a framework of saplings set into the ground, bent over, and lashed together at the top. The living history practitioners at Jamestown Settlement have found that house-building goes much faster when saplings are already curved at their tops. That can be done by bending them into the proper curve soon after cutting and lashing them in that form into the loft of an existing house to cure in the dryness and smoke. Additional straight saplings can be cut at any time to serve as crosspieces and the frames for beds. And on the actual building day, the only jobs left for the women and girls (and possibly males helping) would be digging the small postholes, setting in the curved saplings, adding the crosspieces, climbing them like a ladder and lashing pairs of opposing saplings together at the rooftop, setting in the built-in bed platforms, and lashing on all the mats. It might take a day or two.

John Smith reported that similar but less solid traveling houses could be erected in a couple of hours. That was true, but it was because the women carried ready-made mats and cordage on the trip with them. Where people went frequently, more solid frameworks were erected and left for future visits. In January 1608 John Smith and his escort sheltered under one, put up halfway across the James-York peninsula on a route between Powhatan's capital and Jamestown. If the north-south route involved using Queen's Creek and then College Creek, which cut deeply into the peninsula from opposite sides, then the traveling house's location may have been somewhere in the historic area of Williamsburg.

The last major job Winganuske learned that we need to consider here is farming. The method was recorded in some detail: clear a plot, either by girdling and killing the trees a year in advance or by cutting them down with stone axes; make holes a couple of feet apart, in a gridwork rather than rows; drop in a few beans and corn kernels, and plant squash seeds between the holes; keep the weeds out; part way through the growing season pile soil around the base of the young plants, "like a hop-yard," which helped to keep them from drying out; and begin harvesting the corn when it was still green. Several plots were farmed per year, planted one by one through the spring to produce fresh vegetables all through the late summer and fall.

All of the work after field clearing was done by women and their children of both sexes, according to the English, who felt that the men were too lazy to get involved. However, the men were completely focused on another time-consuming goal, as we shall see. And anyone who has seen a field being farmed by digging-stick horticulture and the plants intercropped (interspersed with each other), as Rountree observed in West Africa, will know that a great deal of food can be produced without removing tree trunks or having to weed extensively once the ground cover (squash vines, in the Powhatans' case) has taken hold. In other words, Powhatan women had to minimize the labor needed in the fields, just as they minimized it around the house, in order to get all their other jobs (like gathering firewood) done.

The women used no fertilizer; extra fish would have had to be caught by somebody. And without fertilizer, fields began to lose their fertility and had to be fallowed after as few as two or three years, which meant a constant shifting of garden plots up and down the waterways. Plow agriculture, requiring clear-cut fields, would have been a waste of time unless fertilizer could be acquired and used, to say nothing of providing pasture or fodder for draft animals (which the Powhatans lacked) to pull the plows. All of that labor, performed by men in the Eastern Hemisphere, would have meant much more work for adults who were already busy.

There was one male job, however, that probably took place in the fields and added to the minimizing-of-labor principle: target practice for boys. Many wild birds and animals, including deer, like to browse on corn as it ripens. Rather than trying to cut fence rails with stone axes and put up fences around fields that were moved every three or so years, Indian mothers could station their young sons around the fields to shoot animal trespassers. The Carolina Algonquian-speakers made "scarecrow huts" for their boys to lurk in, according to John White. The Virginia English are silent on the matter. But the boys got shooting practice, and the proceeds went into the family stewpot.

Winganuske and her womenfolk were the solid bedrock of Powhatan society, producing most if not all of the fuel and much of the food for their households on a reliable, everyday basis. Not only that, but the corn they raised was a high-status food considered necessary in the feasts that chiefs gave to VIPs. Neither ordinary husbands nor chiefs could function without wives (preferably), or sisters or mothers (who might have other men to feed). Men's work was undoubtedly important, but the English estimates of women's "lowly" status are probably far off the mark. The work the women did must have made them autonomous from men, rather than inferior to them. Women's work physically separated them from men for much of every day. Both sexes went outside the village to work, but often in different directions or for activities (like hunting) that did not mix with those of the other sex. The women's interests and conversation would have concerned all that was going on within their very active world, without a great deal of overlap with men's affairs.

Leisure activities, however, brought men and women together, even if they were not conversing. Most evenings there would be singing accompanied by rattles and drums, to which people would dance. The dancing is poorly described in English accounts, but it was active (Henry Spelman likened it to a "Derbyshire hornpipe"), without partners or touching, and men and women both did it. Composing and delivering songs with a message, such as making fun of enemies, was another admired leisure activity among the Powhatans. After 1607, the English became the butt of the satire. There was a gambling game that men and perhaps also women played with reeds, akin to pick-up-sticks, with players guessing the numbers. Men and boys had several games, one a stickball game like the widely reported Indian game of shinny (a cousin of field hockey), another a competition to see who could kick a ball the farthest. But in another active ball game women and boys (probably children in general) competed in kicking a ball to a goal; no fighting or "strik[ing] up another's heels" was allowed.

Boyhood and Manhood

Machumps, meanwhile, was learning to make his way deeper into the world of men, a world focused upon being always prepared to kill animals and enemy people efficiently. Even the men's hairstyle announced publicly that they were expert bowmen: they cut their crown hair into a roach, let the left-side hair grow long for making knots that on dress-up occasions included war trophies like dried enemy hands, and kept the right-side hair shaved so that it did not get caught in their bowstrings (as with us, most Powhatans were right-handed). The effect was not a "Mohawk." In fact, it was condemned criminals who were made to look like Mohawks, for the first thing the Powhatans did in executing a man was to cut off his long left-side hair.

Many of the hunting skills Machumps learned (described by the colonists) would cross over into warring (also described historically) and vice versa. It is therefore logical that each episode of one activity kept the practitioner prepared for the next exploit in the other. Preparation probably went far beyond mere practical considerations among the Virginia Algonquians. Men "lived for war" throughout the Eastern Woodlands, so that ethnographic analogy can come heavily into play in understanding Powhatan males. Europeans occasionally asked Indian men if they could not stop fighting each other. Usually, like the Iroquois men, they answered that they could not even imagine a life without war. Exciting, bloody competition with human beings was only part of the reason. Those same men were using their warring skills to bring down animals that clothed and helped to feed their families, a fact that seems to have been lost on non-Indian observers. Men killed, for the good of their families as well as for themselves. It was as simple, and as all-encompassing, as that.

As a little boy, still called by the baby's name given him by his mother, Machumps's first endeavor was to become proficient as a sharpshooter who could sneak up on animals. His father (or someone acting in that capacity) taught him the essentials, but the practice was up to him. John Smith wrote that fathers did not take their sons along hunting until they were proficient, which simply makes good sense. Men needed to bring in game, even if it involved a long chase. A small, not fully coordinated child had no place in such a scheme. Machumps's mother, however, could egg him on to proficiency: William Strachey heard that Powhatan mothers held back their sons' breakfasts until they had hit a piece of moss or suchlike thrown up in the air. Hitting a target in order to eat was established early in the boy's mind. He would have practiced whenever he was not needed to help his mother carry things back and forth to the village. No small animals, except the village dogs, would have been safe from his and his contemporaries' attacks. And of course, he proudly handed over anything he managed to kill for the family stewpot.

As he got a little older, Machumps understood more of the men's talk he would have heard around the village. Hunting was very strenuous but it came in bursts, followed by rest periods. That "time off" might involve a change of pace, like clearing a new garden plot, building a fish weir, and later harvesting fish from the finished product, things which simply used the muscles of arms and backs more than legs. But real resting, in town, was part of the program. Ironically, that was when most English visitors saw the men, creating an impression of laziness. Machumps would have known better. In-town time was a time for resting and repairing or replacing hunting gear, including stone cutting tools (fig. 3.10). It was also a time to exchange information with other men, which was a necessity. Some of the talk would have been reminiscences of past hunts or raids, which would spur the men on to plan further exploits. Some of it would have been news of possible enemy movements. And some of it may have been simply the reporting of locations the men had noted: where the "scat" (droppings) indicated animal movements, where a promising-

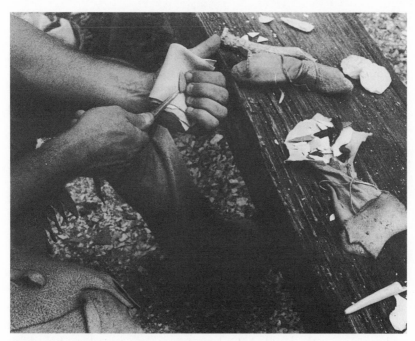

Fig. 3.10. Flint-knapping. Courtesy of Helen C. Rountree.

looking witch hazel tree was growing (to make a fine bow, when needed), and so forth. Boys needed to absorb all of these kinds of things in order to function adequately as men later.

When Machumps was ready, meaning at whatever age he was agile enough, a good enough runner, and an accurate shot with bow and arrow, his father began taking him along on hunting expeditions. The boy would strive to prove himself able, so that his father would give him a boy's name to replace the baby one. That would not be easy, for as English writers attested, hunting was both pleasurable for men and also a deadly serious business. Only in the fall, when a large supply of deer carcasses had to be acquired and processed before winter came, were organized drives employed. During most of the year it was done by stalking, a method that was easier on the deer but harder on the hunter.

Machumps' father, now with his son along, would have to go out from the village to a likely place for deer. This might be the forested edge of an abandoned field, or it might be some "open woods" (woods with occasional clearings) several miles away. Sneaking up on a deer with the help of a stuffed deer's head manipulated by his hand, the hunter approached his quarry until he had a good shot and then let fly as accurately as possible. If he killed the animal, or disabled it and could finish it off right there, then he would only have to retrace his steps to the village carrying the disemboweled carcass. On the other hand, if the shot were less successful, the hunter (and Machumps) would have to chase the creature cross-country until either another shot brought it down or the animal lost consciousness from blood loss or (in summer) overheating. The pursuit might cover quite a few miles, with the hunter running the prey as hard as he could to end the hunt. Deer are built for bursts of speed, while humans are built for distance. Some Native American men in the Northeast were known in Early Contact times to be able to run down deer that had not been wounded at all. The chase part of Indian hunting required the right physical training and also large expanses of land where other humans did not hinder things. Thus the recorded reluctance of the Powhatans and other eastern Algonquian-speakers to draw boundaries out in the forest around their districts. It is hard enough to worry about bringing down a deer without figuring in the issue of trespassing; easier to keep all foraging land in common. Another probable outcome of this kind of hunting was the build of Powhatan men: they must have been built like the cross-country runners they had to be. Modern films that have Indian warriors played by heavily-muscled stuntmen who obviously work out in gyms are simply laughable.

The same skills and weapons that John Smith and others list as being needed in hunting were also needed in war. Only warclubs or tomahawks had to be added for finishing off human enemies. War was fought mainly through lightning raids on enemy communities. It involved sneaking up on the prey, doing as much damage as possible to the men, trying to capture women and children, and then running home, often with enemy men in pursuit. If "home" was a couple of hundred miles away, the men ran the whole distance. There were no horses in pre-European America, and throughout the Eastern Woodlands being captured by enemies meant getting tortured slowly to death, a marvelous incentive to running home rather than walking.

The overall aims in the warfare of Powhatan and other Woodland peoples were to stay alive oneself while inflicting humiliation on male enemies. Captured women and children, who were living proof of their men's failure, were part of the scenario. Their change of venue was both long-term and profitable: dragged home, kept in firm but kindly imprisonment, and gradually brainwashed, they ultimately joined one's own people as wives and adopted children, thereby swelling the working population. "War brides" also brought in useful language skills, if they spoke a language different from the Powhatans' and taught their children to speak it. European traders, as married-in fathers, would do the same thing later in many Eastern Woodlands tribes.

Machumps earned his way into this demanding, frequently exhilarating world as he got older. (He would never have been taken seriously by his brother-in-law Powhatan if he had not.) He may have had to go on a "vision quest," for there is a brief, tantalizing hint of such a quest in William Strachey's writings. It would have meant leaving town, going out to a sacred place (unmarked by the Powhatans except in memory),[2] and there mortifying himself in some way until a spirit took pity on him and communicated with him through a vision. But with or without a guardian spirit, Machumps was still not fully a man until he had been huskanawed, or "made over," into a man.

Boys were expected to go through this initiation rite once they had mastered the needed skilled as hunters. The more able of them demonstrated enough competence by the age of ten; most others by the age of fifteen; a later English account says that others remaining were forcibly put through the mangle in their late teens. It really was a mangle, too, rougher in its way than U.S. Marine Corps boot camp. A recruit occasionally dies at boot camp; one or more candidates *often died* during the annual huskanaw.

The overall intent of the procedure was to "kill" the candidates as boys reared in part by women and then have them "reborn" as men trained entirely by men. English observers never saw more than the first half, which was public. But all Indian people knew something of the other half (Pocahontas did, and she told John Rolfe after she married him), and eighteenth-century writer Robert Beverley was able to learn more details about it. After being mock-killed after a big public dancing and feasting, the boys were taken out into the forest and sequestered there for several months. First they were caged up and drugged to make them "forget" everything about their previous life.[3] This was the dangerous part of the ordeal, especially if it were coupled with food deprivation. If one or two of the weaker boys died, their grieving mothers would be told that the gods had chosen them as a sacrifice. Then the candidates were gradually brought out of their stupor, tested to be sure they had amnesia (or could mimic it successfully, according to Beverley), and then educated all over again, even about eating and shooting, by specially appointed keepers. The keepers were older men of great military prowess who had earned the high honor of retraining the youths. Young men emerging from the ordeal claimed not even to know their own relatives, so focused were they on their hunting and warring duties outside the village. According to Robert Beverley's eighteenth-century account, any boys who slipped up and showed a memory of "childish" things soon after being released were taken back out in the forest and huskanawed again, which usually killed them. Machumps obviously came through the ordeal successfully the first time.

Powhatan Indian men were specifically trained as predators and would remain focused on hunting and war until they were either killed or forced to retire because of advancing age (probably their early to mid-thirties, like today's professional athletes). If they lived to retire from war, they spent their remaining years wrapped up in politics and the doings of younger warriors, while still fishing and doing some hunting and training boys to do the same. A man with great hunting and military exploits behind him could be chosen as a councillor by his village chief, or, farther up the line, by his district chief and even by the great paramount chief Powhatan himself. The decisions he would be consulted on would be primarily military ones, for as we shall see, chiefs' powers over their people were limited.

Virginia Algonquian men stayed, therefore, firmly ensconced in a men's world that was autonomous from the women's world for most of every day. They were "a man's men," for whom women were necessary colleagues but not close associates. Powhatan men got their women's time and attention only if the conditions were right; the men needed the women as much as the women needed the men.

Even a man who had come through the huskanaw was not yet entitled to say much in a war council or to smoke a pipe of tobacco, which occurred not for pleasure but in serious get-togethers. To get those privileges, he had to marry. Thus the last arbiter of whether he had become a "real man," aside from the chiefs' monitoring of their warriors, was likely to be a girl in her early teens.

Womanhood and Marriage to a Chief

Winganuske became marriageable when she began menstruating. This change was symbolized in her clothing and hairstyle. Before puberty, girls went naked and shaved their heads all over except for a long, braided lock at the back; given Powhatan mussel-shell shaving gear, girls' and men's heads probably looked bristly much of the time. Marriageable women donned a deerskin apron and grew their hair out all over, wearing it in various styles: hanging loose, braided into one plait with bangs cut in front, or cut short in a uniform length "as the Irish [do] by a dish." Like girls in many nonindustrial societies, Winganuske had been practicing all her life at what the adult women did, so she had acquired adult-level knowledge and proficiency by the age of thirteen or so. Strachey never mentioned Winganuske's age when he heard of her as a young married woman, but he understood from Machumps that all of Powhatan's current wives were "very young women." He also wrote that Pocahontas began her monthly periods and got married for the first time, to the Indian man Kocoum, in 1610 when she was about fourteen. The activity level required of Powhatan females may have kept her lean enough to delay her menarche, something that often happens to modern female athletes. Pocahontas's younger half-sister, requested as a bride by the English in 1614, was already married to an Indian husband at the age of eleven; it was a diplomatic marriage, so the girl may have been prepubescent still. Nonetheless, Winganuske became a woman and married at an age we consider to be very young for such things.

Winganuske had learned as she grew up that a good husband was a reliable provider of animal carcasses for her to process into usable things. The early English colonists are clear on the matter: the ladies were downright mercenary. They did not expect a romantic attachment and an emotionally close marriage. Such compatibility in a spouse would be welcome if it developed, but expecting it would have been unrealistic, given the different worlds that the two sexes inhabited. So it did not matter to Winganuske or her womenfolks if a prospective groom already had another wife or expected to take an extra wife later, just so long as he showed a promising ability to provide his portion of her and her children's sustenance and a conscientious regard for training his sons properly. Women were not chained to these low-key marriages thereafter: John Smith noted that women could and did get their husbands' permission when they wanted an extramarital dalliance. Strachey added, perhaps from experience, that once the consent was given, the women were "voluptuous" and willing to "embrace the acquaintance of any stranger for nothing [that is, no payment], and it is accounted no offence." In fact, to him it was incredible "with what heat both sexes of them are given over to those intemperances." The marriage bond among the Powhatans was plainly an economic and child-rearing (not child-producing) arrangement for the most part.

Winganuske ended up marrying a man who had a dozen wives *in residence* and others farmed out, as we shall see. Her wedding was also different from the ordinary. But she may have grown up expecting only a run-of-the-mill courtship and marriage, which was the fate of most Virginia Algonquian women. In this scenario, a man would have begun wooing her by bringing her presents of game, fish, and plant foods; he aimed at impressing her and her parents as well. Once marriage had been agreed to, there was the bridewealth to negotiate between the two families. The Powhatans did not have a dowry system as the English did. They calculated female usefulness in the opposite direction: a man had to pay for the privilege of getting a highly valuable wife. Once the bridewealth was accumulated, possibly in the form of shell beads, and the man and his family had prepared cooking gear and bedding for the incoming wife, the couple and their families met for the wedding proper. The couple joined hands, a chain of bridewealth shell beads was broken over their heads, and everyone settled down to a feast. The groom and his family then went home, taking the bride with them. This custom would have caused most Powhatan women to live and work with their in-laws after marriage.

That was the first marriage a girl and a young man could expect to go through, and everyone hoped the first one would last for life. Other marriages were possible afterward, however. The husband could marry additional wives in the same, expensive way if he were a superb hunter. Divorce was permitted, with the children possibly being divided between the parents according to their sex.[4] Powhatan adults could also arrange marriages by contract for a set time period, usually a year, after which they either parted or renewed the contract. Strachey reported that if they missed the deadline, they were shackled together for life, even if they were incompatible. He also wrote as if the Powhatan men had all the power to decide about marrying and staying married, parallel to the power of English husbands over their wives at that time. But from what we have seen of the Indian women's world, and remembering that "dalliances" were frequent, it is likely that marital decisions were mutual, not one-sided.

Winganuske, however, wound up in a situation in which she really did have little power. Chiefs, especially the paramount chief, were special people in Powhatan society. They inherited matrilineally their right to govern, which meant that their mothers' families were set apart. They also had to validate that right through successful military exploits and the canny acquisition of great wealth, which meant they were extremely able individuals. Chiefs could unilaterally choose the women (plural, definitely) that they would marry. They also paid whatever bridewealth they felt like paying to their prospective in-laws, whom they outranked. And they treated their wives with favor or coldness thereafter, as they pleased. Winganuske was chosen out of a lineup of girls when the great chief Powhatan visited her district's capital town (wherever it was), and after the wedding she became part of a household with other young wives in it. She managed to attach and hold Powhatan's affection, according to Strachey, so she must have had some charisma herself. Thus she got to travel around her husband's dominions in his wake, along with the other eleven favorite wives, and she and all his current wives went on display, bejeweled and painted with puccoon, when Powhatan held court at homes (fig. 3.11).

Chiefs' wives probably worked as ordinary women did most days, since their husbands had a prodigious need for corn that may not have been met by the special fields planted by subject districts. Wives would also have been badly needed, along with any other women available, when a feast had to be prepared. There was corn to be reduced to flour, corncakes to be cooked, and game to be roasted. In February 1608, after a drought year and in a month when most families' corn would be running out even after good harvests, John Smith and his escort were presented *before* a feast with fifty pounds of corncakes, freshly made. A mid-seventeenth-century Englishman, Henry Norwood, witnessed a chief's wife pounding up corn in a mortar, preparatory to cooking a meal to feed him as her husband's guest. It is likely that Powhatan's wives did that kind of labor too. Their husband, after all, did some of his own hunting still.

Winganuske nevertheless lived with luxury in her position as Powhatan's wife. She got to share in the food she cooked for feasts, which meant that she could eat cornpone all year (let us hope she liked it). Her

Fig. 3.11. William Hole's engraving of Powhatan holding court, a detail from John Smith's map of 1612.

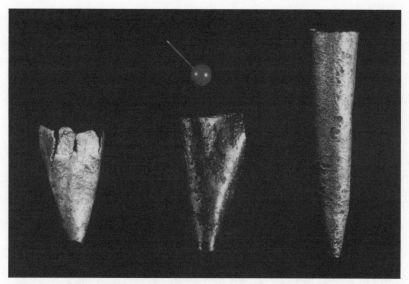

Fig. 3.12. Copper "tinklers," worn to make noise by jangling against one another, from a site in western Virginia. Courtesy of VDHR.

husband received tribute from his subject peoples, and she got to wear some of it: shell beads and ornaments made of links of native copper or "tinklers" of European copper (fig. 3.12); deerskin mantles; puccoon that turned her a luscious mulberry red from the shoulders up; and European glass trade beads, in which Powhatan had been dealing since 1608 (fig. 3.13).

Winganuske may have had other, fancier, clothing too. Embroidery in shells was known among her people. In his "throne" room Powhatan had pillows embroidered with shell beads (English writers called them "coral"). There is also a surviving shell-bead-embroidered mantle, loosely called "Powhatan's Mantle" (fig. 3.14), which may in fact have belonged to any of the chiefs in the Chesapeake region. Virginia English sources are silent about such things, but a Maryland English record of 1639 mentions cloaks that were "oftentimes ornamented with shells in circular rows." Michael Taylor, whose crew made the replica on permanent exhibit at Jamestown Settlement, estimated that nearly 20,000 shells were used on this garment. The little shells are fossil marginellas (*Prunum limatulum*),[5] each one either picked out of an eroding riverside cliff or gathered from the beach beneath. Every shell has had its shoulder

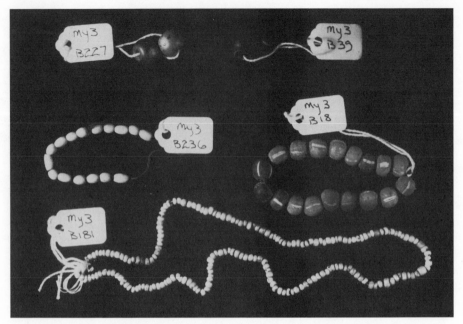

Fig. 3.13. Glass trade beads of various sorts from the Trigg site in western Virginia.
Courtesy of VDHR.

grated away (fig. 3.15) so that sinew thread could be passed through the
opening and out the shell's mouth again. And each shell was individually
sewn on with a fine needle, possibly a metal one acquired by trade, that
did not pierce all the way through the hide, so that the garment when
worn would hang straight, without dimpling. "Powhatan's Mantle" represents a stupendous amount of time and labor, expended for the benefit
of their chief by women who were already very busy. As such, it must
have been of astronomical worth in Indian society. So, too, must have
been the "Virginian Purse," which like the mantle is to be seen today in
the Ashmolean Museum in England and which is elaborately sewn (in a
different technique) with sections of small shells.

     Another luxurious garment, seen by Strachey, belonged to the favor-
ite wife of a deposed district chief named Pipsco (Pepiscunimah). If the
wife of a has-been could have one of these, then so probably could Winganuske. It was another cloak, this time made out of feathers so skill-
fully attached that the garment resembled "a deep purple satin, and is

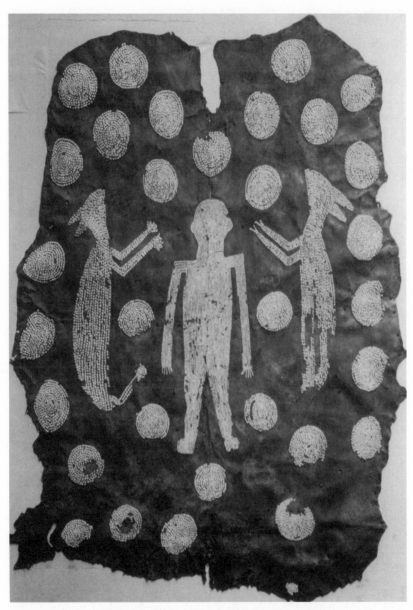

Fig. 3.14. The "Powhatan Mantle." Courtesy of Ashmolean Museum.

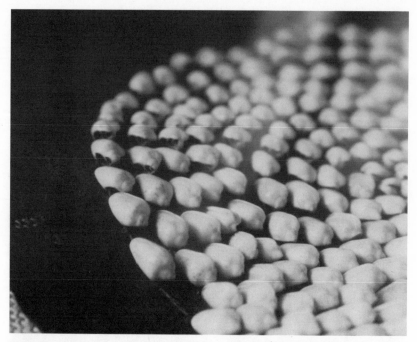

Fig. 3.15. Closeup of shells embroidered onto the "Powhatan Mantle." Courtesy of Helen C. Rountree.

very smooth and sleek." It must have been a sight for people whose clothing usually ranged from beige to brown. The feathers were obviously overlapped, both from row to row and probably from side to side to give a such an overall smooth texture. The question is what bird available to the Powhatans in large numbers has deep purple feathers. The only serious candidate is black ducks, which in today's Chesapeake interbreed freely with and are being replaced by mallards. Mallards' wings have a band, the speculum, with blue feathers; black duck specula are purple. The area of purple (or blue) on each feather is small, about a half inch by two inches: only one side has the color, while the side lying under the adjacent feather is gray. Each wing has seven or eight speculum feathers, and Pipsco's wife's cloak must have had hundreds if it covered her shoulders, thousands if it was longer. So certain feathers from the carcasses of hundreds, perhaps thousands, of black ducks had to be slowly accumulated as Pipsco and his men bagged them, in order for such a beautiful and unusually colored garment to be made for a favorite wife.

Winganuske paid a price for any luxury she enjoyed, however. She had to stay in Powhatan's good graces in the face of considerable competition. She was also not allowed any external interests. Chiefs emphatically did not give permission for dalliances on the part of a wife: that would have reduced their own dignity. Wives out of favor were left behind—under guard—when Powhatan went on trips around his dominions. One of Powhatan's wives, unnamed, managed to slip out and meet someone. Her punishment when the affair was discovered was to spend all twenty-four hours of every third day, for nine days, sitting in full view of everyone on a large rock on her naked bottom. She could eat corn and drink water, but the season (not mentioned) may have made the rock cold.

Although Winganuske lived close to the center of power in her world, it is unlikely that she saw much of the way it worked firsthand. Her husband made his decisions, mainly military in nature, after listening to the advice of priests and expert warriors in a council session to which no others were admitted. The priests, whose family origin and training were never recorded, acted as diviners to determine the identity of criminals and the degree of friendliness of foreigners like John Smith, but they did their divining away from the eyes of laymen (we know of the ceremony only because Smith was the object of it). The priests also met and talked with their local deity, who they said appeared in their temples in human form; but laymen other than Powhatan were not allowed in temples, which seem often to have been placed away from Indian towns anyway. (Big ceremonies, like the green corn thanksgiving one, were held in town, out-of-doors.) The major times that Winganuske would have seen priests at work is when they were doctoring someone, for singing over a patient and sucking out disease was done in the patient's own house with family sitting by. It is possible that Winganuske could sit close enough to overhear some of her husband's haggling and negotiations with foreign visitors, if she were not busy cooking. But she was probably not in her husband's confidence in diplomatic matters because, if nothing else, of the tremendous age difference (he was about sixty, she perhaps fifteen). In any case, her role was to be one of many sexual diversions for Powhatan, not to be an intellectual partner to him in any way.

Later Life

Winganuske's tenure as Powhatan's spouse was limited by custom. Powhatan, and perhaps the chiefs under him, kept wives only temporarily before letting them go and taking new ones—a very effective way to make ever more of his political allies into relatives-by-marriage, while simultaneously creating a new generation of loyal followers. Winganuske remained with her husband until she had had a child by him, which had occurred by 1609–10 when William Strachey came to Virginia. Powhatan had become deeply attached to this wife and, reading between Strachey's lines, he was reluctant to let her go. But custom demanded that he send her and her baby, a daughter, back to her family's village. For the next several years mother and child would be "supported" by Powhatan, with "copper and beads" that she could use to supplement the food she brought in with meat she traded for in the village. Eventually the child, if she survived, would be summoned to join several dozen half-siblings in Powhatan's household (Pocahontas had followed that path), while the mother was divorced. Accounts differ on what could happen after that: cast-off wives were often passed on to favored councillors, who were of course able to support a new wife. Other women remarried as they chose. History is silent about which course Winganuske took. If she married a councillor, who would have been an older man likely to leave her a widow, and if she herself lived into her thirties, when her physical attractions had faded somewhat, she may have entered into a temporary marriage-by-contract in order get a steady supply of meat in her diet. She would probably visit back and forth with her daughter by Powhatan as long as they both lived, for family ties were important to keep up among their people.

Machumps' marital history is unknown. His close connection with Powhatan would fade when his sister was sent away, unless he himself were an unusually able warrior in his own right. He may have aspired to marry a daughter of Powhatan and keep up the connection. Only four sons-in-law of Powhatan are known from historical sources. Pocahontas married first a "private captain" or non-chiefly warrior named Kocoum, followed by her capture and marriage to Englishman John Rolfe. The other two sons-in-law were both prominent men: one was a chief south of Powhatan's dominions who married the eleven-year-old daughter mentioned above. Another daughter named Matachanna married the high-ranking priest Uttamatomakkin (Tomocomo). That husband would have been even more busy with his own life than a chiefly spouse: priests spent most of their time in their temples, away from town and family, keeping the buildings that served as ritual centers, treasure houses, and chiefly tombs, and performing rituals in them. Matachanna may well have been left at home for a year or so (there is no record of her going with them) when her husband accompanied Pocahontas to England in 1616–17 as Powhatan's diplomatic representative. By comparison with those husbands, Machumps was a minor character but still a man with a chance at a political future. The highest position he could aspire to, not being of chiefly lineage anywhere and not being a priest himself, was that of councillor. We do not know if he made the grade.

If either Machumps or Winganuske lived to be "old," which meant in their forties or beyond, they would have gone on inhabiting their separate, gendered worlds—but with less physical activity and at higher levels of respect. They would both have accumulated not only great knowledge about the tasks performed by competent men and women but also experience in watching people carry these out over the years.

Older Powhatan women may, like their better-recorded equivalents in other Woodland groups, have assumed important positions as organizers of female labor. They could also have served as counselors for interpersonal difficulties that must occasionally have arisen among women who had married into the family and who therefore had constantly to work in groups that included non-relatives. They would have seen most, and heard from their elders about the rest, of the possible variants of human contrariness in their own sex and in men as relatives and husbands around the village. Little would surprise them anymore, which would give them a calmness extremely valuable to more volatile young people.

The same was true for the elders in the men's sphere. Their expertise lay in interdistrict and intertribal politics and war, as well as in the techniques of hunting and fishing. They would have seen or heard about most, if not all, of the permutations possible in a world governed either by elders (like the Chickahominies) or chiefs (like the other Powhatans), a world in which men were predators on behalf of their families. Their view would also be a broad, chronologically deep one worth listening to in any judicial matters that arose in their villages.

It is safe to say that Powhatan elders were not considered "old fogeys" to be shunted off to the side, which in modern America contributes to senility and makes their situation worse. In the slow-changing Powhatan world before the English really took over, old people's knowledge about the world and the events of the past was not even remotely out-of-date. What they knew was relevant to the here and now, and like the elders in so many other traditional Native American tribes, they were probably given great respect for it. They would also have been expected to pass their knowledge on, while the younger generations would have been expected to pay attention to it. The oblique "storytelling" done for children would be understood to carry serious messages about what the world was like. The information given to younger adults might also be given a lengthy preface, to set a current matter in perspective, but overall the wisdom would be pertinent. In cultures where old people remain a useful part of society, they do not go senile nearly so often. So if Winganuske and Machumps lived into old age, they may well have kept their mental faculties until death claimed them.

What Good Manners Were Like

Little has been said in this chapter about how the Powhatans kept the peace among themselves. Indian men and women lived surrounded by relatives, in-laws in the case of adult women, under conditions of next to no privacy. That in itself could have put a brake on bad behavior like stealing; knowing the priests could divine the identity of miscreants would help too. The only real privacy people had was in keeping some thoughts and emotions to themselves, and if the emotions were negative, then they definitely should not be acted upon directly.

Many Woodland peoples, including probably the Powhatans, were observed by Europeans to treat one another with astonishingly (to the aliens) respectful manners except when joking together; strangers were kept at a distance with ceremonious gravity. Those manners, of course, were carefully taught from infancy onward, self-control being one of the greatest virtues in the Indian world because it served a functional purpose. Powhatan hamlets had no police to keep the peace. Few people—sometimes not even chiefs—had any right to intervene in quarrels, which could therefore escalate, so it was best to follow the dictum that "proper human beings" were simply not supposed to come into open conflict with anyone among their own people. That meant not letting oneself feel insulted and also adopting a noninterfering, nonpreaching stance to avoid insulting others. The safety valves that released pent-up hostilities were indirect: they went underground through gossip and magic-making, or they were deflected openly onto enemy warriors whom the men fought and who the women and men tortured if they were captured. The respectful gravity shown in public, especially when one did not necessarily like or trust someone, was a social "grease" that Powhatan people and many other traditional Native Americans learned to apply at an early age, especially to non-relatives.

Fellow Indians understood the terms of interaction. Incoming Englishmen did not. They were the products of Shakespeare's England, where neighbors could and did argue in the streets, especially about religion. They therefore took the Indians' polite listening as a sign of agreement (it was not) with their preachings about "superior" English ways (which the Powhatans probably considered rude). It is no wonder, then, that the English colonists in the next few decades would fail to understand a people who appeared to go from one extreme to the other: polite, hospitable acquiescence followed by ferocious attacks. From the Indian point of view, these "extremes" were normal public behavior toward outsiders: you put up with 'em until you can't stand 'em anymore. Indian attacks were not "treachery" against the English; they were the Powhatans' loss of patience with newcomers who did not know how to behave. That back-and-forth swinging between cooperation and raiding would be characteristic of the Powhatan response to the English for as long as they could mount an assault.

Notes

1. William Strachey, himself a member of the English gentry, had served for some months as a diplomatic secretary in Istanbul. He was also a classically trained scholar, able to read ancient Greek and Latin. In his description of Virginia's native people, he often made comparisons between them and other societies he had seen or

read about. Since all those societies left written records, modern scholars can read about their customs to shed some (though not enough!) light on the Powhatan practices Strachey described.

2. Standard American Indian practice is that holy places are marked not with shrines but by being visited and then left unsullied. In non-Indian eyes, such places seem "undeveloped" and therefore meaningless, hence a great many misunderstandings down to the present day.

3. No historical source mentions what drug or drugs were used. One possibility is Jimson weed (*Datura stramonium*), though the date of that tobacco-associated plant's arrival in Virginia is uncertain: it could have been imported in prehistoric times with *Nicotiana rustica* ("native" tobacco, which is actually tropical and not native to North America at all) or in the 1610s with Orinoco tobacco.

4. There is no clear evidence of matrilineality, in which children would belong to the mother's family, or of patrilineality, with children belonging to the father's, in records about the Powhatans. Only chiefly positions are known to have been inherited matrilineally.

5. According to Gary Coovert, the malacologist to whom Rountree and Thomas Davidson sent a videotape made by training a videomicroscope on shells of the mantle while it was on loan to Jamestown Settlement in 1991.

4

The Indian Presence at Jamestown Fort

In 1994 the first English fort on Jamestown Island was located archaeologically. The site had long been regarded as lost to erosion by the James
River, which has steadily eaten away at the upriver end of the island.
However, one early map (the "Zuniga" map of 1608) showed the fort as
being farther downstream, about where the reconstructed church stands.
And that was indeed where the archaeologists hit pay dirt. Most of the
fort and its environs were still there, except for the first few inches
down, which three centuries of plowing had scrambled badly, and also
where a Confederate earthwork had been erected, using soil—and artifacts and human bones, according to nineteenth-century accounts—
scraped out of the ground nearby. Long-term excavation of the site was
begun under the auspices of the Association for the Preservation of Virginia Antiquities, which owns the land, with the cooperation of the National Park Service, which owns the rest of Jamestown Island.

There were vast riches, in archaeological terms rather than monetary
ones, still to be found at the English fort. Most of them say more about
the English than about the Indians amongst whom they were settling. In
this chapter we will, of course, focus on what the fort excavations can tell
us about relations with the Powhatans.

The very fact that there was a fort at all, and that so many of the metal
objects found within it are military in nature, says not only that the English feared reprisals from the Spanish, who laid claim to the region, but
also that they expected from the beginning that the native people would
resent their presence sooner or later. That resentment would be due to
the fact that the English intended to stay, a fact they hid from their Indian
neighbors for quite a while. John Smith and his friends wrote that the
Powhatans were told various tales: the English were refugees from Spanish aggression, they were just curious visitors, and so forth. But the

Fig. 4.1. Full-size model of Indians in a dugout trading with Englishmen in a "barge," from the 1907 Jamestown Exposition.

building of the fort, the armor and weaponry kept within it, and the all-male composition of the first English contingent said otherwise to the local people.

Much of the military gear sent over to Jamestown from England in the first decades of settlement was not state-of-the-art. Writers complaining from Jamestown said so, and the finds of the archaeologists confirm it. Instead the equipment was a congeries of leftover pieces from various dates and campaigns, Dutch and Irish, all of it thought to be sufficient to hold at bay people who were mere "savages." With 20/20 hindsight we can see that the sufficiency was true only up to a point. The gear would have been sufficient if two other conditions had been met: if the colonists had been sent enough food regularly that they did not have to become dependent on the Indians, and if the Powhatan men had not been such experts at guerilla warfare. The English fort did its job only when Englishmen stayed inside it; the arms and armor did their job for the English only as long as they did not have to sell them in order to eat.

There is direct archaeological evidence that the fort and armor did their job. Several hundred stone tools have been found in the excavations at the fort, and most of them are small triangular Late Woodland–style projectile points. (The rest are somewhat larger triangles and could have been hafted and used as knives.) Most of the tools are made from quartz and quartzite pebbles locally available to the Paspahegh people and their neighbors.

The great majority of the projectile points from the fort are broken, half of them with multiple breaks as though they had shattered against English armor. "Burst" is the word used in an eyewitness account of the Paspahegh Indians' first encounter with English steel. It was in May 1607. A wary meeting was taking place between the fort's residents and the chief's emissaries, who had brought a deer carcass as a present. An Englishman set up a wooden shield, which could not be pierced by pistol shot, against a tree and invited a Paspahegh to shoot at it. To the English onlookers' dismay, the arrow pierced the target and stuck out on the other side by a foot. Not to be outdone, the Englishman then set up a shield made of "steele" (iron or steel). The man shot at this target "and burst his arrow all to pieces." The satisfied English looked on while the Indian man "pulled out another Arrow, and bit it in his teeth, and seemed to be in a great rage," after which he left the fort "in great anger." That put the Paspaheghs, and through them the other Powhatans, on notice about English armor.

Military dealings with the Powhatans are not the only kind of intercultural relations that show up in the fort excavations, though. There is evidence of peaceful interaction as well, evidence that falls roughly into two categories: gifts of food to the English during the friendly periods, and a sort of "trading kit" of items Indian people would buy, in exchanges which historical sources tell us happened in both good times and bad.

Deer Given or Sold to the Colonists

A small number of bones, from several deer, have been found so far at the English fort as of this writing. The identifiable bones consist of vertebrae, partial long bones, and pelvis fragments (fig. 4.2). These are all bones adjacent to large muscle masses in the animal, but given the likely Indian origin of any deer carcasses found in a fort dated to 1607–10 (no records mention English gentlemen shooting any deer themselves, though they probably did), there is something unusual about them: the large size of the pieces. At many prehistoric Eastern Woodland sites, deer bones come in small fragments, reflecting the fact that they were broken up to be made into bone tools. No such tool-making treatment was accorded to the deer brought to the fort. The venison was eaten, and the English threw the bones away.

The bones could tell us more if certain expensive tests were run on them. One kind of fine-grained analysis could tell us whether those deer were butchered with stone tools (like the larger triangular tools mentioned above) or metal ones (by Englishmen or by Indians using loaned tools). The English colonists recorded that Indian people were very desirous of metal cutting tools, which lasted longer; their first experience of these may have been on occasions when they brought deer carcasses to the English.

There is more to learn. Every culture has its preferred butchering techniques, which is why the cuts of meat for sale in other countries' markets may look completely unfamiliar to us. The English method of butchering venison probably differed from the Powhatan one and left the bones cut up in different ways (before the Indians reduced theirs to smaller pieces for tool-making). Comparative studies of Early Contact period deer bones need to be done at both Indian and English sites, and compared with the early African-American studies currently underway, to establish preferred cutting techniques of all the early seventeenth-century Virginia ethnic groups (and also to see whether one or another became predominant in the colony later). Then the ethnic identity of the butcher at Jamestown Fort might be established, regardless of whether the knives used were stone or metal ones.

The bones themselves can tell us the "what"; the "when" has to be deduced from the writings of the English colonists. These tell us that deer were presented to the fort's occupants on a number of occasions in 1607

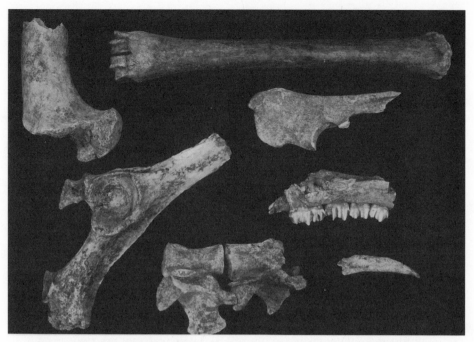

4.2. Large deer bones found in the English fort by archaeologists. Courtesy of APVA Jamestown Rediscovery.

through mid-1609. Those occasions occurred mainly when the native people were both flush with high-status food like corn and also feeling friendly toward their difficult neighbors. An obvious time was immediately after the English landed on Jamestown Island, when the neighboring Paspahegh chief sent word that he would come and "would be merry with us with a fat deer." There was more than just "merriment" at stake, though. Indian hospitality demanded the serving of "important" victuals rather than ordinary foodstuffs like tuckahoe. Thus, in the drought-ridden summer of 1607, while the English were dying of hunger and the local "bugs" while trying to keep their troubles secret, the local Quiyoughcohannocks (called "Tappahannas" by the colonists) seem to have held off bringing meat to their new friends until they could also bring the proper kind of bread with it. Being perhaps unaware of the straits the English were in, they observed the diplomatic niceties. And thus the English saw no Indian gift foods until well into September, when the drought-stricken corn finally began to come in.

Later, after John Smith had made an alliance with the great Powhatan during his captivity, the food flowed toward Jamestown again: deer and other animals plus "bread," meaning cornbread made from the paramount chief's supplies. This flow of food went on through the spring of 1608, until relations went sour again. There was also a time of brief friendliness with the Chickahominies, in the late spring of 1609, when Indian people brought plentiful food to their allies. At other times, the deer brought to the fort may have been purchased from a wary native people and carried to the fort either by Indian sellers or English buyers.

Indian Pottery in Profusion

Amongst the great number and variety of fragmented European vessels found in the fort, thousands of sherds of Indian pottery have been unearthed (fig. 4.3), pottery that definitely came from the fort rather than from any pre-English, Indian occupation level below it. Not only that, but the pieces that could be fitted together indicated that some of the pots had been big ones (the gentleness of the curve of the partial pot's rim is unfortunately not visible in figure 4.3). These were not pretty little pots to trade as "art." These were sizable, utilitarian pots that somehow wound up in a fort manned by foreigners who must have had equally immense metal kettles that they could cook in for themselves. Why would such ceramic vessels be taken into the fort at all?

Part of the answer must be that most of the pots were purchased along with the food that went into them. The accounts of the English colonists tell us that in Jamestown's early years, when supplies from England were skimpy and irregular, they often bought food from the local Powhatans. The written records say what was bought: corn and animal carcasses. Omitted are mentions of the containers in which the corn was brought to the fort. Baskets were the logical items if the kernels were brought overland, but it is more likely that trade even with the Paspaheghs next door (five miles away) was conducted by water. Heavier items could be carried by canoe, including standard Indian conical-bottomed pots propped up against the gunwales. Why not sell the English the pots as well as the corn, in exchange for more trade goods? Both the corn and the pots were constantly being produced by the women; the women may have been active in selling them, though the colonists' writings say only that "savages" did the selling. Some of the benefit of the sales went to the women,

Fig. 4.3. Pottery of various types found in the English fort. Courtesy of APVA Jamestown Rediscovery.

for otherwise Henry Spelman would not have written that by 1612 or so (when he left the colony) the standard women's gardening tool in Virginia was an English iron shovel.

It may be, then, that many of the potsherds in Jamestown Fort represent a seventeenth-century version of an "instant dinner." Englishmen could buy a large potful of corn and some meat from native men and women; put most of the corn into storage; wedge the conical-bottomed pot into the coals of an open fire; add water and the meat to the remaining corn, and cook it up. The stew would come to a boil in a little over half the time required for a flat-bottomed kettle (according to modern Pamunkey Indian women, who have tried it). The Indian women may also have offered to do the cooking—for a fee.

Some of the sherds probably come from pots that were gifts rather than purchases. Here we must consult Indian ideas of hospitality, which were elaborate and aggressively generous. Taking corn and a deer carcass and other delectables to the foreigners may not have been enough, though that was all that English writers saw fit to record about the feasts they enjoyed. A real feast probably meant an Indian visiting party that included women, who would take along a stewpot and cook a meal in it on the spot. Everyone would eat their fill, and then the Indians would go home, carrying English presents but nothing else. John Smith wrote in his first and most detailed account that when guests came to a feast, "this is a general custom, that what they give, not to take again, but you must either eat it, give it away, or carry it with you." In a case of the feast going to the guests, hospitality may have dictated leaving the stewpot behind along with any leftovers.

At least one of the pots, represented by sherds from the fort and shown as dark, separate sherds at the bottom of figure 4.3, was indeed used to cook up meat and corn. Its pieces had enough food residue absorbed into the fabric of the vessel that it could be removed and subjected to a stable isotope analysis. The results point to a mixed stew, containing a vegetable that was almost certainly maize, together with a small amount either of predator's meat (bear, for example) or of more meat from a nonpredator (for example, deer). The deer is most likely, since bears are not mentioned at all by colonists receiving gifts of food.

Who was selling or leaving stewpots in English hands? Most of the sherds found at Jamestown Fort are Roanoke Simple Stamped ware, which is characteristic of Powhatan districts along the lower James River, including the nearby Paspaheghs. There are other pottery types represented, however. Small amounts of Gaston Simple Stamped pottery are also present, a ceramic type associated with the Weyanocks just upriver as mentioned in chapter 2.

The pot actually tested for food residue, however, is a type that is harder to explain at the English fort. It has similarities with Potomac Creek ware, a type discussed in chapter 2 and found near the fall line of both the Potomac and Rappahannock Rivers. It is possible that a woman from that area, a hundred or more miles away from Jamestown Island as the crow flies, was living among the Paspaheghs or other neighbors and making the pots of her homeland. Or a Powhatan group living close to Jamestown may have acquired the pot by Indian-to-Indian trade and then decided to take it to the fort when a feast was planned. Direct trading of the pot to the English by its maker's people seems less likely. English records are detailed for the first three years or so of the colony, and they do not mention any visits at all to Jamestown by people from the Rappahannock or Potomac River basins. There were only two visits by the English to those areas in 1607–10. John Smith's exploratory expedition in summer 1608 took in the Potomac and Rappahannock Rivers, and Samuel Argall made a reconnaissance trip up the Potomac in October 1610, when he retrieved Henry Spelman from the Patawomecks. Either of those visits could have involved the cooking of feasts at Indian towns, at which time the pot could have been obtained and taken to Jamestown. As so often happens in archaeology, this pot has raised more questions than answers. Real pinpointing of the pot's origin would require a spectrographic analysis of the clay used in it and then comparison with other pottery clays available in eastern Virginia and Maryland. Even then, it is possible that we will never know who brought it to Jamestown.

Glass Beads: Important After All

By the time Jamestown was founded, Europeans had made extensive contacts along the Atlantic coast that told them beads would be welcomed as trade items by the native people. Accordingly, beads were sent along with the first batch of Jamestown colonists and also with subsequent groups, though no records tell us in how great a quantity. No evidence, historical or archaeological, has ever come to light that the colony's glassmakers produced beads for the Indian trade. The lack of manufacturing evidence formerly led historians to assume that beads were not very important in the colony's early days, compared with, say, metal tools. Archaeologists had found few glass beads at other early English outposts or Indian sites around Virginia, although it must be admitted that the time and resources allowed for excavation of those sites frequently limited the recovery of small artifacts such as beads.

The bead situation looks different now, thanks to the fine-mesh (1/16–inch) screening used at the Jamestown Rediscovery Project. Glass beads *were* important in the Indian trade, but they were usually small and made back in Europe—various parts of Europe.

Several types of bead found at Jamestown were formerly thought to come from the mid-sixteenth-century movements of the Spanish in Central and South America and in the U.S. Southeast. However, enough beads have been found by now at the English fort, securely dated to

1607–10, and also at other coastal sites as far north as Canada, that the Spanish connection has had to be rethought. It looks instead as though the beads formed a "package" that *many* colonizing Europeans knew would appeal to native peoples, so that sensible explorers and settlers took a selection of beads along with them. The builders of Jamestown Fort appear to have done precisely that (fig. 4.4).

The long, pale, tubular beads in the photograph (two very long ones, six shorter ones) were made in three layers of different colors: usually some shade of blue (either navy or turquoise), then white, then an outer layer of turquoise or cobalt blue. The corners at the ends of each bead were then ground down to reveal the inner two colors. This type is called "Nueva Cadiz," because beads of this kind were first found archae-ologically on an island of that name off the coast of Venezuela, their date being uncertain at first. A number of them have been found in Antwerp, Belgium, in the cesspit of a late-sixteenth-century merchant who dealt regularly with Venice; so the beads of about 1600 may have been Vene-tian. Beads of this type are among the most numerous of those found so far at Jamestown. There is an earlier version of the type as well (not exca-vated at Jamestown), found widely in Spanish sites such as Nueva Cadiz in the New World but hardly at all in Spain or Portugal; its country of origin has not yet been pinpointed.

There are several "chevron beads" in the photograph, called by that name because the ends were ground down and faceted to show the con-centric inner colors in an arrangement of nested "V" shapes. With the two striped beads, the grinding is not readily apparent in the photograph. The outer color of the paler bead is turquoise with a wider red stripe added and then a narrow white stripe within it. The dark bead is navy blue with a white stripe. The grinding shows better in the four short, dark blue tubular beads, one near the top of the photograph and three near the bottom. Chevron beads like these are datable: seventeenth-century ones have five layers, while earlier ones have seven and later ones have four. Both sixteenth-and seventeenth-century versions have been found at the English fort.

Two faceted crystal beads are also shown in the photograph, as is a "gooseberry" bead lying nearly on its side. Gooseberry beads are large, round, and colorless, with varying numbers of opaque white stripes added. In sites from Virginia northward, they usually date just before and after 1600, while in the southeastern United States they were still being

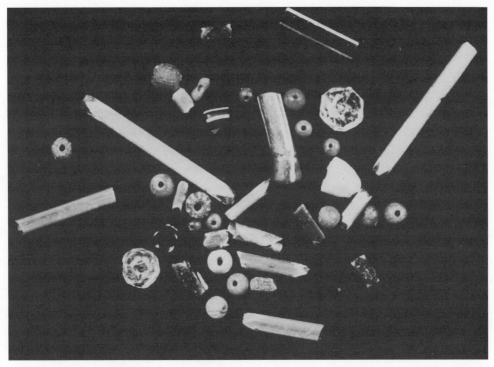

Fig. 4.4. Glass trade beads of various kinds found in the English fort. Courtesy of APVA Jamestown Rediscovery.

traded in the eighteenth century. The other round striped bead, shown end-on, actually has three layers, the innermost white barely showing. The grayish layer was added next during manufacture, and the outermost white layer was added intermittently to produce stripes.

Scattered throughout the photograph are small round or oval beads in single colors of white, dark green, or (most of them) robin's egg blue. Trade beads like these, found in profusion at Jamestown, appear in many early seventeenth-century European sites in North America. Some of them, like the tiny bead nestled below the end-on round striped bead, are downright miniscule (this one is between two and three millimeters in size)[1] and can only be found by fine-mesh water screening. It was blue beads of this type that John Smith foisted off on Powhatan, who was busily raising the price of his corn, in February 1608. Smith initially showed the chief only a few beads, among "many trifles." But once Powhatan showed an interest in *blue* beads, Smith raised the ante: he pretended

> so much the more to affect them [want to keep them] as being composed of a most rare substance the color of the skies, and not to be worn but by the greatest kings in the world. This made [Powhatan] half mad to be the owner of such strange jewels, so that, ere we departed, for a pound or two of blue beads [Smith] brought over my king for 2 or 300 bushels of corn, yet parted good friends.
>
> The like entertainment we found of Opechancanough, King of Pamunkey, whom also he in like manner fitted at the like rates with blue beads, which grew by this means of that estimation that none durst wear any of them but their great kings, their wives, and children.

Whether Smith realized it or not, some groundwork for such a coup had been laid long ago in Indian culture. Blue or purple clamshell beads were much more valuable, because more rare, than the white ones, due to the lesser size of the blue muscle-attachment area compared to the white in the shells. The coup worked both ways, at least for a while: as long as Powhatan and his close relatives monopolized the sky-blue beads, they really *were* valuable as a status symbol in Indian society.

Copper Sheets in the Trading Kit

Copper was highly valued in Woodland Indian society, as the earliest European visitors discovered. Native copper, as it is called, is almost pure copper, containing only miniscule amounts of other elements, so it is relatively soft and useful only for jewelry-making. Native copper is also rather rare in North America, the greatest part of it coming from the Great Lakes area. Some 2,000 years ago, there was a heavy demand for it by the Adena and Hopewell mound-building peoples of the Ohio Valley. Old copper-trade routes remained in use during the Late Woodland period, with additional copper perhaps being produced in localized areas of western Virginia. The demand for the metal was widespread among Native Americans, but in the mid-Atlantic region the chiefs who were making their appearance hoarded it. Consequently most of the copper ornaments found by archaeologists come from burials of high-status people.

And the earliest historical accounts speak of such people wearing large quantities of it, while ordinary folk went without.

Not surprisingly, European exploring expeditions soon began carrying copper as part of their trading inventories. After all, copper was cheap at home, and why not take advantage of "savages" who were "well contented with trifles"? Once a colony was settled, though, the value of the "trifles" would begin a downward slide while corn prices inflated, as we shall see in the next chapter. Meanwhile, the surviving documents say little about the form in which the copper was transported to America. That information has come to us for the first time from the Jamestown Rediscovery Project.

In the first three years of excavation alone, over 1,400 pieces of copper were found in the English fort. The pieces, found in several concentrations within the fort, came from thin sheets of copper alloy and were plainly scraps left over from cutting out ornaments attractive to Powhatan buyers (fig. 4.5). Some of the ornaments consisted of tubular beads made by turning the copper over on itself—with a pair of needle-nosed pliers found nearby. Other ornaments were flat-sheet cutouts, in circles, rectangles, and triangles to judge by the scraps left over. One of the scraps has been drilled to become a pendant itself.

The Jamestown English did not make their sheets of copper at the fort. They came equipped to do so, but the crucibles they had show no signs of having been used. Thus it seems that instead of recycling miscellaneous copper objects, the Jamestown colonists brought quantities of sheet copper, ready for cutting up, across the Atlantic with them.

Ornaments bought from the English made their way immediately into Powhatan society, of course. And they eventually wound up, along with native copper ornaments, in the graves of high-status people. Several such graves were found in the early 1990s in the Paspahegh town described in chapter 2. The copper items from the graves were examined before being reburied with the bones in 1996, and they were compared with the copper from Jamestown Fort and also with prehistoric copper from other sites.

Native (Indian) copper and English copper are somewhat different, so that analysis (specifically proton-induced X-ray emission [PIXE] spectrometry and neutron activation techniques) can show which is which. Native copper has significantly lower levels of the trace elements arsenic,

Fig. 4.5. Pieces of European sheet copper left over after cutting out ornaments for the Indian trade. Courtesy of APVA Jamestown Rediscovery.

lead, and antimony than English copper does. Analysis showed that the copper grave goods found at the Paspahegh town are mostly European in origin, with some native copper also represented. And the European copper at the village matches very closely with the copper found at Jamestown, suggesting that the villagers had gotten the metal by trading with the Jamestown English.

Acquiring pretty "expensive" jewelry to show off was all very well, in Indian minds. But chiefs and commoners alike were even more eager to acquire English iron or steel tools and weapons, which the English preferred to keep for their own uses. It is to that competition, well documented by eyewitnesses but leaving little direct evidence at Jamestown Fort, that we now turn.

Authors' Note

As this book went to press, a small piece of Indian matting was unearthed in the English fort, preserved by the salts from an overlying piece of copper. The species of the reeds and the plant used for the cordage to sew them together have yet to be identified. The mat could have been brought for English guests to sit upon at a feast, though Strachey also wrote that "delicate wrought" Indian mats were "trucked for or snatched up" (during raids) to hang like tapestries in the English houses in the fort. Another recent find was two box turtle–shell cups, probably used as ladles at a feast. The spine and ribs inside both shells were imperfectly smoothed, as though the cups were made on short notice.

Note

1. Shown by comparing it with the rolled-up silver half-groat coin that the photographer placed two beads away. That coin is shown in figure 5.2 with a metric scale that indicates its maximum length to be sixteen millimeters, so the size of all the beads in figure 4.4 can be estimated by comparing them with the half-groat. The longest Nueva Cadiz bead, the one pointing upper left to lower right (northwest to southeast), is about fifty millimeters, or roughly two inches.

5

The First Century of English Occupation

When the English fixed upon Jamestown Island as their headquarters in the Chesapeake, their decision was primarily a military one, a fact not lost upon the Powhatans. The upriver end of the island was a fine place to defend, with its land access in a narrow isthmus (now a paved causeway) and with deepwater anchorage just offshore. But it was a poor place to try to establish a "city" because of the brackish river water and the nearby mosquito-ridden marsh. The Paspaheghs and their ancestors had never used the island as a town site, as far as a detailed archaeological survey of the 1990s shows, so they were probably suspicious of people who tried to settle there.

The newcomers immediately set about building a fort based upon a model they had used elsewhere: triangular in shape and palisaded with tree trunks ("circular or beveled upright timbers") set close together (fig. 5.1). It was a hefty palisade, because the English had metal cutting tools and workmen who did not have to provide other people with food. Fortifications of that sort remained the English goal wherever they settled in Virginia for the first three decades of the seventeenth century. That defensiveness was not lost upon the native people, along with the fact that the first boatload of English were all males.

The Paspaheghs and their fellow Powhatans were well worth the Englishmen's fears. They outnumbered the English colonists—and would continue to do so for several more decades. Their men knew their land intimately and were prepared to defend it with guerilla tactics with which the English were not at ease. The English were also acutely aware of something that we tend to forget four centuries later: no previous English colonization attempt in North America had succeeded. With hindsight we know that the failures were due partly to the resistance of native

Fig. 5.1. Excavated palisade section at the original English fort. Courtesy of APVA Jamestown Rediscovery.

peoples and partly to poor organization among the English. But the Jamestown colonists and their backers were still feeling their way in 1607, which added greatly to the Jamestown denizens' feelings of insecurity. Consequently, the people on both sides of the early English-Indian encounters were superficially friendly to one another, but they were al-

ways wary and prepared for hostilities to break out, which not infre-
quently happened.

Each side hoped to use the other, which kept those apparently friendly
overtures going back and forth for three years. The Powhatans wanted to
make the English into allies against their Indian enemies and also against
any Spanish ships that ventured into the region. (They did not lump the
English and Spanish together into "Europeans" or "white people" at that
time.) They planned to accomplish the alliance while remaining in control of the country and of its varied fighting personnel, a design that was
bound to be thwarted by European ambitions. The English aimed at ex-
ploiting the land for salable commodities (the early accounts are full of
lists of promising things), preferably with the Indians cooperating by
adopting English culture and then helping to provide food and labor (as
employees but not servants, much less slaves—that came later). The
Powhatans, contentedly rooted in a regional culture thousands of years
old, were bound to disappoint such English hopes. The early years of the
English colony therefore witnessed an uneasy seesawing of relations between the two peoples, exacerbated by differing standards of politeness,
by English hunger due to poor supply lines to England, and also by the
droughts that were occurring in those summers.

The Reality of the Early Colony

One myth of early Virginia is that the generous Indians kept the poor,
feckless colonists alive with gifts of food, the gifts often being made by
Pocahontas. Aside from the unlikelihood of *any* eleven-year-old girl in
the Powhatan world being able to command *that* much food to give away,
the myth is terribly oversimplified. The colonists had a minor "starving
time" in the summer of 1607, when drought made the James River less
safe to drink than ever (many men got salt poisoning) and also delayed
the corn crop that the neighboring Indians had promised to share. By
their own accounts, the English stayed penned up in their fort, fearful of
being taken advantage of if their weakness were known. Their isolation
probably prevented still-hopeful Indians like the Quiyoughcohannocks
from assisting their would-be allies with wild, drought-resistant foods
that might have saved them.

Once the corn came in, the revived English became aggressive in trading for it, wearing out their welcome in a number of districts in the James

and York River valleys. Several district chiefs together managed to capture John Smith in December 1607. Smith's canny negotiations with Powhatan (with or without the controversial saving of his life by Pocahontas)[1] renewed the paramount chief's hopes of an alliance, and it was those hopes, not Pocahontas's sympathy, that caused the flow of food into the English fort to resume for a time. Then the wrangling over trade began anew, exacerbated when supplies arrived from England and the colonists needed the Indians less. Indian friendliness shriveled as the English explored the Chesapeake Bay twice in the dry summer of 1608, after which they tried to "crown" Powhatan as an English "vassal" (he saw through it) and then contacted his enemies the Monacans. Nobody wanted to sell food to the English in the fall of 1608. When supplies ran out and the English faced starvation in the winter of 1608–09, John Smith sacked Powhatan's corn supplies, causing the paramount chief to abandon his capital town of Werowocomoco on the York River and move far up the Pamunkey River. That was the end of the visits Pocahontas had made to the English fort—visits she never made alone, always accompanying diplomatic parties of adults. There is fragmentary evidence that she admired John Smith; there is more evidence that he was too preoccupied to have much time for her.

In the summer of 1609, with English supply ships delayed by a hurricane, the Jamestown colonists spent their time not planting corn (they had been taught how) nor patching up relations with the native people—but in trying to establish three satellite forts up and down the James River. Two of these efforts, on prime Indian farmland, were repulsed; the third, on a sandspit at the mouth of the James, survived. By late fall, getting food by trade was impossible, especially after John Smith went back to England (he never returned). The winter of 1609–10 was the famous "starving time" when five-sixths of the colonists died of hunger. A striking symbol of that desperation has been found by the Jamestown Rediscovery archaeologists: two English silver coins (fig. 5.2), which would *immediately* have bought a *lot* of food from English ships had they shown up, were made into ornaments attractive to the Powhatans. Indian people were the only possible source of food that winter, and most of them weren't selling (the coins remained in English hands). The English no longer had goods the local people wanted badly enough.

There was a good reason for the devaluation of trade goods passing into Indian hands. Glass beads and copper ornaments were decorative

Fig. 5.2. English silver coins made into ornaments useful to Indians: a 1602 sixpence clipped into a rectangle and drilled to make a pendant, and a half-groat (minted 1583–1603) rolled into a tubular bead. Courtesy of APVA Jamestown Rediscovery.

items that did not wear out, though they might be lost or buried with the dead. Iron hoes, which colonist Henry Spelman said were standard farming tools for Indian women by 1609–10, also did not wear out readily. Ditto for metal knives, scissors, and other hand tools, as well as for the swords that Indian people wanted and would probably use as machetes. The more easily used-up staples of the Indian trade later in the seventeenth century were not yet being sold: firearms and ammunition, woven cloth, glass bottles (which were knapped into arrowheads with such enthusiasm in the 1620s that a law was passed to stop their sale), and—late in the century—liquor. Those things had to be renewed: guns broke, ammunition was spent, glass arrowheads were lost, cloth wore out, and liquor was drunk up. But early in the century, it was the English who constantly needed to trade: for food and for information on other Indians' movements, things they would continue to purchase throughout the century. The Powhatans, especially those living nearest to Jamestown, had enough English goods by 1609 that they could hold off from trading when they found the English too obnoxious.

The survivors of the dreadful starving time were met as they abandoned their fort by a new and better organized wave of colonists, led by an English lord (the third Baron de la Warr, a first cousin twice removed of Queen Elizabeth I). His lordship refused to truckle with "savages," and his better supplied followers were able to make their expansionist intentions stick. Now the English made attacks on Paspahegh and other towns, where women and children were among the casualties, and the prime Indian farmlands along the James River began to fall into English hands in spite of continual Indian resistance. The territories of the Kecoughtans, Paspaheghs, Warraskoyacks, Quiyoughcohannocks, and Arrohatecks ceased to be Indian-held. The paramount chief never organized a mass attack on English settlements, however (it was his successors who did so), for Powhatan was getting old and desirous of peace. When Pocahontas was captured by the English, he had his excuse to call off hostilities.

Pocahontas was captured during a visit she made to the Patawomeck district in the spring of 1613. Now about seventeen years old, she had been the wife of a "private captain" named Kocoum for two or three years, but English accounts make no mention of the husband's or any children's being with her or feeling bereft at her abduction to Jamestown. She spent a year at the English headquarters, while her father dithered about ransoming her. During that time the English worked hard at trying to convert her to their own culture and religion. The governor, at that time a knight named Sir Thomas Dale, showed her special attention, as did a well-intentioned widower named John Rolfe. Rolfe and Pocahontas became attached to each other, a genuine love-match by all accounts, and wished to marry. They revealed their desire during a trip in which Dale took Pocahontas almost to her father's new capital town, trying to get the old man to make up his mind. Pocahontas saw only some of her half-brothers on that expedition (fig. 5.3), but her father got the message that she was well and wished to divorce and remarry. In the political thinking of both the Powhatans and the English, such a union was a standard way of cementing an alliance. So Kocoum was squared somehow and the couple, back in Jamestown's church, were married about April 5, 1614.

A "golden era" of friendly relations now dawned, darkened somewhat for the Indians by continued English expansion onto their James River

Fig. 5.3. Engraving of captive Pocahontas meeting her brothers. Based on a 1617 original by Georg Keller. Among the many inaccuracies is the drawing of Pocahontas's clothing: she would have worn English attire by then.

lands and occasionally for the English by tiffs with groups like the Chickahominies. Sir Thomas Dale tried to acquire Powhatan's new favorite daughter as another symbol of peace, but the paramount chief had already married her off to another chief. Pocahontas went to England, along with her husband and new son, and she became a seven-days' wonder on the London scene, which was excellent propaganda for the Virginia Company that was paying her bills (fig. 5.4). She died, of unknown causes, on her way back to Virginia, and the son was left to be reared in England. John Rolfe returned to the colony and visited his chiefly father-in-law, who himself had less than a year to live. Nearly a quarter-century later, after the son Thomas Rolfe sailed to Virginia, he, too, would pay a visit to his mother's surviving kin.

The "golden era" was a period of great hope for the English. Pocahontas had converted, and so might other Indian people when they got to know the English world better (fig. 5.5). Powhatan himself had accepted English presents as high-status symbols in the early days. The "English" house begun for him at Werowocomoco on the York was never completed, and we hear nothing of the English clothes and bedstead that were bestowed upon him in 1608. But Henry Spelman mentioned the fake crown as being stored in a temple, and Sir Thomas Dale's emissary in 1614 saw the elaborate "table book," unwritten in, and the bottle of aqua vitae, hardly touched. Yet a chief's acceptance of fancy goods, not useful to him except for showing off, was quite different from ordinary people's acceptance of things that were utilitarian to the English but not easily mixed with Powhatan ways of doing things. Throughout the seventeenth century, the native people in Virginia would show no interest in having

Fig. 5.4. A 1994 oil painting of Pocahontas, based closely upon the Van Der Pas engraving made from life in 1617. This version shows the "Indian" face she really had. Courtesy of Mary Ellen Howe.

Fig. 5.5. Engraving of Indian man Eiakintomino in St. James's Park, 1615. Courtesy of Society of Antiquaries of London.

English-style houses (the one exception being the Mattaponi chief around 1660), English tailored clothes, English livestock (other than pigs, which throve when turned loose in the forest and hunted like game), or English domesticated plants (fruit trees being the exception, possessed by the Weyanock chief in the 1660s and the Chickahominy leader around 1700). As for English land use, social customs, and religion, the Powhatans held off adopting those until well into the eighteenth century.

Ironically, it was Pocahontas's husband who introduced the English colony to the plant that would spell doom for his wife's people. And he did it while his wife was still living in the colony. Orinoco tobacco, less poisonous than the "native" tobacco (both being of tropical origin) that was smoked in small amounts by Native Americans, can be ingested in large enough quantities without nausea and hallucinations that people become addicted to it. Anglo-Virginia planters immediately became enamored of the plant's value as a cash crop. The Virginia colony had always been primarily an economic venture, and in the absence of gold and silver mines, tobacco now became the route to wealth. By the time Rolfe returned, once more a widower, from England, he found the very streets of Jamestown planted with tobacco. The tobacco-growing "boom" would eventually slow down, as tens of thousands of Englishmen crossed the Atlantic, began planting, and gradually flooded the market. By that time, though, there had been two major wars with the Powhatans over the prime waterfront farmlands that tobacco growers were now seizing.

English Expansion at Powhatan Expense

Powhatan's successors, the lame Opitchapam and the next brother, the formidable Opechancanough, continued a superficial peace while organizing a major resistance movement. Powhatan culture did include methods of coordinating attacks and fighting pitched battles when necessary. So in the months leading up to the outbreak, Indian people quietly got themselves organized, while the English welcomed them into their settlements, thinking the conversion process was working at last.

The original date set for the great assault was in 1621, after the ceremony of "taking up Powhatan's bones" and putting them in a final resting place (location unknown, probably in an aboveground temple). However, the assault was to come on the day of a meeting with English leaders in which they were to be poisoned with cowbane (*Cicuta maculata*), a deadly plant that grows more plentifully on the Virginia Eastern Shore than across the bay. Opechancanough sent to the Accomac chief for a supply; the chief leaked the news to the English, who promptly took a defensive stance; and Opechancanough and his brother postponed the assault until March 1622. Spring was a logical season to choose, when the women and children would be foraging away from the towns, safe from immediate reprisals, if any. However, once again the news leaked out. There were at least two Indians, and perhaps more, who had made friends among the English that they did not want to see harmed. One was a man from the Pamunkey River area named Chauco; the other was an unnamed boy working on a plantation across the river from Jamestown. Careless historians in the nineteenth century combined them into a single "enlightened" boy named Chanco. But the result was the same: some English settlements got last-minute warning of the impending onslaught.

On the morning of March 22, all the English settlers along the James suddenly found themselves under attack (fig. 5.6), either by warriors who materialized out of the forest or by Indian people who had been working peacefully alongside them a few minutes before. The settlements that had been warned had prepared defenses; at a few others, such as Ralph Hamor's homestead, the English fought back effectively enough that the warriors cut their losses and broke off the engagement. But some 10 percent of the English in the colony died that day, the carnage being worst at Martin's Hundred, where Carter's Grove Plantation is today. The greater blow, however, was to English pride. The worst fears of the cynics had come true: the "savages" had been treated well (by English standards) but had proved "treacherous" and "ungrateful."

Opechancanough and his brother did not follow up on their assault; there was no more raiding until the next September. Plainly, the Powhatan leadership had its own blinders on and expected their adversaries to react like Eastern Woodland Indians: to collect their survivors and withdraw. The English were too stunned and too short of ammunition to retaliate immediately. But they did not take "hints" like this, for back in England they had a much bigger population upon which to draw. Instead of leaving, they merely sent home for more people and supplies and went on as best they could with their tobacco farming. So while the Powhatan side stood back and waited, the English caught their breath and started planning raids on Indian towns, which were carried out as soon as the ships arrived with more ammunition.

Thus began a war that went on for ten years and that nobody won. English expansion was drastically slowed down, but the Powhatans lost control of the lower York River valley when the Chiskiacks gave up and headed north to the Piankatank River. Indian men sniped at English settlers. English raiding parties burned some Indian towns in the James and York River valleys. The English also staged a great assault of their own, when at Opechancanough's request they met in 1623 for peace talks (his sincerity is very doubtful). A toast was drunk, with some of the Indians getting poisoned wine,[2] after which the English grabbed their weapons

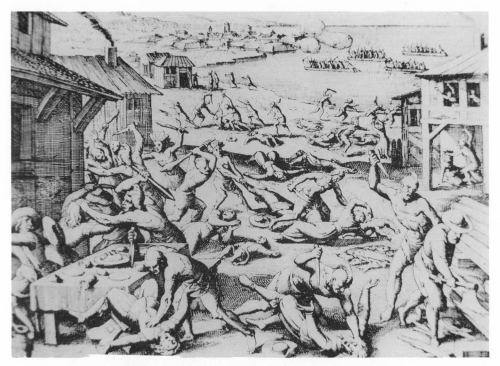

Fig. 5.6. Early seventeenth-century engraving of the great assault of 1622.

and started shooting. *Both* sides perpetrated massacres in the early days of the war.

After a peace was made in 1632 (the text of it is lost), English farmers began pushing outward again, now heading not only farther down the James and along the York but also (beginning in 1640) up the Rappahannock and Potomac Rivers. The settlers did not move smoothly up any of Virginia's rivers from southeast to northwest. Instead they staked their claims to the choicest Indian farmlands first, and as we have already seen in chapter 1, those lay in the inner coastal plain. Later settlers expanded out from there.

Sometimes relations between settlers and Indians were neighborly. One English minister, John Bass, married a daughter of the Nansemond chief and became the ancestor of one of the surviving Powhatan tribes today (fig. 5.7). A few Indian people visited England (fig. 5.8), their way being paid by friendly planters. But at least as often, relations were tense at best.

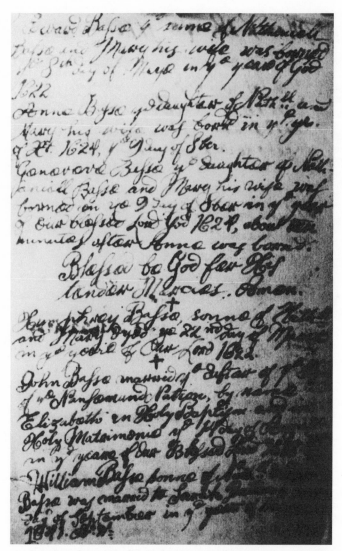

Fig. 5.7. Genealogy page from John Bass's sermon book, recording his marriage with the Nansemond chief's daughter in 1638. Courtesy of Helen C. Rountree.

Land purchases by individual Englishmen were legal until 1656 and continued on the sly afterward. The colony's governing officials wanted to do the negotiating, supposedly to protect the Indians, but since most of those officials were (or became) great landowners themselves, their "insider" status did more for them than for the native people. Neither they

Fig. 5.8. Wenceslas Hollar's engraving of an Indian man from Virginia, 1645. The man was presumably not from a group then warring with the Jamestown English.

nor the English government overseeing them from London believed that non-Christians had a genuine title to the land. For their part, the Powhatans were not accustomed to the kind of permanent ownership that English buyers wanted to acquire, and they were very slow to understand it and quit selling property. Virginia Algonquian ownership was by "usufruct," meaning that one "owned" land only as long as one farmed it, after which it reverted to "public" use. Thus the poorly documented 1630s and early 1640s show only a few of the probably many unpleasant incidents in which Indians "sold" land to planters, saw it being fallowed after a few exhausting years of tobacco cultivation, and assumed that they were free to forage there again. That outraged many trigger-happy English "owners," who were leery of "savages" anyway. Some English farmsteads were palisaded, especially in the 1620s (fig. 5.9), and many of their inhabitants were knowledgeable about firearms. The Indian death toll began to rise.

Fig. 5.9. Artist's conception of the palisaded English settlement at Jordan's Point in the 1620s. Courtesy of VDHR.

Opechancanough still survived, the last of the brothers to be paramount chief, and as he had done before, he kept a superficial peace with the English while organizing another strike at them. It came, as before, in the spring: April 18, 1644. Again about 400 English were killed, but that was a much smaller proportion of an English population that had grown tremendously through migration. Once more Opechancanough and his followers held off following up their victory for six months, but now the English struck back in much deadlier form. They carried their raids farther than before, in 1645 moving up past Opechancanough's Pamunkey River capital town of Menmend and attacking his fort (fig. 5.10). The paramount chief was captured, dying soon afterward at a jailer's hands.

The new paramount chief, Necotowance, signed a treaty in 1646 that made the Powhatans into subjects of the English king. The treaty also supposedly limited English territory (an English reservation!) to the Virginia Peninsula plus an area north of York River downstream from Poropotank Creek, as well as the south bank of the James River down to the Blackwater River's drainage. However, a law passed at the very same session of the Grand Assembly in Jamestown rewrote that clause of the treaty, unknown to the Indians: the governor would give permission later for all lands north of York River to be settled. That permission was given

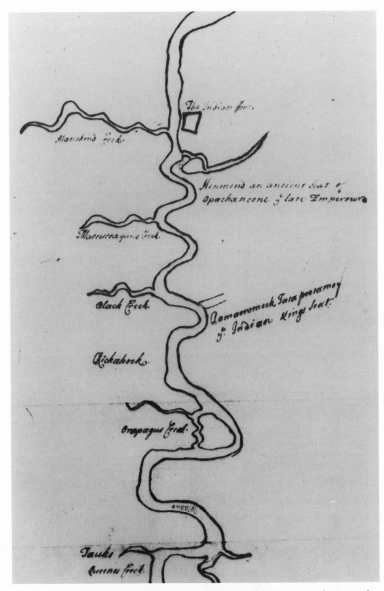

Fig. 5.10. Detail of the Anthony Langston map of York River, showing the upper Pamunkey River, ca. 1662. Courtesy of VDHR.

in 1649, and the rush was on again. By 1665 most of the Virginia coastal plain was in the hands of the English (fig. 5.11). In a very real sense, the Powhatans had lost their lands by being flooded out by settlers, not by being defeated in war.

As the Indian land base shrank rapidly, Indian families through most of coastal Virginia had an ever more difficult time making a living in anything resembling safe conditions. It was a repeat of what had happened along the James before 1622. Most of their waterfront farmland was being gobbled up (the exception was on Pamunkey Neck). They continued to forage in the waterways and marshes and in the forested interiors of the necks, which meant crossing waterfront lands claimed by others who were usually hostile. Once the necks' interiors were patented by Englishmen, the new owners were reluctant to let Indians go there either, even after the passage of a law allowing them to hunt on unfenced patented land. The colony's Grand Assembly also tried to cut down on the death toll by making it illegal to shoot an Indian unless he (only "he's" are mentioned) was engaged in committing an offense directly against an Englishman (usually theft), with testimony from witnesses to the event being required later as well. Even the colony's well-meaning officials were jumpy about receiving Indians on their plantations. In 1662 a new law mandated silver or copper badges for each Indian chief to present when visiting on official business (fig. 5.12).

Native people could be driven off their land by means other than simply preventing their movements while foraging. From the late 1640s it was legal to patent an Indian town's land in advance of the residents' abandoning the site. The law was aimed, naively, at appeasing the settlers' desire to claim choice property. In all too many instances the reality was an English claimant who "assisted" the Indians in leaving early. The push might consist of allowing English cattle to graze in the Indians' corn (unfenced, of course), or it could take the form of an assault on the pigs the Indians had allowed to become feral without first ear-marking them (the English also let them run wild, but *with* earmarks). Laws and ordinances about helping native people fence their corn and so on did little good, judging from the number of Indian complaints to the county courts. In fairness, the Indians themselves were not very cooperative either. Earmarks were required by law for everyone's hogs in 1674, but the Weyanocks had to be forced to comply—for their own good—in 1693.

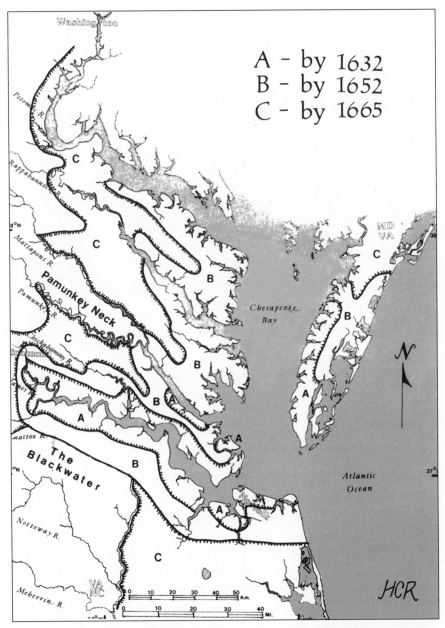

Fig. 5.11. English settlers' claims by 1632, 1652, and 1665. Courtesy of Helen C. Rountree.

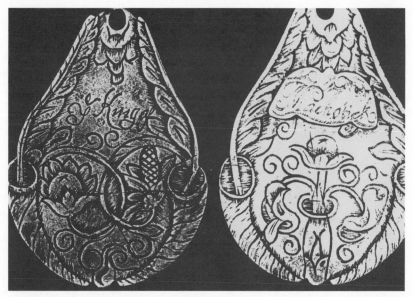

Fig. 5.12. The Machodoc chief's silver badge, 1662. Now owned by the Virginia Historical Society. Courtesy of VDHR.

Still another method of removing the residents of an Indian town was to wait until the populace left, perhaps on their fall hunting and nutting expedition, and then claim abandonment and move in, through a deliberate misunderstanding of the Powhatan seasonal round. Any temporary absence was enough, though, as the Machodocs found out in 1660.

The Machodocs appear on John Smith's map as Onawmanients; their territory stretched up the Potomac River from Lower Machodoc Creek through the Nomini River to Upper Machodoc Creek. Settlers began buying land from the Machodoc segment living on the lowermost creek in the early 1650s, and by 1657 this segment was embroiled in a dispute with the great landowner and later militia colonel Isaac Allerton. The Machodocs did not want trouble; they told Northumberland County investigating commissioners that they were willing to let Allerton stay on the land they had actually sold to him, as long as he did not try to settle tenants on more land, which they had not given up. The issue with Allerton rested there, but other eager neighbors pressed in on them, and in February 1659 two Machodoc men snapped. They murdered two Englishmen and then hid in their town. Their chief and council gave them up to the Northumberland County court, knowing (correctly) that they would be tried and hung. But the group remained so uneasy about English feelings at the time that they left their town and moved in for that farming season with their relatives upriver. The next spring they returned to their town on Lower Machodoc Creek, but they and the English were both so jumpy that the Indians' stance was read as hostile. The Northumberland County court declared the entire town to be accomplices of the two murderers, conveniently forgetting the handing over of the culprits. Men were sent out to drive off the people, burn the houses, and cut the seedling corn, after which English settlers moved onto the land. That section of the Machodocs had to move permanently to Upper Machodoc Creek—where that town (called "Appomattox" by the English) had already been patented by the same landowner-surveyor who "owned" another Indian town's land elsewhere on the Northern Neck.

Pushy, trigger-happy settlers made it increasingly likely that some Indian people would push back, a nightmare for officials trying to govern a frontier in which settlements were widely dispersed. (The Grand Assembly wanted Englishmen to settle densely in towns, but in a region where river transport was so widely available, the settlers would not cooperate, and Virginia had few towns and no cities until late in the eighteenth century.) In fact, by 1660 it is unlikely that the surviving Powhatans could have managed another major strike at the English, especially since the paramount chiefdom had effectively ceased to function by 1650 (Pamunkey leaders would make claims for it into the 1680s). But the fact that the Powhatans still lived in *towns*, while most English people lived on *farmsteads*, probably kept many settlers fearful of concerted Powhatan action on some scale. Another English fear had at least some basis in fact, though events were to prove it exaggerated: English people saw all tribes as "Indians" and assumed that they had an innate sympathy with one another that could lead to joint military action. In reality, though, the Powhatans were caught unhappily between the English and other Algonquians like the Doegs (Tauxenents on John Smith's map), not to mention non-Algonquian groups such as the Tuscaroras, Susquehannocks, and Senecas. Those "foreign" Indians did not trust the Powhatans any more than the English did. Culturally all of these Eastern Woodlands peoples had more in common with one another than with any Europeans, but the Powhatans wanted to stay in their homeland, which meant continuing to get along somehow with the English.

Given all of these pressures, it is surprising that so few Virginia

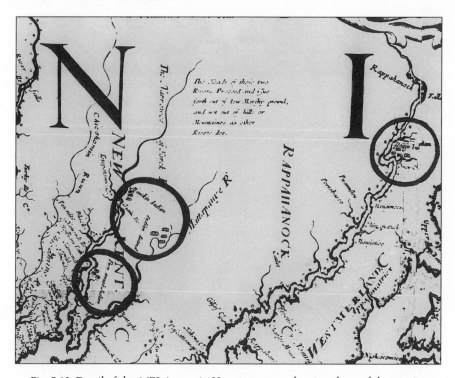

Fig. 5.13. Detail of the 1673 Augustin Herrmann map showing three of the surviv-ing Indian enclaves (circles added).

Algonquian people chose to join English society as detribalized persons. The colonial and county records show very few such people. When they did detribalize, they undertook ownership of livestock and land under the same conditions as their neighbors, a right that was specifically upheld in the case of Edward Gunstocker (probably a Nanzatico [Nandtaugh-tacund]) late in the century. Gunstocker and the few others in the records still kept up ties with their Indian relatives, however, and Gunstocker's heirs had Indian names, not English ones.

Most Powhatan people chose not to give up their traditional ways, even with reduced territories and suspicious and occasionally hostile neighbors. Their populations still declined, due as much to hunger as to disease (there is no record of a major epidemic in Virginia except in 1617, and that disease is unknown), so some of them moved in with other Pow-hatan groups on the land that was left. By 1673, when Augustin Herr-mann drew his map of the Virginia and Maryland colonies (fig. 5.13), there were relatively few islands of tribal territory left. Those islands would be further decreased by the end of the century. Still the Powhatans held on rather than assimilate. Indian people were in fairly constant contact with the English, because of hiring out as hunters (which required a license for the employer) or selling baskets, pots, and wooden trays (these appear in estate inventories of deceased settlers). But they continued to call the Indian towns "home."

Powhatan Refusal to Join English Society

The Virginia colonists never understood why most Powhatans chose to live in straitened but traditional circumstances rather than join the supposedly "superior" English society. Bitterness against the English who took their land would have been only a partial answer. The rest of the answer probably lies in the deep cultural differences that had always existed between the two peoples. Joining the English would have meant living a life in which the material benefits were few and nothing else felt "right." Those Indian people who lived among the English were generally young adults, still fairly adaptable, who were earning wages but not expecting to remain indefinitely. Even then, there seem to have been few such employees until late in the century, when racking poverty overtook the Indian towns.

Workers on seventeenth-century English plantations, whether Indian or English or African, lived at close quarters with the families, often sleeping in the same house. The houses were a far cry from the Georgian brick mansions that the words "Virginia plantation" conjure up for most Americans today. Those mansions were an eighteenth-century phenomenon and were built by a very few owners using slave labor. Most Virginians in any century, and practically all of them in the seventeenth, lived in wooden dwellings with few rooms and fewer embellishments (fig. 5.14). None have survived from the seventeenth century (and very few houses of the rich, either). They would not thrill us if they had: the eyewitness accounts of travelers indicate that given the owners' obsession with tobacco farming, as well as the heavy labor demands made by tobacco plants themselves before the product was salable, most Virginia "planters" threw up their wooden houses hastily and paid little or no attention to upkeep thereafter. That made sense: small farmers knew they would have to move on when tobacco exhausted the soil. Thus most En-

Fig. 5.14. Reconstructed mid-seventeenth-century house at Historic St. Mary's City. Courtesy of VDHR.

glish wooden houses were as "disposable" as Powhatan sapling-and-mat ones, because both peoples were practicing shifting cultivation.

The diet fed to employees was only partially different from what Indian people had at home. It was starchier and mushier than they were used to, for plantation families did little foraging. But at least the mush tasted familiar: as they took up shifting cultivation of tobacco, the English adopted corn (called "Indian wheat") as their major grain source. Real wheat (and oats, barley, and alfalfa) requires the plow-farming of smooth, stumpless fields to produce well, and small-time tobacco farmers rarely had the time and energy for such labor.

English employers expected their workers to be "modest," which in those days meant being covered up almost completely by poorly venti-lated tailored clothing, even in the muggiest weather. The workers may not have complied to the letter in the warm months, but the demands were there—and they were foreign to Indians accustomed to living in breechclouts or aprons. English custom dictated the wearing of hats, too, partly to make shade for pale skin and partly to mark social status, both through the style of the hat and the wearers' ability to keep theirs on while "inferiors" had to doff theirs. (Hat-removal remained a serious matter in Virginia, subject to legislation, at least as late as the 1790s.) The Powhatans did not need the shade, and it is unlikely that they enjoyed any reminders that they were considered inferior by their employers.

The European division of labor was foreign to Powhatan people, which probably made some of the young employees deeply uncomfortable. In the English world, males cultivated plants and cared for the larger farm animals, and females helped at peak times. Powhatan men must have felt like intruders when told to work in the fields, which was "women's busi-ness" at home. In nonharvest seasons, English women's work centered around the house and included making, washing, and mending those heavy clothes the family insisted upon wearing. (At least farm women were not weaving the cloth in those times; nearly all cloth was imported from England in the seventeenth century.) The English did not bathe of-ten, but when they did they used soap, which was usually made on the farm by the women. English people also expected to eat on a schedule, so women prepared several family meals per day rather than reducing the labor by keeping a bubbling stewpot going. (But then, people rarely went out and foraged for wild foods to throw into a stewpot.) Women supplied some food directly, by raising poultry and a garden for herbs and some vegetables. Powhatan women, accustomed to being out and about, must have had to fight "cabin fever" when working for their English counter-parts.

English society was far more hierarchical than the Powhatan one, and that hierarchy made itself felt between families and within families. The Powhatan young people were accustomed to paying deference to chiefs and their relatives, but it is unlikely that they were prepared for the amount of sheer servility in both word and deed that English people expected from their social "inferiors" in those days. Higher-ranking people were supposed to be "better" in all respects, and as such they expected to instruct "lesser" people (who were English as well as non-English) on a wide variety of things, while the lower orders thanked them for the instruction. It would all have been hard to take if one came from a less hierarchical society that also predated the English occupation of the region.

The major income of the family was understood to come from adult male husbandry of plants and animals, and men outranked women and children as a result. Women, being older and more knowledgeable, outranked children. The custom of higher-ranking persons giving orders to and instructing lower-ranking persons applied within the family, with the accepted custom of physical chastisement for mistakes or disobedience thrown in. English childhood differed drastically from the Powhatan one, and Powhatan men and women who went to work for the English, especially if they did it under a seven-year indenture that made them technically servants, must have found living in a status equivalent to "English child" positively galling at times.

The families with whom such employees lived were not constructed like Powhatan families either. Powhatan people lived in extended families, with the men across several generations being related to one another and the women apparently marrying in. English families back home were similar, being extended families but based upon patrilineality (tracing a line of males) with primogeniture (eldest son getting most of the estate) and patriarchy (older males ruling the others) added in. That was the lens through which the English in Virginia saw themselves, and it was the picture they tried to present to the Indians as "superior." The reality, however, was that the English colonists very often lived far apart from their siblings and cousins as they tried to gain riches on the frontier. Not only that, but even a nuclear family, with husband, wife, and their children living and working together until the children were grown, was hard to achieve in the seventeenth century, because so many people died young.

English immigrants lacked immunity to the "bugs" (now unidentifiable) that they encountered in Virginia; new arrivals endured a year or so that came to be called "the seasoning," during which most fell sick and many died. The young age of the people dying at Jordan's Point in the 1620s has already been noted in chapter 2. For the rest of the century, until the majority of the English population came to consist of people born in the colony, about 40 percent of Anglo-Virginian children could expect to have lost both parents before they grew up—if they survived to adulthood themselves. Widowed adults remarried soon, in order to survive economically and get the surviving children reared. Thus the English "nuclear" families that the Powhatans actually saw were collections of adults and children, oftentimes connected to each other rather tenuously (Rountree calls them *menage families*).[3] Pocahontas's only child was in a family situation like that: when Thomas Rolfe grew up and came to Virginia, he was brought over and initially sponsored by his long-dead father's third wife's father. The discrepancy between what the English themselves said was "normal" and how they were living in Virginia would not have been lost upon Indian employees who came from more stable families among longer-lived people.

The English colonists adhered to—and evangelized on behalf of—a religion that differed significantly from the Powhatan one. We can pass over the rudeness, by Indian standards, of pressing one's views upon another. We can also set aside the requirement of weekly church services, so foreign to Powhatan practices of performing rituals as and when they were needed, because many families in the Virginia colony could not manage the time and distance needed to get to weekly services anyway. Family prayers were all that many settlers could come up with. Worshipping one all-powerful deity instead of many less powerful ones would have been understandable to Woodland Indian people, albeit a novel idea. No, the major obstacles to Powhatan understanding of the religion of the English lay elsewhere.

The Anglican religion's holy places were on the other side of the ocean, and its calendar commemorated events in the life of a person who had lived over a millennium and a half earlier. That would have been very confusing to a Powhatan person, reared where holy places were local and the calendar was based upon the seasonal cycle in the here and now. And then the English demand for orthodoxy must have been downright bewildering to the Indians. In English eyes, there was only one right way to believe and worship, and everyone had to conform, just as they conformed to the rule of their fathers at home and their King in public. The only glitch was that the English did not agree among themselves on what version of the Anglican religion was the orthodox or "right" one. They argued about it in public, and back home they had fought a civil war over it in the 1640s. Powhatan people, on the other hand, believed arguing in public was rude, and in any case they were not accustomed to highly authoritarian fathers (at any time) or political leaders (except on ceremonial occasions). They also came from a religious background (according to Pocahontas's second husband, John Rolfe) in which people were free to believe what they wanted without interference. So to Powhatan workers, their employers' insistence upon the "rightness" of their own version of religion, with other Englishmen volubly disagreeing, may have seemed more than a little pigheaded.

The last thing that probably irritated Powhatan youths who worked among the English was the colonists' attitude that fealty to the English King and his officials was the only proper political stance (except, for some, during the 1649–60 period when Parliament and Oliver Cromwell ran the country). The settlers wanted badly for the Indians to be loyal subjects of the King and therefore more or less controllable. Yet as the Indians could see plainly, the settlers themselves were frequently at odds with the royal governors of the colony. The governor and his council (whom Indian leaders met when they paid tribute) and the elected burgesses in the Grand Assembly often found the grassroots colonists out on the frontier impossible to control, especially when those colonists wanted to lay hands on more Indian land. Laws might be passed but not published out in the counties; if published, they might not be enforced. It is unlikely that, while being lectured to by local Englishmen, the Powhatans failed to notice the gap between the ideal of loyalty to king and country and the reality that many colonists practiced, which was that self-interest ruled.

Altogether, the social conditions that young Powhatan employees met, especially as they became fluent in English and understood the talk around them, would have been distasteful to people with their upbringing. And the physical living conditions on the jerry-built plantations were not much better than those in their hometowns. For many Indian people, it was not worth putting up with it all, until actual starvation nipped at their heels.

Harsher English Attitudes toward the Powhatans

Conditions for English families deteriorated in the 1660s and 1670s, which made them more skeptical of their government and more likely to take out their frustrations on the native tribes. In general, the more distant the English governmental body, the more liberal toward the Indians' rights—not from sympathy toward non-English human beings but from a desire to keep the peace. More distant governmental bodies also tried to do things for the colonists' welfare, like getting them to diversify their crops when tobacco prices fell, with which the grassroots would not cooperate (they wanted to beat the odds by somehow raising more tobacco). By the mid-1670s, tobacco prices remained low, there were few "new" Powhatan lands left to take, and incursions by "foreign" Indians from the north began to happen regularly. There were shooting incidents, with the English claiming that the Indians had been the aggressors; we cannot be sure who shot first, for both sides were ill at ease and trigger-happy. The fact that those northern Indians were not allies of the Powhatans, and that some of them, like the Susquehannocks, were under pressure from Iroquoians still farther north, made no difference to many of the Powhatans' neighbors. The government in Jamestown refused to launch a war against all Indians indiscriminately, which caused some colonists to become even more disaffected.

In 1675 an incident with the Susquehannocks triggered the upheaval called Bacon's Rebellion. Nathaniel Bacon Jr. and his followers drove the governor out of his capital and took over the House of Burgesses, where they passed a series of laws including one making all Indian prisoners into slaves-for-life. (This was the first law that mandated slavery for any Indians in Virginia, though a few Indians had been kept as slaves as early as the 1640s.) Bacon and his men attacked two Indian tribes, the Algonquian-speaking Pamunkeys and the Siouan-speaking Occaneechis, neither of whom had actually committed any depredations upon English people. After Bacon himself died suddenly and his forces dispersed, the governor and burgesses returned, to be joined by commissioners sent from England, and began parceling out blame. The only people fully exonerated in the rather chaotic proceedings that followed were the Indians: they had done no wrong to anyone. Instead the commissioners concluded that among the main culprits were the big frontier landowners, many of them on the Northern Neck (Isaac Allerton was one), who had robbed the Indians, complained of the resulting native hostility, and then taken action against the people they had victimized.

To make amends for all that had happened, the commissioners made a treaty on behalf of King Charles II, signed in May 1677 at Middle Plantation (now Williamsburg), which reaffirmed the rights of the Indian signers as loyal subjects of the king. Significantly, "tributary" (tribute-paying) Indians were to have the same civil rights as English people, a point to which we will return repeatedly in chapters 6 and 7 since the treaty is still in force today. Indian people had already been going to the county courts when they had complaints as individuals, but now that right was written down in black and white. Tribal matters were still to be handled by the colony's governor. The surviving tribes were to have perpetual ownership of the land for three miles around their towns, to ensure them enough foraging territory for their small remaining populations; they also had a right to hunt on English patented land if unfenced and also to go into any marsh to gather tuckahoe, cuttanemons, and other things (such as reeds) not useful to the English. The queen of Pamunkey was to have dominion over several of the Powhatan tribes, and as such she received extra presents after the signing, one of which was an engraved silver frontlet (fig. 5.15). Most of the surviving Powhatan tribes signed the treaty, and so did representatives of the Nottoways, Occaneechis, and others.

Ironically, just as the treaty firmed up the Powhatans' civil rights within their communities, the status of Indians off-reservation and of other nonwhites was sliding farther downward in Virginia. Slavery for life had been the official status for Africans entering the colony by sea since the early 1660s; some entering earlier and those who bought or were given their freedom remained in the colony as a small but persistent free negro population. The number of Africans in Virginia had grown steadily and was to increase rapidly after 1690, when the slave trade hit its peak. As the population of obviously non-English people expanded, the English took ever stronger steps to remain in control of the colony. There is little direct evidence of associations between Powhatans and Africans from those decades, but English attitudes toward Africans increasingly colored their attitudes toward the Powhatans. Bacon's law legalizing slavery for Indian prisoners was an example; interestingly, it was repassed by the supposedly anti-Bacon House of Burgesses the next year. It was the 1677 treaty that was unusually liberal for the time.

Fig. 5.15. Silver frontlet presented to the queen of Pamunkey in accordance with the 1677 Treaty of Middle Plantation. Now owned by the Virginia Historical Society. Courtesy of Katherine Wetzel.

Indian tribes remained useful as observant buffers between the English and "foreign" Indians, a notion that began to evaporate during the Seneca attacks on the colony in 1683. In 1691 the law allowing Indian prisoners to be kept in slavery was repealed, but the same year saw passage of an act outlawing all marriages between whites and nonwhites in Virginia. Up until then Indian-white marriages had been legal, though rare (Pocahontas-John Rolfe, John Bass-Elizabeth, and one more in Henrico County in 1688 are all that were ever recorded in the 1600s). Robert Beverley wrote early in the next century that the Powhatans resented the English reluctance to marry, rather than merely mate, with their people, showing a disdain for Indians as potential family members. Now such unions were illegal, and they remained so until the 1960s.

In 1705, just under a century after the English founded the Virginia colony, they proclaimed their superiority over all nonwhites by passing a series of acts that applied to "negroes, mulattoes, and [nonreservation] Indians." Such people were now barred from voting, holding civil or military or religious office, bearing arms, testifying in court in any case whatsoever, and even lifting a hand in opposition to orders from whites. Thus Indian and free black people working under indentures could now be held in servitude beyond the stated time, without having recourse to any court, and they and any other nonwhite employees had to take any physical punishment their masters or any white neighbors loosed upon them. There was also a law that year that set up Virginia's first racial definitions: one-eighth or more African descent made one a mulatto, whether the rest of one's ancestors were European or American Indian. There was no definition of "Indians"—presumably because their communities were small enough to be considered nearly extinct. That was an error, as we shall see in subsequent chapters.

The Powhatans in the Late Seventeenth Century

The last half of seventeenth-century Powhatan history did lead to the impression by 1705 of impending disappearance, though. Let us go down the roster of districts and see why that was so. We have rough counts of "bowmen," or able-bodied men, from a Grand Assembly census of 1669, and a follow-up estimate of community populations made by Robert Beverley in 1705.

In the James River valley, the Nansemonds had split politically into two groups during the 1644–46 war. The anti-English faction, who may be called "traditional" Nansemonds for our purposes, headed southward into "the Blackwater," a region kept off-limits to English settlers for the rest of the century. There they lived in several places, becoming known as "Pochicks," until they got a reservation on the Nottoway River toward the end of the century. Their population held fairly steady: thirty bowmen in both 1669 and 1705. The pro-English faction, which we can call "Christianized" through their association with and later descent from John Bass, remained in the Nansemond River area until either the late seventeenth or early eighteenth century, when they moved to the northern rim of the Dismal Swamp, where some of their descendants still live. In 1669 they had forty-five able-bodied men, but Beverley lost track of them because they lacked a reservation.[4] The Weyanocks headed south just as the traditional Nansemonds did, with fifteen bowmen in their community in 1669. They did not prosper or ever get a reservation, and they ultimately merged with the Nottoways in the mid-1700s. The Appamattucks held on in their homeland, probably because they became established as guides for Englishmen trading with tribes farther southwest. They received a copper badge (now on display at Jamestown Settlement) in 1662 for visiting the English settlements. They had fifty able-bodied men in 1669, a huge population for Powhatan groups still living near the James River, but by 1705 they had shrunk to a few families living, landless, as tenants. The people of Powhatan town, now called "Powhite," had ten bowmen in 1669 and appeared as a community in Henrico County land plats through 1701. They ceased to be an autonomous group after that, being omitted in Beverley's list of survivors. In 1708 one of the Pamunkey councilmen was named "Mister Powhite," so perhaps the people went there.

In the York River drainage, the premier tribe was (and still is, according to its members) the Pamunkeys, who had large landholdings and also royalty throughout the seventeenth century. Opechancanough's successor, Necotowance, had either died or changed his name by 1649, when Tottopottomoy appeared on the scene. After he died in 1656, his wife Cockacoeske succeeded him; both were said to be "descendants" (matrilineal heirs) somehow of Opechancanough. Cockacoeske was the Pamunkey queen who was driven from her town during Bacon's Rebellion and given the silver frontlet afterward. She died in 1686, and her niece (name not recorded) was ratified as her successor by the Virginia colonial council. She either died or changed her name in the early 1700s, for during a few years thereafter the Pamunkey queen appears under the name "Queen Ann," perhaps to honor the new English queen crowned in 1702. After that the Pamunkeys seem to have had no more hereditary chiefs. Their population held steady at fifty bowmen, according to the 1669 and 1705 lists. The neck that bore their name remained off-limits to English settlement (anticipatory patents being permitted) until 1701. In that year the Pamunkeys asked the colony's governor to ratify a number of sales they had made within the three-mile limit specified in the 1677 treaty; the governor complied, but Pamunkey acreage still remained the largest of any Powhatan tribe.

The Mattaponis, ancestors of another Powhatan group surviving down to the present, fled their river in 1646 and took refuge up on the ridge between it and the Rappahannock, at the head of Piscataway Creek.

They remained there as English settlers moved in on them, enduring the burning of their chief's house (complaints to the governor did little good), until they gave up and moved back home around 1667. They built their town on the north bank downstream from modern Walkerton; they had twenty bowmen in 1669. However, their town was captured by the Senecas in 1683, after which the survivors went to live with the Chickahominies and gradually became overshadowed by them—for a time. The Chickahominies, originally from the James River valley, abandoned their homeland in 1646 and moved to the lower Mattaponi River for a while, after which they joined the Mattaponis in Piscataway Creek's headwaters. When the Mattaponis moved back, the Chickahominies went along and established a separate town next door, with sixty bowmen in 1669. They repulsed the Seneca attack and took in the battered Mattaponis, with both groups going to live with the Pamunkeys for five uncomfortable years before moving back to the Mattaponi River. They were assigned reservation land far upriver in 1693 but traded it for the tract on which they had lived in the 1640s and 1650s: the site of the modern Mattaponi Indian Reservation.[5] By 1705 they and the Mattaponis were ensconced there, with sixteen bowmen and, according to Beverley, a growing population.

In the valley of the Rappahannock River and its tributaries, the Chiskiacks had been living on the south bank of the Piankatank River since the late 1620s. They were assigned a reservation there in 1649, which they later exchanged for a nearby tract. They had fifteen able-bodied men in 1669. Their community did not survive much longer, however, for it was gone by the time their land was surveyed for an Englishman in 1683. The Rappahannocks sold off their lands north of the river, retreating upriver and finally giving up altogether and going southward to live on the ridge near the Mattaponis and Chickahominies in the 1660s. After those two groups left, the Rappahannocks stayed on in the face of English settlement until the Seneca attacks brought a crisis. They had had only thirty bowmen in 1669, and they could not defend themselves or, out in the woods, be defended effectively by their English allies. So in 1684 the Rappahannocks "and their corn and lumber [seventeenth-century meaning of lumber: junk]" were moved at Essex County's expense to Portobacco Bay, which had become an Indian refuge area. The Moratticos (John Smith's Moraughtacund, also called Totuskeys) sold out and moved to the headwaters of Piscataway Creek about the same time the Rappahannocks did, making a fourth Indian town there for a time. Like their long-term neighbors, they remained in that area after the Mattaponis and Chickahominies left, in a town that had forty "Totas Chees" bowmen in 1669. They disappeared from the records after that, and probably joined the Rappahannocks in the move upriver. Portobacco Bay seems to have taken its name from a Maryland group of that name (still preserved as a place-name in that state) that moved down into Virginia's Rappahannock drainage in the 1650s to escape the English settlers pouring into their homeland (Maryland began officially encouraging that settlement in 1651). They had sixty fighting men in 1669, but their population decreased, along with that of the tribes that joined them, afterward. By 1705 only a few families were left, according to Beverley, who added that they lived as tenants on English lands. They had, in fact, been pushed off their land the year before, after futilely complaining to the Virginia governor. The English claimant had a patent that dated all the way back to 1650, and he and his family were tired of waiting.

Directly across the Rappahannock from Portobacco Town were the Nanzaticos (John Smith's Nandtaughtacunds). They probably included Pissasecks and upriver Cuttatawomens, groups which do not appear under those names after John Smith's time. The Nanzaticos, together with a second town called "Mattehatique," had fifty bowmen in 1669. The group was in and out of trouble with the English and "foreign" Indians for years, with an expectable diminishment of population through either death or out-migration, until by Beverley's time they had only five men, or so he said. The reality was different. In 1704, with another long-term patent holder pressing in on them and complaints to the governor getting nowhere, several Nanzatico men attacked and killed an entire family of English neighbors (not, sad to say, the patent holders). The Richmond County militia promptly rounded up all forty-nine men, women, and children. Five men were tried—not by jury, as treaty rights would have demanded—and hung. The colonial government (not the county) then invoked a 1665 law that made whole Indian towns responsible for murders committed by one resident until the culprit was found. The culprits in this case had been found and hung, but in a replay of the 1660 Machodoc experience, the community was made into an example. All Nanzaticos over twelve years of age were sold into seven-years' servitude in the Caribbean and forbidden to return to Virginia, while all the children (the youngest being a nine-month-old baby) were bound out to owners of large English plantations in Virginia until the age of twenty-four (the children born to the girls before age twenty-four to be bound out likewise), after which they were forbidden to communicate with any surviving Indian community in the colony. Thus were the Nanzaticos completely wiped out as a tribe, in the first *official* attempt at *social* genocide in Virginia. More attempts would be made in the twentieth century on Indian tribes that had not conveniently died out.

The last Rappahannock valley group, the downriver Cuttatawomens, finished up among the Wiccocomicos by the late 1650s, after holding a reservation briefly in Lancaster County in the early part of that decade. The Wiccocomicos also became the refuge, though not a voluntary one, of the Sekakawons (anglicized to Chickacone, later to Coan) to the northwest of them. The English set up a reservation for the two groups on Dividing Creek, south of the Wiccocomicos' home river, in 1656; they also pushed the Sekakawons (who included some Yeocomicos from Maryland) onto that land and pressured them to accept a joint chief. There were eighty-eight able-bodied men among them in 1656, judging by the surveyed size of the reservation (at fifty acres allowed per bowman), and seventy by 1669. The "Chickacone" name disappeared from the records after the move. The now-multitribal "Wiccocomicos" continued to hold onto their reservation in the face of an English neighbor who nibbled it away and claimed more (the legal fights went on for decades). By 1705 their leader had merely a life-interest in the land, the claimant having won, and Beverley heard that only three men kept up a traditional way of life.

While the Sekakawons went southeast, the other Potomac River groups in Virginia headed southwest. The withdrawal of the Machodocs (John Smith's Onawmanients) from some of their territory has already been described. Their town on Upper Machodoc Creek had only ten bowmen in 1669 and there is no record of their existence anywhere thereafter, except for one tantalizing reference: one of the Nanzatico men shipped to Antigua was called "Mattox Will." If some of the Machodocs joined the Nanzaticos, then they did indeed disappear from Virginia. As for the Patawomecks, they vanish from the Virginia records after about 1665, when the English made war on them and some others in the area. Their chief's silver badge was discovered around 1830 as a surface find at the same Indian town (the Camden site and its environs) where archaeologists unearthed the corresponding badge of the Machodoc chief (both items now owned by the Virginia Historical Society). That site is at Portobacco Bay, which may indicate a merger of both groups with the Portobaccos.

On the lower Virginia Eastern Shore, the Accomacs, now called Gingaskins, had disposed of most of their lands and come to rest on a 630–acre tract on the ocean side of the peninsula. Their chief's sovereignty over the Occohannocks ended by the 1640s, and thereafter they held onto their land in spite of disapproval and occasional open hostility from their English neighbors. They did not sign the treaty of 1677, but because of their never-wavering loyalty, the Virginia government always treated them as though they had. The Occohannocks on the upper Virginia Eastern Shore had sold off most of their land by 1665. From then up through the end of the century they commuted back and forth between their old townsites and the larger, more prosperous Algonquian-speaking communities in Maryland. They retained chiefs and an "empress" past 1700, but according to Beverley most of their populations were dwindling. By that time they had disappeared from the county records.

Except for the Christianized Nansemonds, all of the surviving Virginia Algonquian communities were keeping up a fairly traditional lifestyle in 1705, in spite of much-reduced circumstances. For readers who have studied the history of the Maryland and New England Algonquians, that will not come as a surprise. Coastal Algonquian-speakers were amazingly tenacious of their age-old ways of doing things, if their towns had access to the water resources that had been part of their culture for so long. Losing most of their land did not cause them to alter their culture, by itself. It took that loss plus continuous pressure from the English and the passage of a lot of time to make them change.

Notes

1. Numerous scholars have argued about the incident's validity; Rountree argues against it on both anthropological and historical grounds (see her 1989 and 1990 books in the selected bibliography in this volume). Among other problems, John Smith never mentioned the incident in any of his writings until 1624, when Pocahontas, her English husband, and most of the early colonists who met her were safely dead.

2. The colony's governor later denied that it happened. Meanwhile, the colony's backers, the Virginia Company of London, censured the doctor at Jamestown for having provided the poison.

3. Families of this sort, when organized around a core of cooperating women, are called "matrifocal families" by social scientists; they are a common defense against underemployment and poverty in the modern United States. The seventeenth-century English in Virginia and Maryland had such catch-as-catch-can families because of high mortality, and they were organized around cooperating male-female couples. Hence the need for another term.

4. As this volume was being written, Nansemond Chief Emeritus Oliver Perry received and passed on to Rountree a deed of 1709, never recorded in the official books, that mentions a Nansemond Reservation near Back Bay in Virginia Beach. It was far from where any Nansemonds are ever recorded as living, and it had passed into English hands by 1685.

5. The location of their final reservation, and its identity with the modern Mattaponi one, is a new interpretation (differing from Rountree's published 1990 version) based upon her reexamination of original records during the federal recognition effort of the Chickahominies and Upper Mattaponis in 1999.

6

The Middle Centuries

Between 1705 and the Civil War, the Virginia Algonquians almost disappeared from the historical record, not because they went nearly extinct but because of problems with the record itself. With only a few exceptions, the Powhatans were illiterate until late in the nineteenth century. Almost none of their non-Indian neighbors—the minority who were literate themselves (no mandated public education existing in Virginia until after the Civil War)—found them "exotic" enough to be worth writing about. The exception was Robert Beverley, who in 1705 knew Chickahominies/Mattaponis who were still very traditional. But Beverley plagiarized freely from Captain John Smith, and he also inserted data from other authors writing about "the Indians," the data coming from as far away as Canada, so that it is hard to be sure just what the Powhatans he knew personally were like.

Official records in Virginia present problems too. Indian tribes appear in colonial-level records only if they retained reservations and therefore treaty rights, and then only if they had some sort of difficulty, as the Pamunkeys did in 1706 (fig. 6.1). The frequency of reported difficulties decreased as the eighteenth century wore on, and the surviving reservations increasingly became backwaters inhabited by ever more anglicized Indian people. On the county level, where other kinds of records were being made, individual Indians were forbidden to sue members of the white majority. The only other records kept by counties before the mid-nineteenth century were not the sort that Indians usually appear in: they would have needed to contract Christian marriages (most didn't until late), possess salable or heritable property (most didn't), or get into trouble with the law (most didn't). There is a further problem with county records: some counties with Powhatans living in them lost many or all of their records during the nineteenth century. King William County, containing the Pamunkey and Mattaponi reservations, lost most of its records to fire in 1885. The courthouses in New Kent and Charles City counties, where the Chickahominies returned to live, plus the courthouse in Nansemond County, once home to the Christianized Nansemonds, were all burned by Union soldiers in 1865. The clerk's office in King and Queen County, where some Rappahannock/Portobacco people remained, met the same fate the year before. And Caroline County, where other Rappahannock/Portobacco people lived, budded off in 1728 from Essex County (with intact records) and then lost many of its eighteenth-century books through carelessness, damage from vermin, and so forth. Given the things happening to the Indian communities and the chanciness of records being made about them and then surviving in the eighteenth and nineteenth centuries, it is a wonder that any papers about them are left.

Powhatan-English Affairs in the Eighteenth Century

After the elimination of the Nanzatico tribe and the Rappahannock/ Portobacco reservation in 1705, ending the Indian refuge area on the Rappahannock River, only five Powhatan-descended communities remained under treaty status (not counting the Weyanocks living with the Nottoways on their reservation): the Pamunkeys, the Mattaponi/Chickahominies, the Wiccocomicos, the traditional Nansemonds, and the Gingaskins (fig. 6.2). All of these groups had waterfront reservations, where they could use the fishing and marsh-foraging rights guaranteed to them in the 1677 treaty. These tracts were supposed to consist of the land within a three-mile radius of the people's towns—which was difficult to survey if, like the Chickahominy/Mattaponis, the town consisted of "a row [of houses] at least one mile in length." However, the houses were usually on one side of the river, not both; a law passed in the same year (1705) as the infamous "black code" made it legal for English claimants to take up the land across from the houses, theoretically halving the area of such reservations. The Mattaponi/Chickahominies were probably not affected, being settled by 1705 on their former land that contained the "Cliffs landing." It may have been different for the Pamunkeys, though we cannot be certain thanks to the burning of the records of New Kent County on the other side of the Pamunkey River. But when the Smithso-

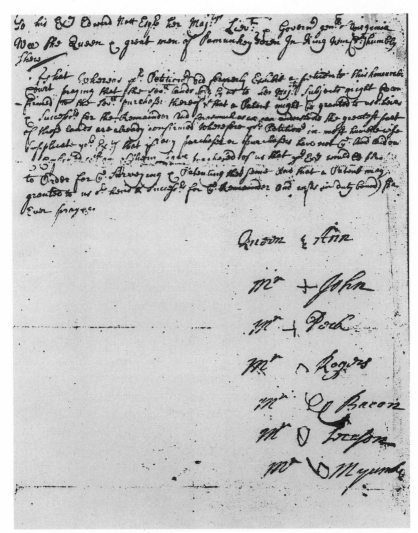

Fig. 6.1. A 1706 petition of the queen of Pamunkey and her council asking that their remaining lands be secured to them by a patent. (Published in 1875 in *Calendar of Virginia State Papers*.)

nian Institution anthropologist Albert Gatschet visited the tribe in the 1890s, he recorded a Pamunkey oral tradition that a century or more before there had been some Indians at Cumberland, across the river to the east of the reservation's peninsula, and that they had perished after a skirmish—with the Pamunkeys. They could have been a dissident faction within the Pamunkeys, forced either to move back or to disappear when the halving law was passed.

The Pamunkeys and the Mattaponi/Chickahominies kept some of their land in spite of ambitious neighbors, including the sons of the planter who had sold the valuable "Cliffs landing" plot back to the Mattaponi/Chickahominies. They lost about half the tract but kept the little plateau containing the landing (see fig. 7.12 in chapter 7). The problem of Indian inability to testify in court was solved in 1748 when white trustees were appointed to oversee Pamunkey land matters (which in those days administratively included those of the Mattaponi/Chickahominies). By the end of the century the trustees had also been given power to assist with making bylaws for the Indians. The Pamunkeys were selling off land as late as 1828, while the Mattaponis endured a condemnation attempt on a bit of their land by a neighbor who wanted to build the abutment for a milldam on Indian Town Creek in 1812.

The Wiccocomicos, on the other hand, were not full-fledged owners of their reservation by 1700. Their last leader, William Taptico, gave up all claim to the land in 1718. The Indians' connection to the land was thus broken, and they therefore ceased to exist as a tribe in the eyes of Virginia's colonial government. Northumberland County did not regard them as Indian anymore either. Their fate becomes very difficult to trace, in the absence of any tribal roll telling us their personal names.

The traditional Nansemonds owned one reservation but after 1744 preferred to live on another among the still-vital Nottoways. By the 1780s there were only a handful of people left with a Nansemond identity, and these asked the colonial government to allow them to sell the reservation that was still officially theirs. After some delays, the sale went through in 1792.

As for the Gingaskins, they clung to their land while their population shrank to the point that they began marrying out rather than commit incest. Their spouses were both whites and free negroes. The free negro connection exposed the Gingaskins to all of the prejudice that local whites felt toward a nonwhite population that was free and therefore incompletely controlled, a prejudice which by the early 1800s had reached paranoiac proportions in Northampton County.[1] The neighbors' attempts to have the reservation eliminated altogether began in 1784, with one major reason given that a reservation population with treaty rights attracted "worthless" people and became a danger to the commu-

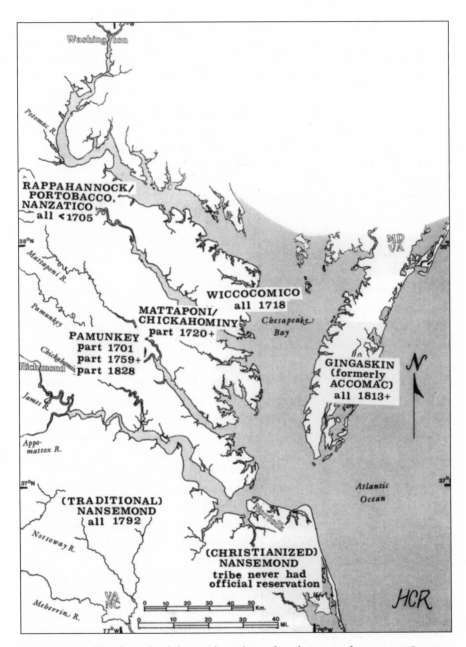

Fig. 6.2. Map of Powhatan lands lost in the eighteenth and nineteenth centuries. Courtesy of Helen C. Rountree

nity. The Indians and their spouses, who according to Rountree's detailed search of the county records were a generally law-abiding group, successfully opposed those efforts. In 1812, however, as the United States moved into another war with Great Britain, a Gingaskin and two free negro spouses of Gingaskins got involved in a slave insurrection plot, after which the tribe surrendered to the pressure and requested that the reservation be divided up and allotted to individual Indians. That was done in 1813, and over the next five decades the allottees and their heirs gradually sold out. Some of their descendants still live in Northampton County.

All Virginia Indian land sales after 1790 were made without reference to any rights of the U.S. federal government in the matter. The federal Indian Non-Intercourse Act of 1790 gave the U.S. government rather than state governments the power to negotiate in land matters (and reap the profits) in "Indian country," which was assumed by everyone at the time to apply only to Indian groups that had not yet made treaties specifically with the United States. Indian peoples like the Powhatans, who had no occasion to make new treaties with anyone, remained officially outside "Indian country" as far as the federal government was concerned. Thus the federal Bureau of Indian Affairs, when it finally came into existence, had no charge to oversee or protect the few surviving Powhatan reservations, much less the groups that had lost their land. The interpretation of what constituted "Indian country" would change in the late twentieth century to include "state" reservations (under treaties with colonies and later states after 1790), and the Pamunkeys would benefit from that change. But before that, no Powhatans had anything resembling "federal recognition" as Indians. And unless they had white trustees and direct access to the state governor (for those on the reservations), or firm friends in the local white community (in the case of nonreservation Powhatan descendants), they were at the mercy of whatever fears and prejudices moved their neighbors.

And where were the missionaries in all this? They weren't in Virginia. Virginia was not a colony founded for reasons of religious freedom; it was founded to give English people a chance to become wealthy. No colonists ever set up "praying towns" in the colony, as was done in parts of New England to educate native people in English culture as well as religion. No Anglican ministers made a special point of evangelizing Indians, not even John Bass (his surviving Sermon Book says nothing whatever

Fig. 6.3. Archaeological exploration of Fort Christanna, 2000. Courtesy of VDHR.

about Indians except on the genealogy pages). In the 1680s John Clayton and John Banister *met* Indians and learned things from "the aborigines," but they were first and foremost the rectors of English parishes. And there was no cleric comparable even to them in the eighteenth century.

The only two attempts to create missions for Virginia Indians were both funded exclusively from England and limited in their extent. Fort Christanna, which existed only for about a decade, was built at the behest of Lieutenant Governor Alexander Spotswood and supported by the bishop of London. It was located along the Meherrin River in the piedmont and served mainly Siouan-speaking Saponis and others. When the bishop's funds ceased, so did the mission; only archaeological remains of it still exist (fig. 6.3). The other enterprise, funded after 1691 by the income from a farm named "Brafferton" in England, consisted of living expenses, classroom space, and a teacher's pay for Indian boys sent to the College of William and Mary (Virginia's only college until Thomas Jefferson's time). The boys could come only from Indian tribes still under a treaty with Virginia. After about 1720, that meant only Pamunkeys and

Nansemonds (Gingaskins never participated), with an occasional Delaware or Shawnee thrown in later. The college did not begin operations until 1693, and no Powhatan boys were turned loose by their parents until in 1711 Lieutenant Governor Spotswood promised to remit their tribute if they would send their sons. That scheme brought in twenty students, a number that tapered off thereafter: to eight boys by 1754, two in 1769. The education consisted of grammar-school work, since the boys were starting from scratch; but then, if we can believe a visitor from Yale, the white boys were not doing real college-level work either at that time. Living accommodations were usually segregated at the college. And in the institution's catalog, which for many years listed the names of students attending, the Brafferton students were clearly labeled as "Indians." Everyone else was white, and the students' fathers were pointed out for snob value if they were prominent (fig. 6.4).

The Indian boys who had attended William and Mary ran up against English people who doubted that they could ever learn enough about "civilization" to be considered worthy of admission to English society. In Spotswood's time, for instance, baptism into the Anglican church was denied even to boys who wanted it after taking classes at the college for several years. Most boys, caught between that kind of prejudice and a native world in which they were out of practice at fitting in, became problems to everyone, including themselves. It is understandable that some treaty Indians such as the traditional Nansemonds continued to go to Williamsburg at the colony's expense to pay their tribute (fig. 6.5) while declining to send any boys to be "educated." It was not until late in the eighteenth century, when the Pamunkeys at home had anglicized a great deal, that a stint at William and Mary would be an advantage to their boys, making them literate and better able to defend their people. But by then no college admission was forthcoming, for the Brafferton Fund moneys had been diverted to the West Indies when the American Revolution broke out (why educate Indians in a rebelling colony?). No one in Virginia stepped in to make up the difference, so William and Mary became completely closed to nonwhites until the fall of 1964.[2]

Major Changes in Indian Lifeways

The Powhatans did finally undergo considerable cultural change in the eighteenth century, after holding out for much of the seventeenth. Los-

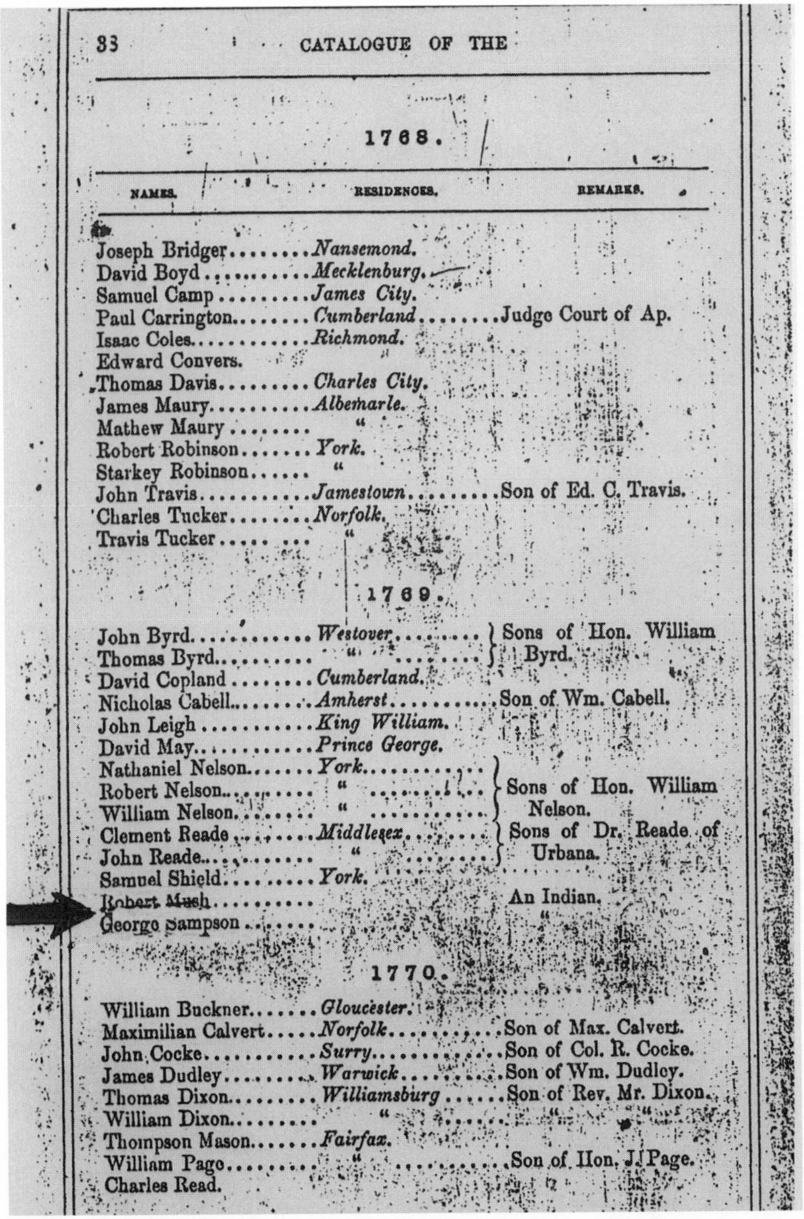

1768.

NAMES.	RESIDENCES.	REMARKS.
Joseph Bridger	Nansemond.	
David Boyd	Mecklenburg.	
Samuel Camp	James City.	
Paul Carrington	Cumberland	Judge Court of Ap.
Isaac Coles	Richmond.	
Edward Convers.		
Thomas Davis	Charles City.	
James Maury	Albemarle.	
Mathew Maury	"	
Robert Robinson	York.	
Starkey Robinson	"	
John Travis	Jamestown	Son of Ed. C. Travis.
Charles Tucker	Norfolk.	
Travis Tucker	"	

1769.

John Byrd	Westover	} Sons of Hon. William
Thomas Byrd	"	} Byrd.
David Copland	Cumberland.	
Nicholas Cabell	Amherst	Son of Wm. Cabell.
John Leigh	King William.	
David May	Prince George.	
Nathaniel Nelson	York	}
Robert Nelson	"	} Sons of Hon. William
William Nelson	"	} Nelson.
Clement Reade	Middlesex	} Sons of Dr. Reade of
John Reade	"	} Urbana.
Samuel Shield	York.	
Robert Mush		An Indian.
George Sampson	"	

1770.

William Buckner	Gloucester.	
Maximilian Calvert	Norfolk	Son of Max. Calvert.
John Cocke	Surry	Son of Col. R. Cocke.
James Dudley	Warwick	Son of Wm. Dudley.
Thomas Dixon	Williamsburg	Son of Rev. Mr. Dixon.
William Dixon	"	
Thompson Mason	Fairfax.	
William Page	"	Son of Hon. J. Page.
Charles Read.		

Fig. 6.4. College of William and Mary catalogue, showing 1768 enrollment list that included Indians (*arrow added*). Courtesy of VDHR.

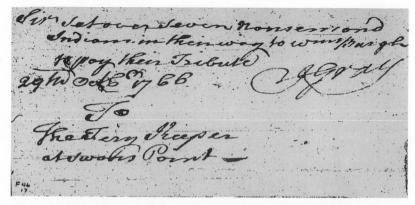

Fig. 6.5. Voucher of 1766, from Nansemond Indians paying their tribute.

ing so much of their lands seems to have been the ultimate cause of their capitulation, but thanks to that stubborn reluctance to change, there was a time lag, especially in the less tangible areas of life. Indian men and women adopted English arms and cutting tools very early, because with those they could go on doing the same work, at the same pace, that they had always done. English clothing was another matter, and during the seventeenth century there are records only about trading cloth, not about made-up clothing being sold to native people. The few late-century eye-witness accounts that mention Indian attire indicate that, among themselves, and sometimes even when Europeans were present, both men and women wore the same deerskin clothing they had always used, even if it offended English sensibilities. Housing remained the traditional sapling-and-mat "cabins" until after 1760, for the English traveler Andrew Burnaby visited the Pamunkeys in that year and described them as wearing English clothing but living in "wigwams." Log cabins replaced those sometime later and went out of fashion only after the mid-nineteenth century. Both "wigwams" (especially if covered with bark rather than mats) and log cabins were made out of materials that came from the adjoining forest without too much preparation; clapboard farmhouses were another matter.

The furnishings in Powhatan "wigwams" may have changed to Anglo styles before housing did. That speculation is based upon an Ezra Stiles drawing from the 1760s of a New England Algonquian wigwam, which had some fairly heavy English furniture sitting in it. No travelers or neighbors described the interiors of Powhatan houses, unfortunately.

Fig. 6.6. Pamunkey Reservation trash pit, with plow zone soil stripped away. Courtesy of VDHR.

The Virginia Department of Historic Resources did, however, excavate a trash pit on the Pamunkey Reservation that dated to the first half of the nineteenth century (figs. 6.6 through 6.10). The pit contained bits of some decidedly Anglo-Virginian things like keys, which implies that the contributor to the pit had something lockable.

The ceramic platters in figure 6.9 may have been made by the Pamunkey women themselves. They adopted European styles and did a brisk sale of pottery to their non-Indian neighbors until the railroad came through in the 1850s. Powhatan women by that time were doing the same house-centered work as their non-Indian neighbors, while their men practiced plow-farming, judging by the household goods and farming tools that Pamunkeys, Gingaskins, and Christianized Nansemonds left in their estates or used for collateral in deeds of trust from the 1820s onward. Men did, however, still take their hunting and fishing far more seriously than did their neighbors. As late as the early twentieth century, Pamunkey men taking out marriage licenses often listed their occupation as "fisherman" rather than "farmer," and the Nansemonds who re-

Fig. 6.7. Pamunkey trash pit, with uncovering of midden under way. Courtesy of VDHR.

Fig. 6.8. Objects emerging from the Pamunkey trash pit. Courtesy of VDHR.

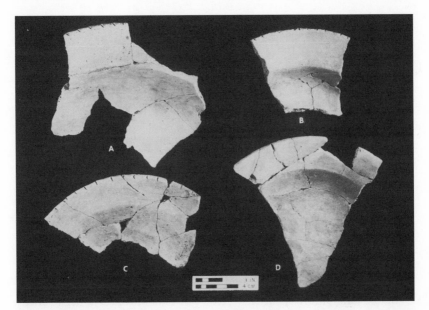

Fig. 6.9. Pieces of the Pamunkey trash pit platters, after cleaning and reassembling. Courtesy of VDHR.

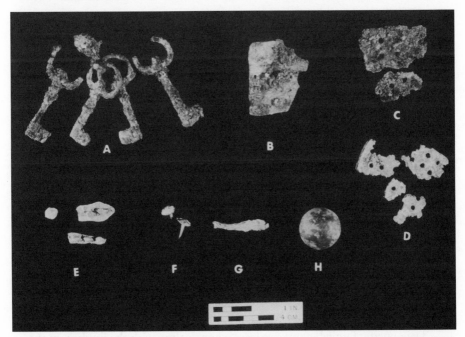

Fig. 6.10. Other items recovered from the Pamunkey trash pit: *A*, keys; *B* and *G*, uncertain; *C* and *D*, strainer fragments; *E*, lead shot and sprue [waste metal from molding the shot]; *F*, furniture tacks; *H*, button. Courtesy of VDHR.

mained on the rim of the Dismal Swamp after some of their relatives had moved to the city in the early 1900s prided themselves on being expert bear hunters (there are still black bears in the Swamp).

On the Pamunkey and Mattaponi Reservations, the settlement pattern remained the old Virginia Algonquian one. English people living in small settlements were apt to align their houses opposite one another and add a gridwork of streets as the population grew. But the reservation people continued spacing their houses out among their fields, with dooryards not meeting and no two dwelling houses exactly across from one another. The pattern shows fairly well in a map of Pamunkey made in 1865 (fig. 6.11), and better in a map made by Rountree, with then-chief William H. Miles's assistance, in 1986 (fig. 6.12). The pattern is currently being followed also at Mattaponi, though less obviously because of a denser population on their limited acreage.

In less tangible areas, the changes in Powhatan life are harder to document. The Pamunkeys were the last group to have chiefs, hereditary or otherwise, and theirs were last mentioned (perhaps posthumously) in 1723. Subsequent petitions sent to the government by the reservation groups were signed by all adult males (Pamunkey) or all adults (Nansemond, Gingaskin). Information about the informal tribal governments that existed are lacking. And no sets of Pamunkey bylaws have ever been made available to outsiders except the one published by John Garland Pollard in 1894, when the political structure on that reservation had formalized considerably. We are likewise in the dark about what the Powhatans' kinship system was like in the middle centuries. Rountree has been able to construct some genealogies for the early nineteenth century (and no farther back), but data are lacking to show whether parents and sets of sons tended to live next to one another, as traditional Powhatan siblings seem to have done. When more detailed federal censuses began to be taken in 1850, the enumerators going from house to house produced lists indicating a fairly random scattering of siblings both on the reservations and off, with parents living in as a third generation when they were both elderly and widowed (a pattern seen among non-Indians as well, before the advent of nursing homes).

The Indians' names, of course, were English by then. Powhatan people began using English names, at least when dealing with the English, in the late seventeenth century. Usually an Indian had only one English name (Sue, for example, the Indian serving-woman married in 1688 at the

Fig. 6.11. Detail from the 1865 Confederate Engineers' map of King William County, showing the two reservations (*arrows added*). Courtesy of VDHR.

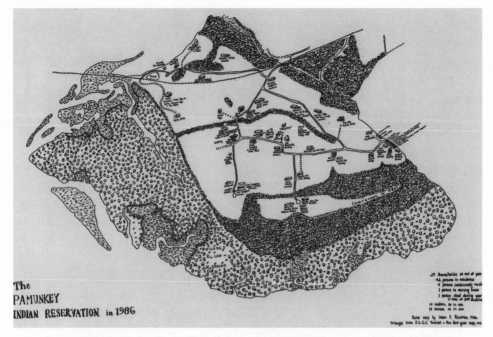

The
PAMUNKEY
INDIAN RESERVATION in 1986

Fig. 6.12. The Pamunkey Indian Reservation in 1986. Courtesy of Helen C. Rountree.

Henrico County court's behest to the Englishman who had made her pregnant). First names and surnames became the norm for Indian people by the mid-eighteenth century and were usually passed down in the father's line, as among the English. The languages people spoke are harder to establish. In 1676 the Pamunkey queen met Governor Berkeley and demanded that they communicate through an interpreter, though she was suspected of being fluent in English. Around 1700 the leading man among the Chickahominies still needed an interpreter. The Nanzatico men accused of murder in 1704 included both older men for whom an interpreter was considered necessary to gather accurate testimony and a young, nearly monolingual English-speaking man whose Nanzatico was so poor that he had not understood what his fellow murderers said to him as they left the scene of the crime.

All Powhatan leaders spoke fluent enough English by 1727 that the Virginia colony discontinued paying official interpreters. The various tribal dialects of the Powhatan language died after that. It takes a large speech-community to keep a language going, one with members representing many occupations so that people use their language in a wide variety of circumstances. Neither the Pamunkeys nor any other Powhatan group had that in the eighteenth century, through no fault of their own. Their populations were small, and they constantly had to deal with English-speaking non-Indians when doing business, commercial or political. By 1800 it is safe to say that all the Powhatan dialects were dead, with only some words and phrases remembered by older people. In 1844 an Episcopal minister tried to collect Indian-language words from the oldest living Pamunkeys, and he got only a dozen or so words, most of which are not identifiable as Powhatan or even Algonquian.[3]

The slowest change of all in Powhatan life was—ironically, for early English hopes—in religion. The Indian groups for whom we have records (excepting the Christianized Nansemonds) retained their temples and the priests to care for them at least until 1700. Sick of being evangelized by individual English people they met, the Powhatans had become close-mouthed about their religion by the late 1600s. The priests steadfastly refused to be interviewed about their practices, as did the common people about their beliefs, except for the one man that Robert Beverley plied with hard cider. The information yielded by this source tallied well with what William Strachey and other early colonists learned from Powhatan people back before they stopped discussing religion with their bossy English neighbors. However, by the seventeenth century's end, the power of Powhatan priests, if not also the deities, was being seriously questioned after so many losses to the English. Sometime after 1700 the last priest died and his temple was allowed to disintegrate. The inner workings of the religion, as well as the herbal knowledge for the more esoteric priestly cures, died too.

The ordinary Indian people who were left seem to have passed into a period of limbo, with the old religion meaning little anymore and the religion of the supercilious English remaining foreign. The Anglican clergy made little effort to win over native people. It is equally doubtful that the Indians would have appreciated their placement had they gone to church: in those lovely Georgian brick churches that still dot eastern Virginia, the seating was based upon class and ethnicity: VIP whites in front, lesser whites farther back in the nave and transepts, and in the far back or, if available, the balconies went the nonwhites (and William and Mary college students of whatever ethnic background).

It was ultimately the Baptists and Methodists who reached the Powhatans. These denominations were new and relatively classless in the late eighteenth century, with a simplified theology and services that appealed to people's deep emotions. The Baptists did not even have church buildings until the 1790s in the area where the Pamunkeys and Mattaponi/ Chickahominies lived. A decade earlier their meetings were held in changing localities—including the Pamunkey Reservation—by itinerant preachers. The appeal to a people living in religious limbo was obvious, and not only Indians but other people, nonwhite and lower-level white, joined up. Over the next century, all the Powhatan descendants became Baptists, except for the Christianized Nansemonds, for whom the Methodists built a mission church in 1850. Before the Civil War, all of a locality's Baptists attended the same church together. The seating arrangements are hard to determine today, and the church rolls, like that of Lower College Baptist Church where the Pamunkeys went in the 1790s, may have been segregated into whites and free nonwhites. But the church was a community church, not an ethnic one. Ethnic Baptist churches were a post–Civil War phenomenon.

The reason we know that the Pamunkeys joined a Baptist congregation with itinerant preachers in the 1780s is that one Pamunkey, the same Robert Mush (later spelled Mursh) who was a William and Mary student in 1769, married another Pamunkey in a semitraditional, semi-Baptist manner that later caused them both some trouble. And trouble generated records. The date was 1783, and the way they married was as follows: The couple and her parents agreed that a marriage should take place; the couple borrowed an Anglican custom and had the next three Baptist preachers passing through announce the impending marriage (parallel to Anglican ministers "publishing the banns"), after which the couple were considered married and immediately moved in together. That was an incomplete marriage by both Anglican and Baptist standards. Members of the Anglican Communion used the banns to unearth possible impediments to a marriage, after which a formal wedding would take place; the Baptists also insisted upon wedding ceremonies. So in the eyes of whites, the Murshes were not fully married. That presented Robert with a problem when he wanted to become a Baptist minister; he had to marry Elizabeth again in 1797. Robert was also a Revolutionary War veteran: like a number of other Powhatan men, he fought on the side of the Americans. After he died in 1837, Elizabeth tried to collect a veteran's widow's pension, but she was denied for twelve years because the legality of her first marriage to Robert was questioned. It is from all the papers she submitted over those twelve years that we know about the itinerant preachers' activities and also how her people were conducting their marriages in the 1780s. The papers included the genealogy page from the Murshes' family Bible (fig. 6.13), showing that once Robert and Elizabeth converted, they wrote the same things in their Bible that non-Indians did.

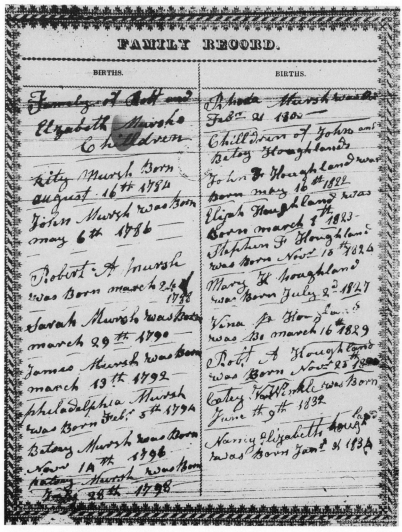

Fig. 6.13. Genealogical page from the Pamunkey Mursh family Bible. Courtesy of VDHR.

Hardening Attitudes Toward Nonwhites

Literate man that he was, with a war record on the "right" side in the Revolution, Robert Mursh did not choose to live for the rest of his life in Virginia, where non-Indians were becoming yet more intolerant of nonwhites. He moved his family to the Catawba Reservation in South Carolina soon after 1800, though he and later his son John continued to visit the Pamunkeys and take part in their political life occasionally through 1812. A few other Pamunkey families accompanied the Murshes, but all the other Powhatan remnants stayed where they were, both then and later. No state- or county-level politicians ever suggested putting the surviving reservation tribes through a "removal" such as the one that caused the infamous "Trails of Tears" for the Cherokees and other "Civilized Tribes" in the late 1830s. Instead the anti-Indian contingent in Virginia took note of the fact that the Powhatans had become so culturally similar to their neighbors that they could be declared no longer to be "real" (that is, pidgin-English-speaking, feather-and-deerskin-wearing) Indians. Once that declaration was carried through legally, the Powhatans would disappear as Indians, bloodlessly, in what a modern scholar has called "genocide through census redefinition." The group they were expected to "melt" into was the free negro population, and it was those people that the white lawmakers hoped would leave the state, preferably taking the Powhatans with them.

Virginia was definitely becoming a harsher place for nonwhites to live. Anglo-Virginians had not paid too much attention to controlling nonwhites other than slaves before the Revolution; in the eighteenth century they seem to have felt they had enough to do first to repulse French efforts to seize the British colonies and then to shake free of British sovereignty itself. But a considerable number of slaves had been freed after the Revolution, as a reward for loyal service during the war. And the number of mulattoes, free or enslaved, continued to grow because white men still regarded nonwhite women, and their own female slaves in particular, as sexual prey and were able to get away with predation.[4] (There were also matings between white women and nonwhite men, but on a lesser scale.) Virginia's population, in fact, was developing a sizable "middle" population, whose ancestry and/or physical appearance varied between African-right-off-the-boat and European-right-off-the-boat. Those "middle" people who were free were waiting expectantly for the kind of citizenship promised in the Bill of Rights. So after a "liberal" period following the Revolution, during which the racial definition of "mulatto" was made one-quarter or more African instead of one-eighth, the white people who wanted to keep power in their own hands began clamping down on the movements and rights of free nonwhites, which included any Powhatan descendants not living under a treaty.

Interestingly enough, the lawmakers did not go about the enterprise by tightening up the racial definitions and making it more difficult to be "white" and impossible to be "Indian"; that came in the twentieth century. The one-quarter African blood quantum remained on the books from 1784 to 1910. The "one-drop rule," by which anybody with even one "drop" of African "blood" (meaning, in practice, biological ancestry plus various other social qualities) became "colored," did not become Virginia law until 1923. The "rule" gained currency, however, in Anglo-Virginians' minds long before that. By the mid-nineteenth century, many white Virginians had become so sensitive about possible nonwhite "blood" in their families that even the mention of descent from obviously nonwhite Pocahontas could start a fight. That sensitivity, coupled with resistance to the efforts of historians in northern states to discount Jamestown's contributions to the founding of an English-American nation, caused the resurrection by Southern historians of John Smith's 1624 "Generall Historie," with its already revisionist view of Pocahontas. During the rest of the nineteenth century the legend, more like a myth, of Pocahontas would grow apace. The irony was not lost upon the surviving Powhatans: Pocahontas was made into a saint, while they themselves were considered either "savages" or "riffraff."

The racial laws made in nineteenth-century Virginia before the Civil War concentrated not upon defining racial categories but upon controlling people's actions. In the mid-1790s some counties passed ordinances requiring freeborn nonwhites to get certificates stating that fact; it became a state law for the cities about the same time. That probably explains why William Bass, one of the Christianized Nansemonds, got a county certificate declaring his English-Indian ancestry in 1797 (fig. 6.14); he was being harassed as he went about his business. In 1806 it was made illegal for free nonwhites to carry guns without a license from their county, and all slaves given their freedom from henceforward had to leave the state (even if it meant leaving still-enslaved spouses and children behind). There was a spate of laws after that: all free nonwhites had

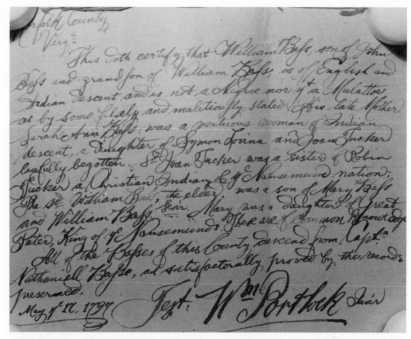

Fig. 6.14. William Bass certificate of Nansemond Indian ancestry, 1797. Courtesy of Helen C. Rountree.

to register with their counties and get certificates to carry around with them, or otherwise they could be arrested and sold as slaves; they also had to get permission from the county court to leave their county. They were forbidden to become river pilots (that is, boat captains); they had to get a license to sell agricultural produce, or otherwise it was considered to have been stolen; they could be sold into temporary servitude for debt; and if they were indigent after all these economic disabilities, their children could be bound out as laborers to other people without their permission—and it was illegal for the employers to teach those children to read. It got worse after 1830, and the Nat Turner Slave Insurrection of August 1831 only speeded up the passage of discriminatory laws. Slaves freed by well-meaning owners were to be sold directly back into slavery. No nonwhites at all were to be taught to read and write (one Norfolk woman who did it anyway for some neighborhood children was sent to prison for a year—and wrote a book about it afterward in protest). Nonwhites, whether slave or free, were to have oyer and terminer trials only (three judges in a "bench trial," in today's parlance); they were not to have any access to firearms; and they were not to assemble among themselves, even for church services (only mixed services, with white preachers, allowed).

The strategy was obvious: keep them unable to communicate with each other in writing (*literacy is power*); keep them under such close supervision that they could not talk freely face-to-face with friends; make it so that even a minor misstep could lead to forcible separation from family and friends; and keep these theoretically isolated families so hungry that they would decide to leave the state out of sheer self-preservation.

The reality, out in the counties at least, had to be somewhat different. Even in the 1830s, which saw the closest thing to a mass exodus of free nonwhites pouring out of Virginia, fewer than a third of the target population left most counties (Northampton, home to the Gingaskins, with its county-funded program for repatriation back to Africa, got rid of 43.4 percent of its free people of color). Manumitted slaves continued to turn up in the legislative petitions, sometimes years after being freed, asking to be officially allowed to remain in the state—and sometimes getting permission. It depended upon the attitudes of the most powerful local whites, who were not always hateful, and upon the nonwhites' demeanor and ability to win allies among those whites. Enforcement of the laws was spotty in rural areas, where transportation was slow and people knew their neighbors well. It is probable that nobody in the Anglo-Virginian population expected strict enforcement all the time of laws like the one forbidding firearms to nonwhites. In rural districts, every working-class family shot squirrels, raccoons, and opossums for the pot; it might be the only fresh meat the family tasted for weeks at a time.

Trouble for Indians, Too

Tough laws were a useful tool to keep "uppity" nonwhites in line—and to threaten nonwhite strangers who showed up. That helps explain why the Pamunkey man Cooper Langston got his tribe's trustees to make out a certificate of free birth for him (fig. 6.15) when he had business off-reservation in 1834. He lived and worked in New Kent County, across the Pamunkey River, for long periods of time, and he did not want trouble. The Christianized Nansemonds, on the other hand, went a different

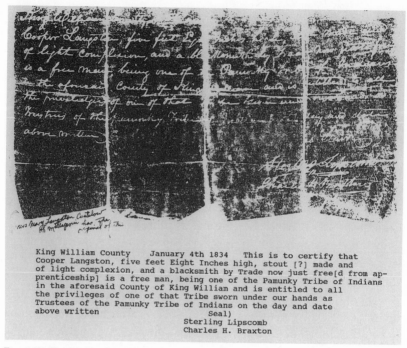

Fig. 6.15. Cooper Langston certificate of Pamunkey tribal membership, 1834. Preserved in the James R. Coates papers; transcription by Helen C. Rountree. Courtesy of Helen C. Rountree.

route: probably at their instigation, the representative from Norfolk County to the Virginia House of Delegates introduced a bill, and saw it through passage, that set up a new racial category in Virginia: "Persons Of Mixed Blood, Not Being Free Negroes Or Mulattoes." The category had no quick-and-easy label, like "Indian"—there was still no legal definition of "Indian" in the state—and it could have been applied in some cities to people with ancestry from other parts of the world. Nonetheless, the Nansemonds were immediate and knowledgeable beneficiaries, for they promptly trooped over to the courthouse and got certificates as POMBNBFNOMs. That may in turn have prompted local Methodists to set up a mission for them in 1850, named Indiana Methodist Church. It was the first ethnic Native American church in the Commonwealth.

Trouble could still arise, even for reservation Indians living under treaty rights, when they met whites who were determined to enforce the letter of the law on all nonwhites. As political pressures built up just before the Civil War, some King William County whites confiscated some Indian guns. The Pamunkeys promptly lodged a complaint with the governor of Virginia, who in early 1857 instructed their trustees to take the matter to the county court and point out that the tribesmen clearly had a right to carry firearms. The men losing their guns may actually been from the tiny Mattaponi Reservation, where hunters going after deer in order to pay their tribute had to do it off-reservation, unlike the Pamunkeys proper. The Mattaponis were administratively combined with the Pamunkeys until 1893, when they got their own trustees and their separate history becomes clearer. It is safe to say that they were always at more risk from local whites' ill will because their small land base put them into more contact with outsiders.

Sometime between the mid-eighteenth and the early nineteenth century, while the doings on the Mattaponi Reservation were still decidedly ill-recorded, there occurred the exit of the ancestors of three of the Powhatan tribes that survive today: the Upper Mattaponis and the two sectors of the Chickahominies. When anthropologist Frank Speck began questioning them seriously just after World War I, the Upper Mattaponis had an oral tradition of connections with the "Pamunkeys" and the Chickahominies (still one group) recollected migrating back to their original homeland some generations (an indeterminate number) before. The departure was probably from Mattaponi, since the U.S. censuses show a fairly stable population at Pamunkey but a changing one on the smaller reservation. The Upper Mattaponis, who would be given their "tribal" name by Speck for geographic reasons, headed upriver to an area near where their last colony-appointed interpreter had lived; his surname (Adams) was also the most common surname among them. The move may therefore have taken place sometime in the eighteenth century, when the interpreter or his children or grandchildren were still on the scene to help them settle in. The Chickahominy move, on the other hand, may have been later. Their nucleus, several families named Adkins, appears in the 1830s in Charles City County, south of the river where their ancestors had lived. The adults had to get county certificates of free birth, which put them into that county's Free Negro Register, in order to go shopping at the nearest market town: Richmond, in an adjacent jurisdiction. But once on friendly terms with their neighbors—and they were hard-working people who soon began buying plots of farmland—they were able to live out from under the curious, occasionally jealous, scrutiny that reservation Indians with treaty rights must endure.

Over on the Pamunkey Reservation, the 1850s saw another difficulty with whites. A railroad was built connecting West Point (at the confluence of the Pamunkey and Mattaponi Rivers) with Richmond, and it ran though the northern part of the reservation, as figures 6.11 and 6.12 demonstrate.[5] No permission was asked of either the Pamunkeys or the Commonwealth of Virginia, which was supposed to protect their land; no purchase or rental moneys were forthcoming. The railroad simply came through, shattering the privacy of the Pamunkeys and, since it brought an influx of manufactured goods to King William County, drastically reducing the women's income from pottery-making.

It was primarily because of the railroad, and the bridge that crossed the Pamunkey River on the west side of the reservation, that the Pamunkeys suffered more than any other Powhatan group during the Civil War. No Indians had it easy, since Anglo-Virginians considered them, rightly or wrongly, to be sympathizers with Union abolitionists. Most Powhatan people lay low; some Chickahominies left and took refuge with Ojibwas in Canada; several Pamunkey men surreptitiously joined the Union Army; and a couple of Rappahannock families sympathized enough with the South to name their sons after Confederate generals. But the Pamunkeys caught flak from both sides. In 1861 some of their young men were conscripted, along with local negroes, to work on the fortifications outside Richmond; they managed to get released from that labor because it violated their treaty rights. Toward the end of the war, the reservation was occupied by Union troops pushing toward Richmond. The soldiers did what soldiers in those days always did in occupied territory: they lived off the local people by confiscating the farmers' crops and slaughtering their animals to eat, using the rails from people's fences for tent poles and cooking fires. They were arrogant but not unruly, according to accounts given later by Pamunkeys who sought—and got—damages from the U.S. government. But Pamunkey pride was high, and their defensiveness was higher after the pressures of the prewar decades, so the advent of the soldiers must have been a thoroughly unpleasant experience.

New Defensive Strategies

The years before, during, and after the Civil War showed the Powhatans that they would have to pull together among themselves in order to survive; there would always be neighbors who refused to get along with them, however anglicized they became. They would also need to have leaders to represent their interests when difficulties arose with outsiders. The Pamunkeys led the way. They already had "headmen" in the early nineteenth century, people who could write letters to the governor when things went wrong. After the Civil War they began electing a leader whom they denominated their chief ("chief" is not a derogatory term in Virginia, as it has become among American Indians in the western United States). When the Mattaponis separated administratively from the Pamunkeys, they followed the same practice. Both reservations followed the Anglo model current at the time by providing in their bylaws for male suffrage only, a practice they retained through the end of the twentieth century. By the time the nonreservation Powhatans organized formally in the twentieth century, votes for women were the law in American society, so chiefs and their councils were elected by all adults in those tribes.

In the Reconstruction era, the harsh laws that made people drastically inferior even if they lived cheek by jowl with whites were gone, replaced (for a time) by equal access to jury trials and so forth, and also by opportunities for nonwhites to hold office. Many formerly powerful Anglo-Virginians became nonpersons politically until they gave in and signed an oath of allegiance to the federal government. White Virginians' attitudes toward nonwhites did not ameliorate, however; they merely went into abeyance until power could be regained, which happened by the end of the century. In the meantime, there were serious enough differences of opinion, and bitterness about the past on the part of whites, that many institutions became segregated in fact, though not yet in law. Many churches like Colosse (formerly Lower College) Baptist in King William County no longer had three ethnic groups in their congregations. African-American members budded off into their own congregations. The Pamunkey members of Colosse asked for and got their Letters of Dismissal in 1866, after which they built their own church on the reservation (fig. 6.16), named it Pamunkey Indian Baptist Church, and arranged with a white minister to preach there. Mattaponi and Upper Mattaponi people traveled up to ten miles each way to attend it. Other churches saw the whites withdraw from the old church, leaving the nonwhites behind, as happened at Cedar Grove Baptist where the Chickahominies went. Feeling they had to keep their own ethnic distance to remain Indians, the Chickahominies found a church building in 1888 in which they could set up their own Indian congregation, naming it Samaria Indian Baptist Church when they formally organized their tribe in 1901. Their ministers were white, too, until well into the twentieth century, when a man from the Mattaponi Reservation was ordained and became their pastor.

Public education was now mandated for all children in Virginia, replacing a prewar system that was poorly administered and benefited only whites. However, feelings in the white population were such that the counties set up separate schools from the beginning. That made two school systems, a "white" one and a "colored" one (meaning African-American). Everyone including the Indians understood that anyone going to the "colored" schools forfeited any right to be called "Indian." "Real" Indians were considered to be people who held themselves apart from other nonwhites, even at the price of getting no schooling for their children at all, a sentiment that was acted upon legally during World War II when some Rappahannock men, who had attended a "colored" school rather than remain illiterate, were sent to prison for refusing to serve with negro troops. Indian parents now had to begin working toward getting the Commonwealth (for the reservations) or the counties (for the enclaves) to spend the money to create a third set of schools. The Pamunkeys got a school first, around 1890, but they rejected the first teacher of it because she was not white. "Guilt" through *any* public association was a deadly serious matter for people whose credibility as "real Indians" was so low. Some of the major efforts made by Indian communities in the twentieth century would be getting separate *grade* schools with qualified white or Indian teachers.

The Pamunkeys were visited in the late 1890s by two anthropologists from the Smithsonian Institution, Albert Gatschet and James Mooney, both of whom had worked with Native American tribes elsewhere in the country. Mooney in particular was impressed with how American Indian the Pamunkeys still looked, and in 1899 he arranged for a Smithsonian photographer, Delancey Gill, to visit them and the Chickahominies and Nansemonds, with whom he had also made contact. Gill's photographs show us that on a day-to-day basis Powhatan people at the turn of the

Fig. 6.16. Pamunkey Indian Baptist Church (established 1866, photographed 1970). Courtesy of Helen C. Rountree.

century were Indians who were living like their neighbors in many ways. They wore "ordinary clothes," new ones for dress-up and old ones for work or play (fig. 6.17), only the very rich having a different outfit for each activity in those days. Their houses, usually made of clapboard by that time, had picket fences in front of them and ordinary chairs and tables inside them. Houses had curtains in the windows and contained family Bibles that were treated with great respect (fig. 6.18). Hard physical work still made many Indian women wiry, even in old age, but moments of leisure included playing with pets, like the kitten that made the blur in figure 6.19. The old days of having only dogs and dogs being only for work were long gone.

The county records of the late nineteenth century show that all of the Powhatan groups were law-abiding people who did not get into scrapes with outsiders and who managed any conflicts among themselves with discretion. On the reservations, people could be banished by the tribal council for misbehavior, and that was considered by the residents to be a terrible fate. Anglicized as they were, the Powhatans considered their In-

Fig. 6.17. Some of the Nansemond Basses in 1899. Courtesy of Delancey Gill, National Anthropological Archives, Smithsonian Institution (NAASI).

dian communities to be "home." These were the people from whom they drew spouses if humanly possible; otherwise, they married into other Indian tribes—and even then, reservation women who married those "semioutsiders" could not bring them, much less non-Indian husbands, to live on the reservation. Indian people lived, worked, went to church, and banded together in times of need primarily within their own communities, while trying to maintain friendly if distant relations with non-Indians.

The last-named goal was not easily attained. The African-American community resented the distance the Indians wanted to keep in order to retain an "Indian" label; that division made the nonwhite population in general less able to pressure the whites to be less discriminatory. The Anglo-Virginian community had members who were sympathetic with

Above: Fig. 6.18. A family of Allmonds at Pamunkey in 1899. Courtesy of Delancey Gill, NAASI.

Left: Fig. 6.19. Keziah Langston Dennis, a Pamunkey woman, in 1899. Courtesy of Delancey Gill, NAASI.

Fig. 6.20. Pamunkeys reenacting Pocahontas's rescue of Captain John Smith, at the 1907 Jamestown Exposition. *Standing, left to right:* unknown (holding axe), George M. Cook (in headband), Theophilus Dennis (holding spear), Otigney Cook, unidentified boy (perhaps a son of George M. Cook), John Dennis (in headdress), Peter Cusey (Tuscarora, holding bow). *Below:* Helen Collins (Pocahontas), unknown (Captain John Smith).

Indian aims and others who regarded the Powhatans as "fakes" for not speaking the language and not wearing feathers all the time. The latter group of whites could be embarrassingly vocal about their doubts, which led to a new response by the Indians.

Powhatan people began their still-held policy of "playing Indian to be Indian" (in another scholar's words) on certain *public* occasions in the 1890s, and as usual the Pamunkey Reservation people, always under more scrutiny from outsiders, led the way. James Mooney had encouraged them to send a representative to the World's Columbian Exhibition of 1893; the man who went was one of the tribe's Union Army veterans. He and some of his fellow tribesmen soon began donning "Indian" regalia—based upon more covered-up models than traditional Powhatan dress, to avoid being arrested for indecent exposure—and putting on a play. The play, of course, was a reenactment of the saving of Captain John Smith by Pocahontas, a legend both known to most Americans by then and one that excited spectators' sympathy toward at least one Indian. The message in the play was that peace had been made between the Powhatans and the English, and the up-to-date Pamunkeys were willing to continue the peace. The play was performed as late as 1907, at the Jamestown Exposition in Norfolk, Virginia, marking the 300th anniversary of the founding of the English colony (fig. 6.20).

It is ironic that just as some of the nonreservation Powhatans were organizing, as the Mattaponis were enjoying their first decade of autonomy, and as the Pamunkeys were mastering the art of impressing a public ignorant about Indians, that same public's lawmakers were preparing to make it much more difficult for the tribes to survive as "Indians" in Virginia. The first half of the twentieth century would in subtle ways prove to be the most racist period that the Powhatans had to endure.

Notes

1. For the documentary evidence for this statement, see chapter 5 of Rountree and Davidson's *Eastern Shore Indians of Virginia and Maryland*.

2. Rountree was a junior at the college that year, and she remembers the "token black" sophomore, grudgingly admitted.

3. There have been several attempts since 1970 among the Powhatan descendants to revive the Powhatan language. Those efforts have come to naught so far and are likely to fare no better in the future. Rountree has scoured the old documents and collected all the versions of words (several hundred), place-names, and personal

names in them. She has consulted three leading Algonquian linguists (Ives Goddard, David Pentland, and the late Frank Siebert) in the matter, and all have told her that without more *sentences* having been recorded in Powhatan, it is impossible to resurrect the Powhatan language with any accuracy. None of the surviving Algonquian languages is closely enough related to it to use as a model, according to the three linguists.

4. John Mercer Langston (born 1829), one of the founders of the Law Department at Howard University, was the product of two such liaisons: he was the son of a slave mother and a white master, who manumitted her before the baby's birth so that he would be freeborn. His mother was the daughter of an African slave mother and a Pamunkey Indian master, who sold his own offspring away. Indians were not automatically in sympathy with African slaves, as some writers have alleged; as individuals they could be as cold- or as warm-hearted as any other people.

5. The triangular, flat-topped mound next to the tracks at the end of the Pamunkey River bridge may have been a by-product of the tracks' construction. No authenticated Indian mounds have been found anywhere else on the Virginia coastal plain, and the Mississippian culture, which featured flat-topped rather than conical (rounded, like the mounds in the Ohio Valley) mounds, seems not to have reached coastal Virginia except in a few trade goods like the maskette found at Patawomeck (fig. 2.10). Twentieth-century Pamunkeys, however, have insisted to outsiders that the mound is the burial place of early seventeenth-century chiefs. In Frank Speck's time, the claim was made for Opechancanough (who was probably buried near Jamestown, where he died). Nowadays it is Powhatan himself who is supposed to have been buried there (instead of inside an aboveground temple).

7

A Century of Public Struggle

The first half of the twentieth century presented the Powhatan groups with legal challenges that were in many ways more difficult to survive than anything that had happened in preceding centuries. First came the segregation by "race" of all public places and all state, city, and county records in Virginia. Then there was a legal tightening up—to a ludicrous extent—of racial categories, which nearly squeezed the Indians out. And pushing both these issues straight into Indian homes, which had *not* often happened in earlier centuries, was the increasingly pervasive nature of "bigger" government, which grew tremendously during a half-century that saw the Great Depression and the fighting of two world wars. Between 1923 and the 1960s, the laws on the books in Virginia added up to a requirement that a person's racial identity be ascertained for every single dealing he or she had with government agencies or public facilities—dealings that occurred weekly if not daily. And in the minds of most of the people running those institutions and facilities, there was no "Indian" category in Virginia. Thus while the Powhatans were expected to—and willing to—participate in twentieth-century Virginia life, they were being told they could not remain "Indians" if they did so.

A Legal and Bureaucratic Struggle

De jure segregation happened first, in 1900. Now there had to be separate "white" and "colored" schools, hospitals, seating sections on steamers and trains and buses, waiting rooms and ticket counters for those steamers and trains and buses, restrooms and drinking fountains in public places, etc., etc. The public facilities were supposed to be "separate but equal," but in fact the "colored" ones normally were grossly underfunded compared to the white ones.[1] The Pamunkeys, with a railroad running through their reservation, and the Chickahominies, who had to ride another railroad to shop in Richmond (to this day, their market town), both lodged immediate protests against riding in "colored" sections on public transportation; they won (and so did the protesting Chinese community in Richmond).

In 1910, a new law made it easier to be "colored" in Virginia: one-sixteenth African ancestry was enough. Then in 1923, the "one-drop rule" became law: "any ascertainable trace" of African ancestry made one "colored"—a ridiculous law to try to enforce, since most Virginians of *any* racial persuasion could not ascertain all of their ancestry back very far due to the limited nature of Virginia's historical record (see the beginning of chapter 6). Nonetheless, the Racial Integrity Law went into force in 1924 and required that identities be established for all Virginia citizens and registered. There had to be racial labels attached to all people appearing in public records such as tax books, voter registration books, and marriage registers, not to mention certificates of birth and death.

The head, or Registrar, of the state's Vital Statistics Bureau was a medical doctor interested in eugenics, and he willingly shouldered the burdens not only of registering people throughout the state but also of seeking out the "proper" registrations of "suspicious" people who might try to "pass" as white. (It may have occurred to those in power that maintaining third-rate facilities for the "colored" population would merely induce more people to try to "pass," but they brushed the idea aside, feeling that "inferiors" did not deserve better.) Dr. Walter Ashby Plecker took a little time at first to gear up, during which he countersigned a few birth certificates that read "Indian" (fig. 7.1). But once he hit his stride, his activities in searching out "mongrels" (his usual word for the Indians) and his willingness to be vocal about his two-races-in-Virginia opinions, would blight the lives of many Powhatan people for decades.

Perhaps not coincidentally, it was in the years between the segregation laws and the Racial Integrity Law that several Powhatan groups organized formally: the Chickahominies in 1901 (with the Eastern Division separating in 1925), the Rappahannocks in 1921, and the Upper Mattaponis in 1923. James Mooney and the Pamunkeys had encouraged the Chickahominies; it was University of Pennsylvania anthropologist Frank G. Speck, along with Pamunkeys again (fig. 7.2), who got the others motivated. All these nonreservation groups organized legally in a way that Plecker and his followers could never challenge: they incorporated under

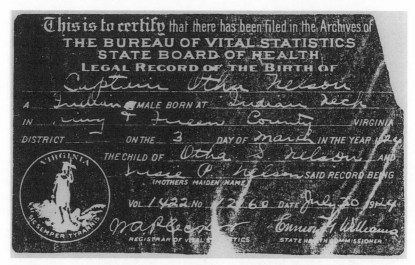

Fig. 7.1. Birth certificate that bore the "Indian" label even after the Racial Integrity Law was passed.

the Virginia State Corporation Commission, with bylaws, presidents (called chiefs), vice presidents (called assistant chiefs) and boards of directors (called councilmen). Outsiders might not agree with the word "Indian" and "tribe" in the new corporations' titles, but the Powhatans had to use the legal rights that were available to them. When the Christianized Nansemonds formally organized as late as 1984, they went the same route. Property held in common, which the members think of as "tribal," is safely, legally theirs when under their corporation's ownership. And nowadays, "property held in common" applies to land.

The two reservations remained exempt from state taxes as long as they paid their tribute, and that exemption was extended to military service in 1917. The U.S. Armed Forces drafted Pamunkey and Mattaponi men, who protested that as reservation Indians they were not full citizens. They won their special "Indian" point—and then volunteered. When all American Indians were declared U.S. citizens in 1924, the Pamunkeys and Mattaponis became draftable. The reservations' land was supposed to be protected as long as they paid their tribute, but that protection proved more limited. The Mattaponis had the greater problem, for their community contained the major landing along that part of the right (southwestern) bank of the Mattaponi River. King William and adjacent counties had then and still have timber cutting as one of the major

Fig. 7.2. Pamunkey Chief George M. Cook and Rappahannock man Robert Nelson during the time the Rappahannocks were organizing. Courtesy of Frank G. Speck, NAASI.

industries for miles around; the paper mill using the timber is at West Point, at the confluence of the Mattaponi and Pamunkey Rivers. Only Indians were entitled to use the reservation's landing, but that did not prevent some of the tough loggers in the area from horning in anyhow. Things came to a head in July 1917, and the way in which they were handled (in accordance with the people's treaty rights) shows how slowly justice could move:

> It appears from a statement furnished this office [the state's attorney general] by Chiefs Arthur Allmond and George F. Custalow that the Chesapeake Pulp and Paper Company, Inc., with headquarters at West Point, and various agents of this corporation[,] have been guilty of coming upon the reservation over the protest of the chief of the tribe, and using the wharf belonging to the reservation and property adjacent thereto for the purpose of piling cord wood, which is later removed on boats on the Mattaponi river [*sic*] and transported to the plant of this company. I am informed by these chiefs that they have repeatedly protested against these acts of tres-

pass, and have forbidden the agents of the company to come upon the reservation, or to deposit any wood thereon, which protests have been repeatedly disregarded, and that almost daily acts of trespass are being committed upon the reservation. . . .

If the Chesapeake Pulp and Paper Company, Inc., and its agents have come upon the reservation without the consent of the tribe, I am of the opinion that a right of action [lawsuit] exists in the trustees [i.e., the trustees can undertake that lawsuit] for the benefit of the tribe against such persons, and that the mode of procedure, if for a single trespass, will be an action of tort [damages] for the trespass. If these acts are so frequently repeated, that an action at law would afford no adequate redress, I am of the opinion that the proper procedure would be by a bill in equity to restrain the continuing tort, in which proceeding the damage suffered by the tribe could be ascertained and awarded.[2]

The same year saw the Mattaponis and Pamunkeys successfully protest against having to pay county taxes on personal property, including the general store that Chief George Custalow ran. Before that time, King William County had taxed the Indians unimpeded, even though their reservations were technically not part of the county.

Frank Speck prodded all the nonreservation Powhatans to organize legally, seeing even more clearly than they did that if they were to survive the new pressures brewing for them, they would need both legal rights and leaders who could represent them forcefully to the public. That need is still true for tribes not tied to the U.S. Bureau of Indian Affairs. The leaders needed, like the Pamunkeys' George Major Cook (fig. 7.3), to be articulate public speakers and literate writers of letters. (Today's Virginia Indian leaders are often both computer-literate and media-savvy.)

Indian people other than the leaders had to become even more image-conscious than they already were, and Speck showed them ways to do it. He put them in touch with other Indian communities with which he worked in Maryland and Delaware, helping them begin holding gatherings to which all of them were invited. He encouraged them to revive pottery making and begin "Indian"-style dancing again, while wearing regalia similar to that adopted by the Pamunkeys thirty years earlier. He photographed them, sometimes in stances that emphasized the hunting background of the men (fig. 7.4). He published books and articles about

Fig. 7.3. Pamunkey chief George M. Cook and wife and daughter as representatives of their tribe, in regalia and prepared to speak to the public (1926). Mrs. Cook was the daughter of Mrs. Dennis in figure 6.19. Courtesy of Probably DeMenti Studio, Richmond.

how the tools they used in hunting, fishing, and farming resembled aboriginal ones. With his encouragement, the Mattaponi Reservation organized its own church, the Upper Mattaponis set up Indianview Baptist Church, and the newly split-off Eastern Chickahominies established Tsena Commocko Indian Baptist Church (a Powhatan-language name, recorded only by then-lesser-known colonist William Strachey, and so almost surely supplied to them by Speck) to serve their communities. The new Indian congregations joined the Dover Baptist Association, a collection of white churches that had admitted the Pamunkeys back in the 1860s and that saw to it that all its member congregations were supplied with (white) preachers. The Indian members took things a bit further: where other Baptist churches simply chose a summer Sunday for a "homecoming," the Indian churches staggered their homecoming Sundays (they still do) so that intertribal visiting could take place.

Tribal organizing also heightened the need for separate Indian schools for the children, as public markers of the families' Indianness. As things stood in 1900, most of the groups had in effect been told that if they wanted literacy for their children, they would have to cease being "Indian" by going to "colored" schools. The Powhatans chose to struggle along their own path instead. The Mattaponi Reservation got its own school soon after the landing-trespass incident in 1917; before that, their

Fig. 7.4. Nannie and Powhatan Major, Mattaponis, photographed by Frank Speck in the 1920s. Courtesy of Frank G. Speck, NAASI.

children went to Pamunkey if they went anywhere. After about two decades of sporadic help from King William County, the Upper Mattaponis
finally got a small, stable school for their children in the same year,
though for many years thereafter it remained even more of a stepchild in
the county system than the black ones were. The Chickahominies had
managed in 1922 to get Charles City County to help them pay the teachers in a school they built themselves soon after organizing in 1901. The
Nansemonds had a school briefly in the 1890s, but their neighbors' attitudes hardened enough that by 1922 they had to go all the way to the
attorney general of Virginia to get backing for a school of their own
again.

"Genocide by census redefinition" became a literal fear for the Powhatans in the late 1920s. The U.S. Census of 1930 loomed ahead of them.
They knew that Dr. Plecker would do his best to prevent their being listed
as "Indian," unlike the censuses of 1900 and 1910 in which nonreservation groups first publicly (and successfully) claimed an Indian identity
in a federal enterprise. The Indians would have been dismayed to know
that Plecker had begun pressuring the Census Bureau back in 1925, but
heartened to hear that the Bureau had blandly but steadfastly refused to
take sides. Washington bureaucrats claimed that the census would be
used "for statistical purposes only," which shows how little they ac-
knowledged of what was going on to the south of them. Ethnic legitimacy
was at stake, as far as both Plecker and the Indians were concerned, and
the enumeration of families in the summer of 1930 caused a war of words
that sucked in the Census Bureau in spite of itself. Ultimately the Bureau
mandated a compromise: the Powhatans would be listed as "Indian*"—
and the asterisk meant that some people questioned the designation. In
the 1940 census, Plecker won out, and suddenly Virginia had many fewer
Indians without much emigration having taken place. (Many families
had, in fact, moved earlier, during the agricultural depression in the
1920s, to northern cities like Philadelphia, where they lived concentrated
close together.) The lesson to researchers: census labels and census tabu-
lations should not be taken as absolute, especially when dealing with
people who for two centuries had not fallen neatly into the major categories.

When the United States entered the next world war in 1941, the men
of all the Powhatan groups were eligible for the draft. A new challenge
faced them: the nation's armed forces were segregated into "white" and

"colored" units. The Indians wanted to help fight Japan and Germany (they remain intensely patriotic down to the present day), but they were told in effect that in order to fight, they would have to be cease being "Indians." Dr. Plecker decreed that they must serve with blacks, which would earn them a permanent "colored" label in the state. For its part, the Selective Service tossed Indian cases around among its staff like a hot potato. In the end, Indian men went various places, usually after a row. The Nansemonds served with whites, as did the Pamunkeys, Mattaponis, and Upper Mattaponis after a tussle about which day ("white" or "colored") they would report for induction. Men from both Chickahominy tribes were inducted with blacks, after which they refused to leave the barracks until their chief pulled some strings in the army to allow them to serve with whites. One Eastern Chickahominy man living away from his tribe fought tooth and nail with his draft board (which included Rountree's pro-Plecker paternal grandfather) and was finally classified as "nationality unknown," after which he served with whites. (When he first met and heard the surname of the anthropologist granddaughter in 1976, there was another explosion.) Some of the Rappahannock men (including a future assistant chief of the tribe) went to prison when serving with blacks was the only other option, as mentioned in chapter 6. Through Frank Speck's efforts and those of a sympathetic Petersburg lawyer, they were eventually released, as "conscientious objectors," to serve in hospitals instead.

During these struggles, the Rappahannock and Chickahominy chiefs both appealed to the federal Bureau of Indian Affairs for assistance in combatting Dr. Plecker's influence. Then-Commissioner John Collier told them that since they lacked a treaty giving them "federal recognition" (a more recent term), the Bureau had no power to intervene; he did, however, write to Plecker questioning his methods. Plecker was not deterred. In fact he subsequently issued a circular to all public health personnel in the state, listing the surnames, county by county, of people suspected of having African ancestry while claiming a white or Indian identity. To Plecker, Indian status was merely a "way-station" (his word) to "passing for white." For some people outside the tribes, it may have been. But for the Powhatans it was not—as is proved by their continuing to claim an Indian identity in the 1960s and 1970s, after segregation ended but before there came to be so great a monetary advantage to qualifying for federal "Indian" status. Meanwhile, another white friend

of the Indians, James Coates, helped them compile tribal rolls and affida-
vits from neighbors about their ancestors' credibility (fig. 6.15 was one
document unearthed during that effort). Tribal chiefs also sought out
friends in high places, one being the head of the Medical College of Virginia, who announced publicly that Indian people were welcome as pa-
tients in his ("white") hospital.

The pressure from Plecker's Bureau of Vital Statistics eased after the
Registrar retired at the age of eighty-six in 1946; a real change occurred
after his protégé-successor retired in 1959. By then the Cold War was in
full swing, and that may have deflected some people's animus against the
Powhatans: the "reds" they were looking for weren't Indians anymore.
With the pressure easing, the Powhatans could turn their attention from
continual self-defense and begin to work again for better education for
their children, most of whose Indian schools went only through the
grammar-school grades, if that.

Through James Coates's efforts, the Bureau of Indian Affairs was per-
suaded to allow some Virginia Indian children to attend the federal high
school in Cherokee, North Carolina, for a few years; one of those, a
Mattaponi, later went on to become a medical doctor and return to practice in his home state. The Pamunkey Reservation school closed by 1950,
since so few children lived on that reservation due to out-migration to
northern cities (the Reservation is mainly a retirement community even
today). The Mattaponi Reservation school took them in (that tribe has
long had numerous people of all generations living on it), and high school
classes were gradually added in the late 1950s, before which most ambitious Mattaponi students went over to Chickahominy.

The two Chickahominy tribes, sharing a school with ten grades in
Charles City County, made a deal with that county in 1950 whereby their
youngsters who wanted high school work beyond the tenth grade would
get tuition money and a one-way ticket to Bacone College in Bacone,
Oklahoma, run by the Baptists for Indian students needing both high
school and college classes. Several Chickahominies made the trip, staying
on for the junior-college work and returning to become teachers in their
own tribal elementary and high schools. The eleventh grade offerings
were begun about 1954 by a white teacher, who told Rountree years later
that she had been so unpopular with local whites for doing it that somebody had once shot out the front window in the house in which she was

living. The music teacher for the school and church, Dick Griffith, did not face that problem: for decades he commuted on weekends from Richmond.

Understandably, after struggling so long to get that far in educating their children, the Powhatan tribes were very reluctant to see their schools closed in the 1960s when desegregation consolidated all students into a single system in all Virginia counties and cities. Indian children continued to do well in the county schools, for education is valued very highly in the tribes, but one of the major physical symbols of their Indianness had been taken from them. Their churches remained; there would be tribal centers built later to fill in the gap.

A Public Relations Struggle

The Chickahominies, who by 1950 had replaced the Pamunkeys as the most publicly activist of the Powhatan groups, started a new trend in 1951: the annual tribal festival. Other nonreservation groups would follow suit after state recognition in the 1980s. The Chickahominy Fall Festival followed a set formula until 1990, when all the Virginia tribes adopted pan-Indian powwow customs. Speeches by dignitaries in support of the tribe were interspersed with dancing in regalia. The regalia resembled that of the early twentieth century, though the men were probably relieved at not having to cover up so much anymore in the hot September weather. The dances were "theme" ones such as the Welcome Dance, the Green Corn Dance, and the Courtship Dance (fig. 7.5), as well as dances borrowed (with tribal names proudly announced) from other tribes like the Nanticokes. The Chickahominies took considerable flak in the first couple of decades for putting on such a publicly "Indian" show. Rountree began attending in 1968, and she remembers white-driven pickup trucks driving by the schoolyard where the gathering was then held and people leaning out the windows, whooping Hollywood-style. That sort of jeering ended soon after, as the Civil Rights movement made itself thoroughly felt and the Powhatans profited by it. When ethnic heritage festivals, and festivals held for any and all excuses, exploded onto the scene after the 1976 Bicentennial, Chickahominy and other tribal dance teams and potters from Pamunkey (fig. 7.6) and Mattaponi began to receive more invitations than they could accept. Now, at last,

Fig. 7.5. The Chickahominy Redmen Dancers performing the Courtship Dance, 1974. Courtesy of Helen C. Rountree.

there were many outsiders who concurred with and appreciated their being "Indian" almost as much as they themselves did.

Before the mid-1970s, Powhatan participation in pan-tribal organizations, other than the informal network that Frank Speck assisted them with, had been limited. The one exception was the National Congress of American Indians, of which Chickahominy chief Oliver Adkins was a member from its inception. His tribe and many of the other Powhatan ones began joining other pan-Indian groups after 1970, including a short-lived one that was specifically eastern, the Coalition of Eastern Native Americans. Two Mattaponis also served on the board of the Native American Rights Fund in the 1970s and 1980s. Meeting with people from other tribes vastly increased the Powhatans' knowledge of how similar their history was to that of other eastern coastal tribes; it also increased their savvy in dealing with government bureaucracies. When more federal monies became available for improving minority education, several tribes applied for and got grants for things like math books—which they sometimes donated to the local schools' libraries to share the largesse. The Indian communities also got grants to improve their housing standards, a useful addition to the gradual improvements they were making themselves as they and their children got more education and better jobs. The Pamunkeys also launched a land case, citing the lack of federal involvement under the Indian Non-Intercourse Act of 1790, to get reparations for the taking of some of their land by the railroad (several railway companies in succession had owned the tracks). After a number of years of litigation through the Native American Rights Fund, they won their case in 1980, and along with reparation funds they were to receive lease money thereafter. The railroad, which nowadays carries freight to and from the Chesapeake Corporation's paper mill in West Point, still runs through Indian land.

The Virginia state government still did not officially recognize any

Fig. 7.6. Pamunkey pottery makers selling their wares at the Dragon Run Folk Festival, 1980. *Left to right:* Katy Bradby Southward, Daisy Stewart Bradby, and Bernice Bradby Langston. Courtesy of VDHR.

Fig. 7.7. The bill recognizing four "citizen" Indian enclaves is signed into law by Governor Charles Robb, March 8, 1983. Courtesy of Office of the Governor, Richmond, Va.

tribal organizations other than the "reservated" (their term) Pamunkeys and Mattaponis, because they still had reservations under the treaty of 1677. In the early 1980s, a North Carolina Lumbee-led pan-tribal organization in northern Virginia guided the nonreservation "citizen" (their term) Powhatan tribes in seeking state recognition. After a Joint Committee from both houses of the legislature examined the historical evidence presented by the tribes and heard testimony from their leaders (and also from Rountree), state recognition was granted to the two Chickahominies, the Upper Mattaponis, and the Rappahannocks in 1983 (fig. 7.7). The Nansemonds received recognition in 1985, the Monacans (descended from the historic Siouan-speakers) in 1989.

The Virginia Council on Indians was created by the recognition law. It consists of a representative from each recognized "citizen" tribe, a position allowed for representatives from each of the two reservations (neither has made much effort to keep the position filled), one "at large" Indian person to speak for the many members of non-Virginia tribes who live and work within the state today, and a representative each from Virginia's Senate and House of Delegates. The Council is therefore a state agency, under the Department of Health and Human Services, which ironically includes Dr. Plecker's old bailiwick, Vital Statistics. Therefore, through the Council, the Virginia tribes with or without reservations now have a direct pipeline to the governor, the attorney general, and the legislature. The Council examines and makes recommendations on petitions from other Indian descendants for recognition as historical tribes (an onerous job, if done thoroughly); it also acts as an information clearinghouse between the Indians and any organizations or individuals who wish to make contact with them. Meanwhile, the "citizen" Indians' recognition effort spawned another, parallel organization with similar aims but no ties to the state bureaucracy or representation from non-Virginia people: the United Indians of Virginia, Inc., formally organized in 1988.

The 1980s and 1990s also witnessed the building or refurbishing of several tribal centers, where meetings could be held, crafts classes conducted, and public events staged. The Mattaponis got a grant to renovate their former schoolhouse on the reservation; their annual powwow, featuring their Wahunsunacok "drum" (drumming and singing team), began to be held adjacent to it in 1996. They already had a museum and an educational trading post, both privately owned. The Pamunkeys got a grant to build a new structure that also includes a small but professionally produced museum that covers Indian prehistory as well as history. The Chickahominies built a big center, where the multitribal Thanksgiving Dinners are held annually, and through very active fund-raising they paid off the loan for it in about three years. They then turned to acquiring adjacent land for a cemetery extension and a ball field, where the Fall Festivals are now held, along with a new event: a midsummer crab feast/music festival. Their dance team, the Chickahominy Redmen Dancers, has been a fixture of powwows in Virginia and adjacent states for decades now. The Upper Mattaponis petitioned and got back their schoolhouse from King William County in 1982, renovating it for a center and then buying and developing land across the road into an elaborate public-

Fig. 7.8. Traditional women dancers from Virginia tribes. Courtesy of Helen C. Rountree.

meeting ground. Their annual powwow has been held there since the mid-1990s, as is their new music festival. (Both the tribal music festivals are "American" rather than "American Indian" in nature, and everybody wears casual clothes while listening to pop or country or gospel music.) The Rappahannocks built a grant-funded tribal center in the late 1990s and began holding their powwow there rather than in adjacent towns. There have been Rappahannocks involved in dance groups and a drum since the 1980s. The Nansemonds are working toward a tribal center at this writing, but they are hosting two powwows a year, the August one (put on since 1986) in Suffolk on the bank of the river bearing their name, and now a June one at the request of the City of Chesapeake. Both powwows take place in city parks. The dancing at all the Powhatans' pow-wows today is pan-Indian in regalia and dance steps (fig. 7.8). Indian and Indian-descended people from a wide variety of tribes in the United States participate actively (fig. 7.9).

Since the early 1990s, the Powhatan tribes have accomplished another goal that reaches deep into their emotions: the repatriation (reburial) of bones and artifacts excavated from Indian graves. The Powhatans' rela-tions with the archaeological establishment have been cooperative in Vir-ginia, and a standard repatriation procedure has been agreed upon.

Nowadays in Virginia, the archaeological excavation of human re-mains, whether they be Native American or not, generally occurs only when they are threatened with unavoidable disturbance or destruction. After Indian bones and grave goods come out of the soil, scholars typi-cally have two years in which to analyze them in nondestructive ways; an

Fig. 7.9. Fancy dancers and others, most of them guests from tribes outside Virginia. Courtesy of Helen C. Rountree.

exception can be made for tiny amounts of bone and other materials for very informative methods such as carbon-14 testing (for age), stable isotope analysis (for elements of the person's diet),[3] and so forth. Then the items are reburied, preferably near to where they were excavated but in a more protected place: that means creating a new cemetery. The reburial is carried out by the tribe(s) most nearly related to the bones' former owners; for the Great Neck Site's bones, that meant the Nansemonds. At Paspahegh, early in the reburial program, multiple tribes were involved in setting the policy and in burying the bones, on land donated by the developer (see chapter 2). For bones too old for historical identification, a central Indian cemetery is currently being negotiated for by the United Indians of Virginia.

Bones and associated artifacts to be reburied are grouped together as they were when they lay in the ground, then wrapped in red biodegradable fabric (analogous to the trade cloth that replaced deerskins in Indian culture), and laid in a wide, deep pit dug with modern machinery. The depth is for protection; the width is due to the strong Indian feeling that all Indian people present should be able to see in fairly easily (non-Indians are invited to stand behind them). In the Great Neck repatriation, the pit was in First Landing State Park, which has very sandy soil, so a scaffold had to be erected around the pit for people to stand on during the ceremony (fig. 7.10). The ceremony itself is a prayer service in pan-Indian style, though the Nansemond service had Cheyenne overtones because the leader was an Oklahoma Southern Cheyenne living in Virginia Beach. When the prayers end, the onlookers walk around the pit throwing in pinches of tobacco, after which the pit is covered over. Later on, a historical marker is raised at the site. The Nansemonds also paid for plantings on and around their filled-in pit; the site, adjacent to a public parking lot, is now a place for visitors to meditate. All repatriation ceremonies held at this writing (there have been four) were closed to everyone except Indians and a few non-Indian friends (like Turner and Rountree).

Being a Powhatan Indian Today

There are, at this writing, seven state-recognized Powhatan-descended tribes (fig. 7.11), with descendants of some other Powhatan groups still living in Virginia and elsewhere. (More tribal groups may be recognized

Fig. 7.10. Officiants at the repatriation of human remains from the Great Neck site, 1997. *Left to right:* Chief Ronnie Branham (Monacan), Chief Leonard Adkins (Chickahominy Tribe), Chief Emeritus Oliver Perry (Nansemond), Chief Webster Custalow (Mattaponi), John Minerich, and Fred Bushyhead (Southern Cheyenne). Courtesy of Anthony Belcastro.

in the future.) Each of the recognized groups has a residential core, shown on figure 7.11, with fewer than 500 (often fewer than 100) living in the "home" area. There are also many more members and people genealogically eligible for membership living and working in Virginia cities and also out-of-state. The total number of enrolled Powhatans today is around 1,500, whether they live "at home" or live in a nearby city and commute "home" on weekends. Three or four times that many are conscious of being eligible but are not enrolled for various personal reasons.

Tribal membership can be onerous. Members have to pay dues and are expected to do the following as well: attend tribal meetings, usually held monthly in the "home" area; serve as unpaid tribal officers when asked; work to put on tribal events like festivals; belong to the tribal church if it is feasible; see that their children grow up knowing about their people's history and learning, if possible, about still-existing crafts ("Saturday

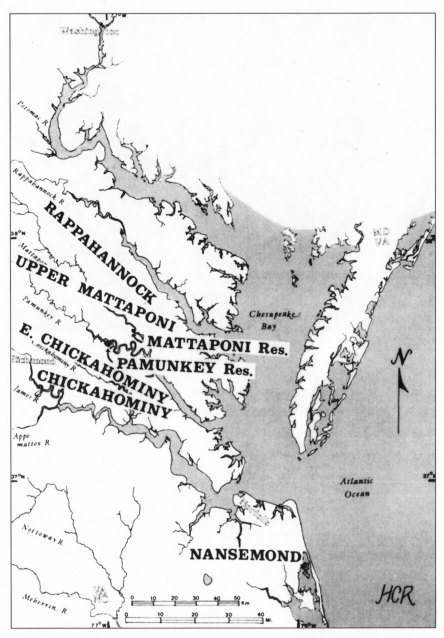

Fig. 7.11. Map of the Powhatan tribes today. Courtesy of Helen C. Rountree.

schools" are run at some tribal centers); represent the tribe at the Virginia Council on Indians, the United Indians of Virginia, and/or at other tribes' powwows, without pay; answer questions *knowledgeably* and, when possible, accept some of the many speaking invitations arriving from civic and school groups; live up to a good-citizen image at all times as representatives of their tribes and of Indian people in general (efforts to counteract negative stereotypes are ongoing). All of this is a tall order for people who are simultaneously living a modern American life, with high employment on a blue-collar and increasingly on a white-collar level. Virginia's Indian people are *very busy*.

The two Powhatan reservations follow a modern American lifestyle with the addition of the rights and difficulties brought them by their treaty status. They are exempt from state and local taxes if they live at least six months per year on the reservations, but they cannot sell their dwellings there to non-Indians—unless they live in mobile homes, which some of them do. The reservations are miniature towns that have to keep up their community's sanitation, building code standards (necessary for home improvement grants), and the like. They used to have to keep up their own roads as well; paving and state maintenance only came when they leased the roads' land to the state, which the Mattaponis did in the 1950s, the Pamunkeys in the 1980s. Passing the maintenance to the state brought a disadvantage: anyone can drive through the reservations on those paved roads. The two tribes can no longer shut their reservations off to the public. The Mattaponi reservation is small (fig. 7.12), and with a population that has always included many children, they have long needed and wanted to maintain good relations with their neighbors. The Pamunkey Reservation is eight miles from the nearest highway, making daily commuting a chore, so from the mid-twentieth century onward many Pamunkey families with children have lived off-reservation. That tribe's land is far more extensive than the Mattaponis,' and since it includes considerable low woods and marsh (fig. 7.13), the men do not have to go off-reservation to hunt for game with which to pay their annual tribute.

Being "Indian" in Virginia today is partially a matter of formal membership in an organized tribe, as described above. It is also some other things that come from spending much of one's life in an "Indian" community. Being Indian is feeling an allegiance firstly to one's own tribe; secondly to the other Virginia tribes, some of whose members one may

Fig. 7.12. Aerial view of the Mattaponi Reservation, March 1992. The cleared land *is* the reservation; a pulp mill owns the forest beyond it. Courtesy of Helen C. Rountree.

Fig. 7.13. Aerial view of most of the Pamunkey Reservation, March 1992. Courtesy of Helen C. Rountree.

have known since infancy; thirdly to Native Americans elsewhere in the continent; fourthly to the local and state communities in which one lives; and fifthly to the United States of America (during wartime, American citizenship ranks much higher in the Indian people's consciousness, as it does for non-Indian Americans).

Being "Indian" is being acutely aware that everybody else is descended from immigrants; that is true even if the Indian person has a lot of Eastern Hemisphere ancestors too. Indians were here first, no matter how proprietary some whites may feel if their ancestors landed in North America in the very early seventeenth century. Indians look upon such people as descendants of "late" arrivals: how can four centuries compare with over twelve millennia (the archaeologically *certified* length of human occupation in Virginia)?

There is also the special bitterness of having been conquered in one's own homeland. Even Native American people who cannot cite specific dates or events or tribal customs are vividly aware that their ancestors used to "own" all of the land and live upon it in age-old ways that were intimately adapted to it. When non-Indians make even passing belittling remarks about those customs, the people's hackles rise ("scalping" and "massacre" are especially hated words in Virginia). The tribes' members have the defensiveness that goes with the territory of being a minority, whose feelings are often unknowingly trampled by the majority (Indians are likely, though, to see it as deliberate). But their defensiveness is combined with a special attitude to American land and American history, since their side of the story is not so often told.

Powhatan Contributions to America

America would be the poorer if the Powhatans had not left a mark upon its history and culture. North American literature would have lacked the legend, or rather the mythology, surrounding Pocahontas. Another Indian girl might have served as John Smith's savior, had he needed one, for as other scholars have pointed out, Smith portrayed himself as having a knack for getting saved by sympathetic females. But it was the unusually strong (for North America) chiefly power of Pocahontas's father that made her important enough to capture as a hostage and worthy of a public-relations campaign afterward, when she went to England. There lay the real core of the legend, and that core, at least, was a historical reality.

Anglo-Virginian culture ultimately overtook the Powhatan and other native cultures, but not before those ways of life had a few effects upon the evolving English culture in the colony and later the state (there are parallels in other eastern states, from contact with other Woodland tribes). The Indians' guerilla style of fighting among themselves was suited to people living in a forested environment in small, scattered settlements. When the English came to North America, their ideas of warfare were based upon intensive agriculture that produced large, open areas to serve as battlefields and that supported large populations of people from whom to draw soldiers to fight in pitched battles. European warfare did not work well on this side of the Atlantic until the late eighteenth century, when the countryside and population of the colonies had come to resemble those of Europe. Before then, Euro-Americans had to fight their enemies, Indian and European, in Indian style, after a learning process that began in Powhatan-English engagements in Virginia in 1607.

Another effect of Indian fighting ways is still with us today. Male Powhatans were always prepared to shoot, whether at animal prey or at human enemies. English settlers on the Virginia frontier soon learned that in order to hold what was "theirs" against Indian resistance, all males and some females had to be proficient in using firearms, which they would keep within easy reach. Back home in England, many (lower-class) people were legally forbidden to bear arms; in America, that law had to change if the colony were to succeed. By the end of the seventeenth century, when Powhatan men did not consider themselves fully dressed without their guns, many Englishmen in the colony felt similarly. That feeling did *not* begin on the better-documented eighteenth-century frontier of Daniel Boone's time. After appearing from necessity in the early seventeenth-century Virginia colony, the right of all free people (later, only whites and reservation Indians) to bear arms gradually became embedded in the American consciousness as being particularly "American." It is still so regarded by many, in spite of the very changed conditions under which most urban and suburban Americans (including Indian ones) live today.

The Powhatans' language gave to all North Americans two place names that have become famous: the Potomac (formerly Patawomeck) River that flows past Washington, D.C., and the name Appomattox (formerly Appamattuck) that is still applied to the river and was later given to the piedmont town where General Lee surrendered at the end of the American Civil War. Powhatan words have also been "borrowed" into English under certain special circumstances. Terrapin (*torepew*) was an Algonquian word for large turtles of various kinds, but in English it came to be used for the aquatic ones found in the many Virginia waterways. Two North American animals, the raccoon (*araughcoon*) and the opossum (*aposum*), had no counterparts at all in the Eastern Hemisphere, so when the English had the first extended contact with them in Virginia, they adopted the Powhatan words for them. The same thing happened with a larger number of native wild plants: chinquapin (*chechinquamin*, a cousin of the chestnut); hickory (*powcohicora*); maypop (*maracock*, or native passionflower plant); pecan (*pakawn*, "nut" to the Powhatans, but applied by the English to hickory nuts and later one kind of hickory nut [the pecan]); persimmon (*pushemin,*); puccoon (*pohcoon*); tuckahoe (*tockawhogh*, preserved in the names of numerous plantations); and wicopy (*wikepi*, fibrous inner bark to the Powhatans, used as the common name of several trees today). Some Woodland Indian–made items also entered the American English vocabulary through Powhatan words: moccasins (shoes in general to the Powhatans, soft-soled shoes to us), tomahawks (hatchets in general to the Powhatans, fighting hatchets to us), and roanoke (mussel-shell beads, preserved nowadays in place names).[4]

Two more borrowed Powhatan words reflect the fact that the English first learned to cultivate corn in North America from the Powhatans, not from the Massachusetts to the north: hominy (*usketahamen*, "beaten with an instrument") as a way of preparing the kernels, and pone or cornpone (*apone*, "bread") for bread made from cornmeal rather than from other kinds of flour. Modern America—and many other parts of the world today—would be hungrier if the invading Europeans (Spanish and English) had not adopted corn agriculture, which can be tremendously productive in feeding human populations. We United Statesians take it farther: one distinguishing feature of on-the-go North American "junk food," as opposed to snacks in Old World countries, is that so much of ours is based upon corn: chips, curls, popcorn, and now, borrowed from

Mexican cuisine, tortillas. It was the Powhatans who first introduced *Zea mays* to hungry Englishmen in Virginia, and we should thank them for it.

Notes

1. Rountree can still remember how different the various grade schools looked in her hometown of Hampton in the late 1940s and early 1950s: the "colored" ones got much less maintenance. And Rountree's mother, a native of Kansas, never forgot her embarrassment upon entering the town's train station to buy a ticket and seeing the station's one and only clerk immediately cease serving several black customers at the "colored" window in order to serve the new arrival at the previously customerless "white" window. The people on the *receiving* end of such cavalier treatment would never forget it either.

2. Opinions of the Attorney General of Virginia, 1917, pp. 161, 163.

3. Stable isotope analysis was the analytical method that won over some members of tribes, when the policy was still in the making and the recognized Powhatan tribes were being asked to vote on how much destructive analysis they felt was permissible. Stable isotope analysis can show that their ancestors' diet was heavy on corn—and that therefore those Indians were *not* nomads.

4. Other Algonquian-language words were borrowed from native peoples north of Virginia: wigwam, wampum, powwow, toboggan, and quahog (a kind of clam).

Places to Visit

Pamunkey Reservation Museum, north of West Point, Va.

Mattaponi Reservation Museum, north of West Point, Va.

Mattaponi (Reservation) Educational Trading Post, north of West Point, Va.

Jamestown Settlement: a Living Museum

Jamestown Rediscovery archaeological site, on Jamestown Island

Various tribal powwows (May through September): watch for listings in newspapers or go online and call up the websites of the tribes or of the Pepperbird Foundation.

Bibliography

Archer, Gabriel. *See* Haile, *Jamestown Narratives.*

Axtell, James. *The Rise and Fall of the Powhatan Empire: Indians in Seventeenth-Century Virginia.* Williamsburg: Colonial Williamsburg, 1995.

Banister, John. *John Banister and His Natural History of Virginia, 1678–1692.* Ed. Joseph and Nesta Ewan. Urbana: University of Illinois Press, 1970.

Berkeley, Edmund, and Dorothy S. Berkeley, eds. *The Reverend John Clayton.* Charlottesville: University of Virginia Press, 1965.

Berry, Brewton. *Almost White.* New York: Macmillan, 1963.

Beverley, Robert. *The History and Present State of Virginia* [1705]. Ed. Louis B. Wright. Chapel Hill: University of North Carolina Press, 1947.

Billings, Warren M. "Some Acts Not in Hening's Statutes: The Acts of Assembly, April 1652, November 1652, and July 1653." *Virginia Magazine of History and Biography* 83 (1975): 22–76.

Blanton, Dennis B., Veronica Deitrick, and Kara Bartels. "Brief and True Report of Projectile Points from Jamestown Rediscovery as of December 1998." *Journal of the Jamestown Rediscovery Center* 1 (2001). Available from <http://www.apva.org/resources/jjrc>.

Blanton, Dennis B., Stevan C. Pullins, and Veronica Deitrick. *The Potomac Creek Site (44ST2) Revisited.* Report series no. 10. Richmond: Virginia Department of Historic Resources, 1999.

Blume, G.W.J. "Present-Day Indians of Tidewater Virginia." *Quarterly Bulletin of the Archeological Society of Virginia* 6, no. 2 (1950): 1–8.

Bridenbaugh, Carl. *Vexed and Troubled Englishmen, 1590–1642.* New York: Oxford University Press, 1967.

Burnaby, Andrew. "Travels Through the Middle Settlements in North America, in the Years 1759 and 1760. . . ." In *Voyages and Travels,* ed. John Pinkerton, vol. 13, 701–52. London: Longman, Hurst, Rees and Orme, 1812.

Campbell, Mildred. *The English Yeoman under Elizabeth and the Early Stuarts.* Yale Historical Publications no. 14. New Haven, 1942.

Canner, Thomas. "A Relation of the Voyage Made to Virginia in the Elizabeth of London . . . in the Yeere 1603." In *New American World: A Documentary History of North America to 1612*, ed. David B. Quinn, 163–66. New York: Arno Press, 1979.

Commissioners Appointed Under the Great Seale of England for the Virginia Affairs. "Articles of Peace between the most Mighty Prince . . . Charles the II . . . And the severall Indian Kings and Queens &c . . . the 29th day of May: 1677. . . ." *Virginia Magazine of History and Biography* 14 (1906): 289–96.

Crosby, Alfred. *The Columbian Exchange.* Westport, Conn.: Greenwood Press, 1972.

Dent, Richard J., Jr. *Chesapeake Prehistory: Old Traditions, New Directions.* New York: Plenum Press, 1995.

Durand de Dauphine. *A Huguenot Exile in Virginia . . . from the Hague Edition of 1687.* New York: Press of the Pioneers, 1934.

Earle, Carville V. "Environment, Disease, and Mortality in Early Virginia." In *The Chesapeake in the Seventeenth Century: Essays on Anglo-American Society*, ed. Thad W. Tate and David L. Ammerman, 96–125. Chapel Hill: University of North Carolina Press, 1979.

Egloff, Keith T., and Deborah Woodward. *First People: The Early Indians of Virginia.* Charlottesville: University Press of Virginia, 1992.

Egloff, Keith T., Mary Ellen N. Hodges, Jay F. Custer, Keith R. Doms, and Leslie McFaden. *Archaeological Investigations at Croaker Landing, 44JC70 and 44JC71.* Research Report series no. 4. Richmond: Virginia Department of Historic Resources, 1988.

Fausz, J. Frederick. "The Powhatan Uprising of 1622: A Historical Study of Ethnocentrism and Cultural Conflict." Ph.D. diss., College of William and Mary, 1977.

———. "Fighting 'Fire' with Firearms: The Anglo-Powhatan Arms Race in Early Virginia." *American Indian Culture and Research Journal* 3, no. 4 (1979): 33–50.

———. "Opechancanough: Indian Resistance Leader." In *Struggle and Survival in Colonial America*, ed. David G. Sweet and Gary B. Nash, 21–37. Berkeley: University of California Press, 1981.

———. "Anglo-Indian Relations in Colonial North America." In *Scholars and the Indian Experience: Critical Reviews of Recent Writing in the Social Sciences*, ed. W. R. Swagerty, 79–105. Bloomington: Indiana University Press, 1984.

———. "Patterns of Anglo-Indian Aggression and Accommodation along the Mid-Atlantic Coast, 1584–1634." In *Cultures in Contact: The European Impact on Native Institutions in Eastern North America, a.d. 1000–1800*, ed. William W. Fitzhugh, 225–68. Washington: Smithsonian Institution Press, 1985.

———. "Middlemen in Peace and War: Virginia's Earliest Indian Interpreters, 1608–1632." *Virginia Magazine of History and Biography* 95 (1987): 41–64.

———. "The Invasion of Virginia: Indians, Colonialism, and the Conquest of Cant: A Review Essay on Anglo-Indian Relations in the Chesapeake." *Virginia Magazine of History and Biography* 95 (1987): 113–56.

————. "'An Abundance of Blood Shed on Both Sides': England's First Indian War, 1609–1614." *Virginia Magazine of History and Biography* 98 (1990): 3–56.

Feest, Christian F. "Powhatan, a Study in Political Organisation." *Wiener Volkerkundliche Mitteilungen* 13 (1966): 69–83.

————. "The Virginia Indian in Pictures, 1612–1624." *Smithsonian Journal of History* 2 (1967): 1–30.

————. "Seventeenth-Century Virginia Algonquian Population Estimates." *Quarterly Bulletin of the Archeological Society of Virginia* 28 (1973): 66–79.

————. "Virginia Algonquians." In *Handbook of North American Indians*, vol. 15, *Northeast*, ed. Bruce G. Trigger, 253–70. Washington: Smithsonian Institution Press, 1978.

————. "'Powhatan's Mantle' and 'Skin Pouch'" [the "Virginia Purse"]. In *Tradescant's Rarities*, ed. Arthur MacGregor, 130–37. Oxford: Clarendon Press, 1983.

————. "Pride and Prejudice: The Pocahontas Myth and the Pamunkey." *European Review of Native American Studies* 1, no. 1 (1987): 5–12.

————. *The Powhatan Tribes*. New York: Chelsea Press, 1991.

————, ed. "Another French Account of Virginia Indians by John Lederer." *Virginia Magazine of History and Biography* 83 (1975): 150–59.

Fleet, Henry. "A Brief Journal of a Voyage Made in the Bark *Virginia*, to Virginia and Other Parts of the Continent of America" [1631–32]. In *The Founders of Maryland*, ed. Edward D. Neill, 19–37. Albany, N.Y.: Joel Munsell, 1876.

Gallivan, Martin D. "Spatial Analysis of John Smith's Map of Virginia." *Journal of Middle Atlantic Archaeology* 13 (1997): 145–60.

Gatschet, Albert S. Notebook. MS 1449. Washington, D.C.: National Anthropological Archives, Smithsonian Institution.

————. Post-1893 Pamunkey Notebook. MS 2197. Washington, D.C.: National Anthropological Archives, Smithsonian Institution.

Gleach, Frederick W. *Powhatan's World and Colonial Virginia: A Conflict of Cultures*. Lincoln: University of Nebraska Press, 1997.

Glover, Thomas. *An Account of Virginia, Its Scituation, Temperature, Inhabitants and Their Manner of Planting and Ordering Tobacco, etc.* [Originally published in Philosophical Transactions of the Royal Society, 1676.] Oxford: B. H. Blackwell, 1904.

Goddard, Ives. "Eastern Algonquian Languages." In *Handbook of North American Indians*, vol. 15, *Northeast*, ed. Bruce G. Trigger, 70–77. Washington, D.C.: Smithsonian Institution Press, 1978.

Haile, Edward W., comp. *Jamestown Narratives: Eyewitness Accounts of the Virginia Colony: The First Decade: 1607–1617*. Champlain, Va.: RoundHouse.

Hantman, Jeffrey L. "Between Powhatan and Quirank: Reconstructing Monacan Culture and History in the Context of Jamestown." *American Anthropologist* 92 (1990): 676–90.

Hening, William Waller, comp. *The Statutes at Large, Being a Collection of All the Laws of Virginia from the First Session of the Legislature*. 13 vols. New York: R. & W. & G. Bartow, 1809–23.

Herrman, Augustin. *Virginia and Maryland as it is Planted and Inhabited this Present Year 1670, Surveyed and Exactly Drawne by the Only Labour & Endeavour of Augustin Herrman Bohemiensis*. London, 1673. [Copy in Virginia State Library, Richmond.]

Hodges, Mary Ellen N. *Native American Settlement at Great Neck: Report on VDHR Archaeological Investigations of Woodland Components at Site 44VB7, Virginia Beach, Virginia, 1981–1987*. Research Report series no. 9. Richmond: Virginia Department of Historic Resources, 1998.

Jefferson, Thomas. *Notes on the State of Virginia, 1787*. Ed. William Peden. Chapel Hill: University of North Carolina Press, 1954.

Johnson, Robert C., ed. "The Indian Massacre of 1622: Some Correspondence of the Reverend Joseph Mead." *Virginia Magazine of History and Biography* 71 (1963): 408–10.

Jones, Hugh. *The Present State of Virginia* [1724]. Ed. Richard L. Morton. Chapel Hill: University of North Carolina Press, 1956.

Kelso, William M. *Jamestown Rediscovery I: Search for 1607 James Fort*. Richmond: Association for the Preservation of Virginia Antiquities, 1995.

———. *Jamestown Rediscovery II*. Richmond: Association for the Preservation of Virginia Antiquities, 1996.

Kelso, William M., Nicholas M. Luccketti, and Beverly A. Straube. *Jamestown Rediscovery III*. Richmond: Association for the Preservation of Virginia Antiquities, 1997.

———. *Jamestown Rediscovery IV*. Richmond: Association for the Preservation of Virginia Antiquities, 1998.

———. *Jamestown Rediscovery V*. Richmond: Association for the Preservation of Virginia Antiquities, 1999.

Kelso, William M., and Beverly A. Straube. *Jamestown Rediscovery VI*. Richmond: Association for the Preservation of Virginia Antiquities, 2000.

Kingsbury, Susan Myra, comp. *Records of the Virginia Company of London*. 4 vols. Washington, D.C.: Library of Congress, 1906–35.

Kupperman, Karen Ordahl. *Settling with the Indians: The Meeting of English and Indian Cultures in America, 1580–1640*. Totowa, N.J.: Rowman and Littlefield, 1980.

———. *Indians & English: Facing Off in Early America*. Ithaca: Cornell University Press, 2000.

Lamb, H. H. "On the Nature of Certain Climatic Epochs Which Differed from the Modern (1900–1939) Normal." In *Changes of Climate: Proceedings of the Rome Symposium*, 125–50. Paris: UNESCO, 1963.

Lane, Ralph. "Discourse on the First Colony." In *The Roanoke Voyages, 1584–1590*, ed. David B. Quinn, ser. 2, vol. 104, 255–94. Cambridge: The Hakluyt Society, 1955.

Langston, John Mercer. *From the Virginia Plantation to the National Capitol* [1894]. New York: Arno Press, 1969.

Lewis, Clifford M., and Albert J. Loomie, comps. *The Spanish Jesuit Mission in Virginia, 1570–1572.* Chapel Hill: University of North Carolina Press, 1953.

Lippson, Alice Jane, and Robert L. Lippson. *Life in the Chesapeake Bay.* Baltimore: Johns Hopkins University Press, 1984.

Luccketti, Nicholas M., Mary Ellen N. Hodges, and Charles T. Hodges, eds. "Paspahegh Archaeology: Data Recovery Investigations of Site 44JC308 at the Governor's Land at Two Rivers, James City County, Virginia" (1994). Report on file. Richmond: Virgina Department of Historic Resources.

Lurie, Nancy Oestreich. "Indian Cultural Adjustment to European Civilization." In *Seventeenth-Century America: Essays in Colonial History,* ed. James Morton Smith, 33–60. Chapel Hill: University of North Carolina Press, 1959.

MacCord, Howard A. Sr. "Camden: A Postcontact Indian Site in Caroline County." *Quarterly Bulletin of the Archeological Society of Virginia* 24, no. 1 (1969): 1–55.

Mathew, Thomas. "The Beginning, Progress and Conclusion of Bacon's Rebellion in Virginia in the Years 1675 & 1676." In *Tracts and Other Papers,* ed. Peter Force, vol. 1, 8. New York: Peter Smith, 1947.

McCartney, Martha W. "Seventeenth-Century Apartheid: The Suppression and Containment of Indians in Tidewater Virginia." *Journal of Middle Atlantic Archaeology* 1 (1985): 51–80.

———. "Cockacoeske, Queen of Pamunkey: Diplomat and Suzeraine." In *Powhatan's Mantle: Indians in the Colonial Southeast,* ed. Peter Wood, Gregory Wasilkov, and Thomas Hatley, 173–95. Lincoln: University of Nebraska Press, 1989.

McCary, Ben C. "The Virginia Tributary Indians and Their Metal Badges of 1661/62." *Quarterly Bulletin of the Archeological Society of Virginia* 38 (1983): 182–96.

McClure, N. E., ed. *Letters of John Chamberlain.* Memoir 12, parts 1 and 2. Philadelphia: American Philosophical Society, 1939.

McIlwaine, H. R., comp. *Journal of the House of Burgesses.* 13 vols. Richmond: Virginia State Library, 1915.

———. *Legislative Journals of the Council of Colonial Virginia.* 3 vols. Richmond: Virginia State Library, 1918.

———. *Executive Journals of the Council of Colonial Virginia.* 6 vols. Richmond: Virginia State Library, 1925–66.

———. *Minutes of the Council and General Court of Virginia, 1622–1632, 1670–1676.* 2d ed. Richmond: Virginia State Library, 1979.

McLearen, Douglas C., and L. Daniel Mouer. "Jordan's Journey II: A Preliminary Report on the 1992 Excavations at Archaeological Sites 44PG302, 44PG303, and

44PG 315." Report on file. Richmond: Virginia Department of Historic Resources.

———. "Jordan's Journey III: A Preliminary Report on the 1992–1993 Excavations at Archaeological Site 44PG307." Report on file. Richmond: Virginia Department of Historical Resources.

Merrill, William L., and Christian F. Feest. "An Exchange of Botanical Information in the Early Contact Situation: Wisakon of the Southeastern Indians." *Economic Botany* 29 (1975): 171–84.

Miller, Christopher L., and George R. Hamell. "A New Perspective on Indian-White Contact: Cultural Symbols and Colonial Trade." *Journal of American History* 73 (1986): 311–28.

Mooney, James. "The Powhatan Confederacy, Past and Present." *American Anthropologist*, n.s., 9 (1907): 129–52.

Morgan, Edmund S. "The First American Boom: Virginia, 1618 to 1630." *William and Mary Quarterly*, 3d ser., 28 (1971): 169–98.

Morgan, Tim, Nicholas M. Luccketti, Beverly Straube, S. Fiona Bessey, and Annette Loomis. "Archaeological Excavations at Jordan's Point: Sites 44PG151, 44PG300, 44PG302, 44PG303, 44PG315, and 44PG333" [1995]. Report on file. Richmond: Virginia Department of Historical Resources.

Mouer, L. Daniel. "Powhatan and Monacan Settlement Hierarchies." *Quarterly Bulletin of the Archeological Society of Virginia* 36 (1981): 1–21.

Mouer, L. Daniel, Douglas C. McLearen, R. Taft Kiser, Christopher P. Egghart, Beverly J. Binns, and Dane T. Magoon. "Jordan's Journey: A Preliminary Report on Archaeology at Site 44PG302, Prince George County, Virginia, 1990–1991." Report on file. Richmond: Department of Historic Resources.

Murray, Paul T. "Who Is an Indian? Who Is a Negro? Virginia Indians in the World War II Draft." *Virginia Magazine of History and Biography* 95 (1987): 215–31.

Norrisey, Mary Ellen. "The Pamunkey Indians Retrieve Their Past." *Notes on Virginia* 20 (1980): 24–27.

Norwood, Col. "A Voyage to Virginia by Col. Norwood" [1650]. In *Tracts and Other Papers*, ed. Peter Force, vol. 3, no. 10. New York: Peter Smith, 1947.

Nugent, Nell Marion, comp. *Cavaliers and Pioneers: Abstracts of Virginia Land Patents and Grants, 1623–1800.* Vols. 1–3. Richmond: Dietz Press, 1934, 1977, 1979.

Ortner, Donald J., and Robert S. Curruccini. "Skeletal Biology of the Virginia Indians." *American Journal of Physical Anthropology* 45 (1976): 717–22.

Painter, Floyd E. "The Great King of Great Neck: A Status Burial from Coastal Virginia." *The Chesopiean* 18, nos. 3–6 (1980): 74–75.

Palmer, William P., Sherwin McRae, and Henry W. Fluornoy, eds. *Calendar of Virginia State Papers, and Other Manuscripts, 1652–1781.* 11 vols. Richmond, 1875–93.

Pargellis, Stanley, ed. "The Indians of Virginia" [1688; author possibly John Clayton]. *William and Mary Quarterly*, 3d ser., 16 (1959): 228–53.

Peebles, Christopher S., and Susan M. Kus. "Some Archaeological Correlates of Ranked Societies." *American Antiquity* 42 (1977): 421–48.

Percy, George. *See* Haile, *Jamestown Narratives.*

Pfaus, Mrs. Fred. *Our Indian Neighbors.* Richmond, Va.: Dover Baptist Association, ca. 1947.

———. *Our Debt to Virginia Indians.* Richmond, Va.: Dover Baptist Association, 1949.

Plecker, Walter Ashby. *Eugenics in Relation to the New Family and the Law on Racial Integrity, Including a Paper Read Before the American Public Health Association.* Richmond, Va.: Superintendent of Public Printing, 1924.

———. *Reports of the Bureau of Vital Statistics.* Richmond, Va., 1924 and succeeding years.

Pollard, John Garland. "The Pamunkey Indians of Virginia." *Bulletin of Bureau of American Ethnology* 17. Washington, D.C.: U.S. Government Printing Office, 1894.

Potter, Stephen R. "Indian-White Relations in Virginia, 1607–1646." *Quarterly Bulletin of the Archeological Society of Virginia* 27 (1973): 192–97.

———. "Early English Effects on Virginia Algonquian Exchange and Tribute in the Tidewater Potomac." In *Powhatan's Mantle: Indians in the Colonial Southeast,* ed. Peter Wood, Gregory Waselkov, and Thomas Hatley, 151–72. Lincoln: University of Nebraska Press, 1989.

———. *Commoners, Tribute, and Chiefs: The Development of Algonquian Culture in the Potomac Valley.* Charlottesville: University Press of Virginia, 1997.

Puglisi, Michael J. "Controversy and Revival: The Chickahominy Indians Since 1850." In *Charles City County, Virginia: An Official History,* ed. James P. Whittenburg and John M. Coski, 97–104. Salem, W.Va.: D. Mills Genealogical Publishing Co, 1989.

Purchas, Samuel, comp. and ed. *Purchas His Pilgrimes.* 3d ed. London, 1617.

———. *Hakluytus Posthumus or Purchas His Pilgrimes* [orig. pub. 1625]. 20 vols. Glasgow: James MacLehose and Sons, 1904–6.

Quinn, David Beers. *Set Fair for Roanoke: Voyages and Colonies, 1584–1606.* Chapel Hill: University of North Carolina Press, 1985.

Reinhart, Theodore R., and Mary Ellen N. Hodges, eds. *Early and Middle Archaic Period Research in Virginia: A Synthesis.* Archeological Society of Virginia Special Publication 22. Richmond: Dietz Press, 1990.

———. *Late Archaic and Early Woodland Research in Virginia: A Synthesis.* Archeological Society of Virginia Special Publication 23. Richmond: Dietz Press, 1991.

———. *Middle and Late Woodland Research in Virginia: A Synthesis.* Archeological Society of Virginia Special Publication 29. Richmond: Dietz Press, 1992.

Reinhart, Theodore R., and Dennis J. Pogue, eds. *The Archaeology of Seventeenth-Century Virginia.* Archeological Society of Virginia Special Publication 30. Richmond: Dietz Press, 1993.

Reinhart, Theodore R., and J. Mark Wittkofski, eds. *The Middle and Late Woodland Period in Virginia: A Synthesis*. Richmond: Dietz Press, 1992.

Robinson, W. Stitt. "Indian Education and Missions in Colonial Virginia." *Journal of Southern History* 18 (1952): 152–68.

Rountree, Helen C. "Powhatan's Descendants in the Modern World: Community Studies of the Two Virginia Indian Reservations, with Notes on Five Non-Reservation Enclaves." *The Chesopiean* 10 (3) (1972): 62–96.

———. "Indian Land Loss in Virginia: A Prototype of Federal Indian Policy." Ph.D. diss., University of Wisconsin, Milwaukee, 1973.

———. "The Indians of Virginia: A Third Race in a Biracial State." In *Southeastern Indians Since the Removal Era*, ed. Walter L. Williams, 27–48. Athens: University of Georgia Press, 1979.

———. "Ethnicity among the 'Citizen Indians' of Virginia, 1800–1930." In *Strategies for Survival: American Indians in the Eastern United States*, ed. Frank W. Porter III, 173–209. New York: Greenwood Press, 1986.

———. *The Powhatan Indians of Virginia; Their Traditional Culture*. Norman: University of Oklahoma Press, 1989.

———. *Pocahontas's People: The Powhatan Indians of Virginia Through Four Centuries*. Norman: University of Oklahoma Press, 1990.

———. "Indian Virginians on the Move." In *Indians of the Southeastern United States in the Late 20th Century: An Overview*, ed. J. Anthony Paredes, 9–28. Tuscaloosa: University of Alabama Press, 1992.

———. "Powhatan Priests and English Rectors: Worldviews and Congregations in Conflict." *American Indian Quarterly* 16 (1992): 485–500.

———, ed. *Powhatan Foreign Relations, 1500–1722*. Charlottesville: University Press of Virginia, 1993.

———. *Young Pocahontas in the Indian World*. Yorktown, Va.: J & R Graphics Services, 1995.

———. "A Guide to the Late Woodland Indians' Use of Ecological Zones in the Chesapeake Region." *The Chesopiean* 34, nos. 2–3 (1996).

———. "Powhatan Indian Women: The People Captain John Smith Barely Saw." *Ethnohistory* 45 (1998): 1–29.

———. *Beyond the Village: A Colonial Parkway Guide to the Local Indians' Use of Natural Resources*. Yorktown, Va.: J & R Graphics Services, 1999.

———. "Pocahontas: The Hostage Who Became Famous." In *Sifters: Native American Women's Lives*, ed. Theda Perdue, 14–28. New York: Oxford University Press, 2001.

Rountree, Helen C., and Thomas E. Davidson. *Eastern Shore Indians of Virginia and Maryland*. Charlottesville: University Press of Virginia, 1997.

Rountree, Helen C., and E. Randolph Turner III. "On the Fringe of the Southeast: The Powhatan Paramount Chiefdom in Virginia." In *The Forgotten Centuries: The Southeastern United States in the Sixteenth and Seventeenth Centuries*, ed.

Charles Hudson and Carmen Tesser, 355–72. Athens: University of Georgia Press, 1994.

———. "The Evolution of the Powhatan Paramount Chiefdom in Virginia." In *Chiefdoms and Chieftaincy: An Integration of Archaeological, Ethnohistorical, and Ethnographic Approaches*, ed. Elsa M. Redmond, 265–96. Gainesville: University Press of Florida, 1999.

Rutman, Darret B., and Anita H. Rutman. "Of Agues and Fevers: Malaria in the Early Chesapeake." *William and Mary Quarterly*, 3d ser., 33 (1976): 31–60.

Sainsbury, W. Noel, J. W. Fortescue, and Cecil Headham, comps. *Calendar of State Papers, Colonial Series*. 60 vols. London: Longman, Green and Roberts, 1860–1926.

Schmitt, Karl, Jr. "Patawomeke: An Historical Algonkian Site." *Quarterly Bulletin of the Archeological Society of Virginia* 20 (1965): 1–36.

Shepherd, Samuel, comp. *The Statutes at Large of Virginia . . . Being a Continuation of Hening.* 3 vols. Richmond: privately printed, 1835.

Sherman, Richard B. "'The Last Stand': The Fight for Racial Integrity in Virginia in the 1920s." *Journal of Southern History* 54 (1988): 69–92.

Siebert, Frank T. Jr. "Resurrecting Virginia Algonquian from the Dead: The Reconstituted and Historical Phonology of Powhatan." In *Studies in Southeastern Indian Languages*, ed. James M. Crawford, 285–453. Athens: University of Georgia Press, 1975.

Smith, Gerald P. *The Hand Site, Southampton County, Virginia*. Special Publication no. 11. Richmond: Archeological Society of Virginia, 1984.

Smith, J. David. *The Eugenic Assault on America: Scenes in Red, White and Black*. Fairfax, Va.: George Mason University Press, 1993.

Smith, [Captain] John. *See* Haile, *Jamestown Narratives*.

Smits, David D. "'Abominable Mixture': Toward the Repudiation of Anglo-Indian Intermarriage in Seventeenth-Century Virginia." *Virginia Magazine of History and Biography* 95 (1987): 157–92.

Sneyd, Charlotte Augusta, trans. *A Relation, or Rather a True Account, of the Island of England, with Sundry Particulars of the Customs of these People, and of the Royal Revenues under King Henry the Seventh, About the Year 1500.* London: Printed for the Camden Society by John Bowyer Nichols & Son, 1847.

Speck, Frank G. *The Rappahannock Indians of Virginia*. Indian Notes and Monographs 5, no. 3, 1925.

———. *Chapters on the Ethnology of the Powhatan Tribes of Virginia*. Indian Notes and Monographs 1, no. 5, 1928.

Speck, Frank G., Royal B. Hassrick, and Edmund S. Carpenter. "Rappahannock Herbals, Folk-lore and Science of Cures." *Proceedings of the Delaware County Institute of Science* 10 (1942): 7–55.

Spelman, Henry. *See* Haile, *Jamestown Narratives*.

Spotswood, Alexander. *The Official Letters of Alexander Spotswood, Lieutenant-*

Governor of the Colony of Virginia, 1710–1722. Vol. 1 of 2. Collections of the Virginia Historical Society. Richmond: Virginia Historical Society, 1882.

Stahle, David W., Malcom K. Cleaveland, Dennis B. Blanton, Matthew D. Therrell, and David A. Gay. "The Lost Colony and Jamestown Droughts." *Science* 280: 564–67.

Stanard, W. G. "The Boundary Line Proceedings, 1710." *Virginia Magazine of History and Biography* 4 (1896–97): 30–42, 5: 1–12.

———. "Indians of Southern Virignia, 1650–1711: Depositions in the Virginia and North Carolina Boundary Case." *Virginia Magazine of History and Biography* 7 (1900): 337–52, 8: 1–11.

Stern, Theodore. "Pamunkey Pottery Making." *Southern Indian Studies* 3 (1951).

———. "Chickahominy: the Changing Culture of a Virginia Indian Community." *Proceedings of the American Philosophical Society* 96 (1952): 157–225.

Stewart, T. Dale. "Excavating the Indian Village of Patawomeke (Potomac)." In *Explorations and Fieldwork of the Smithsonian Institution in 1938,* 87–90. Washington, D.C.: Smithsonian Institution, 1938.

———. "Further Excavations at the Indian Village Site of Patawomeke (Potomac)." In *Explorations and Fieldwork of the Smithsonian Institution in 1939,* 79–82. Washington, D.C.: Smithsonian Institution, 1940.

———. *Archaeological Exploration of Patawomeke: The Indian Town Site (44ST2) Ancestral to the One (44ST1) Visited in 1608 by Captain John Smith.* Contributions to Anthropology no. 36. Washington, D.C.: Smithsonian Institution, 1992.

Stiles, Ezra. *Extracts from the Itineraries and Other Miscellanies of Ezra Stiles, D.D., Ll.D., 1765–1794, With a Selection from his Correspondence.* Ed. Fanklin Bowditch Dexter. New Haven: Yale University Press, 1916.

Stone, Lawrence. *The Family, Sex and Marriage in England, 1500–1800.* New York: Harper and Row, 1977.

Strachey, William. *See* Haile, *Jamestown Narratives.*

Stuart, Karen A. "'So Good a Work': The Brafferton School, 1691–1777." M.A. thesis, College of William and Mary, 1984.

Tanner, Helen Hornbeck. "The Land and Water Communication Systems of the Southeastern Indians." In *Powhatan's Mantle: Indians in the Colonial Southeast,* ed. Peter Wood, Gregory Waselkov, and Thomas Hatley, 6–20. Lincoln: University of Nebraska Press, 1989.

TIME-LIFE Books. *Algonquians of the East Coast.* Alexandria, Va.: TIME-LIFE Books, 1996.

Turner, E. Randolph III. "An Archaeological and Ethnohistorical Study on the Evolution of Rank Societies in the Virginia Coastal Plain." Ph.D. diss., Pennsylvania State University, 1976.

———. "An Intertribal Deer Exploitation Buffer Zone for the Virginia Coastal Plain—Piedmont Regions." *Quarterly Bulletin of the Archeological Society of Virginia* 32, no. 3 (1978): 42–48.

———. "Population Distribution in the Virginia Coastal Plain, 8000 B.C. to A.D. 1600." *Archaeology of Eastern North America* 6 (1978): 60–72.

———. "A Reexamination of Powhatan Territorial Boundaries and Population, ca. A.D. 1607." *Quarterly Bulletin of the Archeological Society of Virginia* 37 (1982): 45–64.

———. "Socio-Political Organization within the Powhatan Chiefdom and the Effects of European Contact, A.D. 1607–1646." In *Cultures in Contact: The Impact of European Contacts on Native American Cultural Institutions, a.d. 1000–1800*, ed. William W. Fitzhugh, 193–224. Washington, D.C.: Smithsonian Institution Press, 1985.

———. "Difficulties in the Archaeological Identification of Chiefdoms as Seen in the Virginia Coastal Plain During the Late Woodland and Early Historic Periods." In *Late Woodland Cultures of the Middle Atlantic Region*, ed. Jay F. Custer, 19–28. Newark: University of Delaware Press, 1986.

———. "The Virginia Coastal Plain during the Late Woodland Period." In *Middle-Late Woodland Period in Virginia: A Synthesis*, ed. Theodore R. Reinhart and J. Mark Wittkofski, 97–136. Archeological Society of Virginia Special Publication 29. Richmond: Dietz Press, 1992.

———. "Native American Protohistoric Interactions in the Powhatan Core Area." In *Powhatan Foreign Relations, 1500–1722*, ed. Helen C. Rountree, 76–93. Charlottesville: University Press of Virginia, 1993.

Turner, E. Randolph III, and Antony F. Opperman. "Archaeological Manifestations of the Virginia Company Period: A Summary of Surviving Powhatan and English Settlements in Tidewater Virginia, ca. A.D. 1607–1624." In *The Archaeology of Seventeenth-Century Virginia*, ed. Theodore R. Reinhart and Dennis J. Pogue, 67–104. Archeological Society of Virginia Special Publication 30. Richmond: Dietz Press, 1993.

———. "Searching for Virginia Company Period Sites: An Assessment of Surviving Archaeological Manifestations of Powhatan-English Interactions, A.D. 1607–1624." Richmond: Virginia Department of Historic Resources, forthcoming.

Ubelaker, Douglas H. "Reconstruction of Demographic Profiles from Ossuary Skeletal Samples: A Case Study from the Tidewater Potomac." *Smithsonian Miscellaneous Collections* 18 (1974).

———. "Human Biology of Virginia Indians." In *Powhatan Foreign Relations, 1500–1722*, ed. Helen C. Rountree, 53–75. Charlottesville: University Press of Virginia, 1993.

Underdown, D. E. "The Taming of the Scold: The Enforcement of Patriarchal Authority in Early Modern England." In *Order and Disorder in Early Modern England*, ed. Anthony Fletcher and John Stevenson, 116–36. Cambridge: Cambridge University Press, 1985.

Virginia Museum of Natural History. *Virginia Indians: An Educational Coloring Book*. Martinsville, Va., 1991.

Waselkov, Gregory A. "Indians of Westmoreland County." In *Westmoreland County, Virginia, 1673–1983*, ed. Walter Biscoe Norris Jr., 15–33. Montross, Va.: Westmoreland County Commission for History and Archaeology, 1983.

Washburn, Wilcomb Edward. *The Governor and the Rebel: A History of Bacon's Rebellion in Virginia*. Chapel Hill: University of North Carolina Press, 1957.

———. "The Moral and Legal Justifications for Dispossessing the Indians." In *Seventeenth-Century America: Essays in Colonial History*, ed. James Morton Smith, 15–32. Chapel Hill: University of North Carolina Press, 1959.

———. *Red Man's Land/White Man's Law*. New York: Charles Scribner's Sons, 1971.

Waugaman, Sandra F., and Danielle Moretti-Langholtz. *We're Still Here: Contemporary Virginia Indians Tell Their Stories*. Richmond, Va.: Palari Publishing, 2000.

William and Mary, College of. "Bursar's Book" (manuscript), 1754–70.

———. "Bursar's Book (manuscript)," 1763–69.

———. "Bursar's Book (manuscript)," 1770–77.

———. *A Catalogue of the College of William and Mary in Virginia, from its Foundation to the Present Time*. Williamsburg, 1859.

Williamson, Joel. *New People: Miscegenation and Mulattoes in the United States*. New York: The Free Press, 1980.

Wilson, Theodore Brantner. *The Black Codes of the South*. Southern Historical Publications no. 6. Norman: University of Oklahoma Press, 1965.

Winfree, Waverly K., comp. *The Laws of Virginia, Being a Supplement to Hening's Statutes at Large, 1700–1750*. Richmond: Virginia State Library, 1971.

Wingfield, Edward Maria. *See* Haile, *Jamestown Narratives*.

Wittkofski, J. Mark, and Theodore R. Reinhart, eds. *Paleoindian Research in Virginia: A Synthesis*. Archeological Society of Virginia Special Publication 19. Richmond, Va.: Dietz Press, 1989.

Index

Helen Rountree is retired professor of anthropology at Old Dominion University. She is the author of *The Powhatan Indians of Virginia: Their Traditional Culture* (1989), *Pocahontas People: The Powhatan Indians of Virginia through Four Centuries* (1990), and, with Thomas Davidson, *The Eastern Shore Indians of Virginia and Maryland* (2000).

Randolph Turner is director of the Portsmouth Regional Office for the Virginia Department of Historic Resources. A Late Woodland/Contact period specialist, he has written over fifty articles on Virginia archaeology.